Izabela Kazejak

JEWS IN POST-WAR WROCŁAW AND L'VIV

Official Policies and Local Responses in Comparative Perspective, 1945-1970s

Bibliografische Information der Deutschen Nationalbibliothek
Die Deutsche Nationalbibliothek verzeichnet diese Publikation in der Deutschen Nationalbibliografie; detaillierte bibliografische Daten sind im Internet über http://dnb.d-nb.de abrufbar.

Bibliographic information published by the Deutsche Nationalbibliothek
Die Deutsche Nationalbibliothek lists this publication in the Deutsche Nationalbibliografie; detailed bibliographic data are available in the Internet at http://dnb.d-nb.de.

ISBN-13: 978-3-8382-1802-1
© *ibidem*-Verlag, Stuttgart 2023
Alle Rechte vorbehalten

Das Werk einschließlich aller seiner Teile ist urheberrechtlich geschützt. Jede Verwertung außerhalb der engen Grenzen des Urheberrechtsgesetzes ist ohne Zustimmung des Verlages unzulässig und strafbar. Dies gilt insbesondere für Vervielfältigungen, Übersetzungen, Mikroverfilmungen und elektronische Speicherformen sowie die Einspeicherung und Verarbeitung in elektronischen Systemen.

All rights reserved. No part of this publication may be reproduced, stored in or introduced into a retrieval system, or transmitted, in any form, or by any means (electronical, mechanical, photocopying, recording or otherwise) without the prior written permission of the publisher. Any person who does any unauthorized act in relation to this publication may be liable to criminal prosecution and civil claims for damages.

Printed in the EU

Soviet and Post-Soviet Politics and Society (SPPS)   Vol. 269
ISSN 1614-3515

General Editor: Andreas Umland,
Stockholm Centre for Eastern European Studies, andreas.umland@ui.se

Commissioning Editor: Max Jakob Horstmann,
London, mjh@ibidem.eu

EDITORIAL COMMITTEE*

DOMESTIC & COMPARATIVE POLITICS
Prof. **Ellen Bos**, *Andrássy University of Budapest*
Dr. **Gergana Dimova**, *Florida State University*
Prof. **Heiko Pleines**, *University of Bremen*
Dr. **Sarah Whitmore**, *Oxford Brookes University*
Dr. **Harald Wydra**, *University of Cambridge*

SOCIETY, CLASS & ETHNICITY
Col. **David Glantz**, *"Journal of Slavic Military Studies"*
Dr. **Marlène Laruelle**, *George Washington University*
Dr. **Stephen Shulman**, *Southern Illinois University*
Prof. **Stefan Troebst**, *University of Leipzig*

POLITICAL ECONOMY & PUBLIC POLICY
Prof. **Andreas Goldthau**, *University of Erfurt*
Dr. **Robert Kravchuk**, *University of North Carolina*
Dr. **David Lane**, *University of Cambridge*
Dr. **Carol Leonard**, *University of Oxford*
Dr. **Maria Popova**, *McGill University, Montreal*

FOREIGN POLICY & INTERNATIONAL AFFAIRS
Dr. **Peter Duncan**, *University College London*
Prof. **Andreas Heinemann-Grüder**, *University of Bonn*
Prof. **Gerhard Mangott**, *University of Innsbruck*
Dr. **Diana Schmidt-Pfister**, *University of Konstanz*
Dr. **Lisbeth Tarlow**, *Harvard University, Cambridge*
Dr. **Christian Wipperfürth**, *N-Ost Network, Berlin*
Dr. **William Zimmerman**, *University of Michigan*

HISTORY, CULTURE & THOUGHT
Dr. **Catherine Andreyev**, *University of Oxford*
Prof. **Mark Bassin**, *Södertörn University*
Prof. **Karsten Brüggemann**, *Tallinn University*
Prof. **Alexander Etkind**, *Central European University*
Prof. **Gasan Gusejnov**, *Free University of Berlin*
Prof. **Leonid Luks**, *Catholic University of Eichstaett*
Dr. **Olga Malinova**, *Russian Academy of Sciences*
Dr. **Richard Mole**, *University College London*
Prof. **Andrei Rogatchevski**, *University of Tromsø*
Dr. **Mark Tauger**, *West Virginia University*

ADVISORY BOARD*

Prof. **Dominique Arel**, *University of Ottawa*
Prof. **Jörg Baberowski**, *Humboldt University of Berlin*
Prof. **Margarita Balmaceda**, *Seton Hall University*
Dr. **John Barber**, *University of Cambridge*
Prof. **Timm Beichelt**, *European University Viadrina*
Dr. **Katrin Boeckh**, *University of Munich*
Prof. em. **Archie Brown**, *University of Oxford*
Dr. **Vyacheslav Bryukhovetsky**, *Kyiv-Mohyla Academy*
Prof. **Timothy Colton**, *Harvard University, Cambridge*
Prof. **Paul D'Anieri**, *University of California*
Dr. **Heike Dörrenbächer**, *Friedrich Naumann Foundation*
Dr. **John Dunlop**, *Hoover Institution, Stanford, California*
Dr. **Sabine Fischer**, *SWP, Berlin*
Dr. **Geir Flikke**, *NUPI, Oslo*
Prof. **David Galbreath**, *University of Aberdeen*
Prof. **Frank Golczewski**, *University of Hamburg*
Dr. **Nikolas Gvosdev**, *Naval War College, Newport, RI*
Prof. **Mark von Hagen**, *Arizona State University*
Prof. **Guido Hausmann**, *University of Regensburg*
Prof. **Dale Herspring**, *Kansas State University*
Dr. **Stefani Hoffman**, *Hebrew University of Jerusalem*
Prof. em. **Andrzej Korbonski**, *University of California*
Dr. **Iris Kempe**, *"Caucasus Analytical Digest"*
Prof. **Herbert Küpper**, *Institut für Ostrecht Regensburg*
Prof. **Rainer Lindner**, *University of Konstanz*

Dr. **Luke March**, *University of Edinburgh*
Prof. **Michael McFaul**, *Stanford University, Palo Alto*
Prof. **Birgit Menzel**, *University of Mainz-Germersheim*
Dr. **Alex Pravda**, *University of Oxford*
Dr. **Erik van Ree**, *University of Amsterdam*
Dr. **Joachim Rogall**, *Robert Bosch Foundation Stuttgart*
Prof. **Peter Rutland**, *Wesleyan University, Middletown*
Prof. **Gwendolyn Sasse**, *University of Oxford*
Prof. **Jutta Scherrer**, *EHESS, Paris*
Prof. **Robert Service**, *University of Oxford*
Mr. **James Sherr**, *RIIA Chatham House London*
Dr. **Oxana Shevel**, *Tufts University, Medford*
Prof. **Eberhard Schneider**, *University of Siegen*
Prof. **Olexander Shnyrkov**, *Shevchenko University, Kyiv*
Prof. **Hans-Henning Schröder**, *SWP, Berlin*
Prof. **Yuri Shapoval**, *Ukrainian Academy of Sciences*
Dr. **Lisa Sundstrom**, *University of British Columbia*
Dr. **Philip Walters**, *"Religion, State and Society", Oxford*
Prof. **Zenon Wasyliw**, *Ithaca College, New York State*
Dr. **Lucan Way**, *University of Toronto*
Dr. **Markus Wehner**, *"Frankfurter Allgemeine Zeitung"*
Dr. **Andrew Wilson**, *University College London*
Prof. **Jan Zielonka**, *University of Oxford*
Prof. **Andrei Zorin**, *University of Oxford*

---

* While the Editorial Committee and Advisory Board support the General Editor in the choice and improvement of manuscripts for publication, responsibility for remaining errors and misinterpretations in the series' volumes lies with the books' authors.

Soviet and Post-Soviet Politics and Society (SPPS)
ISSN 1614-3515

Founded in 2004 and refereed since 2007, SPPS makes available affordable English-, German-, and Russian-language studies on the history of the countries of the former Soviet bloc from the late Tsarist period to today. It publishes between 5 and 20 volumes per year and focuses on issues in transitions to and from democracy such as economic crisis, identity formation, civil society development, and constitutional reform in CEE and the NIS. SPPS also aims to highlight so far understudied themes in East European studies such as right-wing radicalism, religious life, higher education, or human rights protection. The authors and titles of all previously published volumes are listed at the end of this book. For a full description of the series and reviews of its books, see www.ibidem-verlag.de/red/spps.

Editorial correspondence & manuscripts should be sent to: Dr. Andreas Umland, Department of Political Science, Kyiv-Mohyla Academy, vul. Voloska 8/5, UA-04070 Kyiv, UKRAINE; andreas.umland@cantab.net

Business correspondence & review copy requests should be sent to: *ibidem* Press, Leuschnerstr. 40, 30457 Hannover, Germany; tel.: +49 511 2622200; fax: +49 511 2622201; spps@ibidem.eu.

Authors, reviewers, referees, and editors for (as well as all other persons sympathetic to) SPPS are invited to join its networks at www.facebook.com/group.php?gid=52638198614 www.linkedin.com/groups?about=&gid=103012 www.xing.com/net/spps-ibidem-verlag/

Recent Volumes

260 David Dalton
The Ukrainian Oligarchy After the Euromaidan
How Ukraine's Political Economy Regime Survived the Crisis
With a foreword by Andrew Wilson
ISBN 978-3-8382-1740-6

261 Andreas Heinemann-Grüder (Ed.)
Who are the Fighters?
Irregular Armed Groups in the Russian-Ukrainian War in 2014–2015
ISBN 978-3-8382-1777-2

262 Taras Kuzio (Ed.)
Russian Disinformation and Western Scholarship
Bias and Prejudice in Journalistic, Expert, and Academic Analyses of East European, Russian and Eurasian Affairs
ISBN 978-3-8382-1685-0

263 Darius Furmonavicius
LithuaniaTransforms the West
Lithuania's Liberation from Soviet Occupation and the Enlargement of NATO (1988–2022)
With a foreword by Vytautas Landsbergis
ISBN 978-3-8382-1779-6

264 Dirk Dalberg
Politisches Denken im tschechoslowakischen Dissens
Egon Bondy, Miroslav Kusý, Milan Šimečka und Petr Uhl (1968-1989)
ISBN 978-3-8382-1318-7

265 Леонид Люкс
К столетию «философского парохода»
Мыслители «первой» русской эмиграции о русской революции и о тоталитарных соблазнах XX века
ISBN 978-3-8382-1735-2

266 Daviti Mtchedlishvili
The EU and the South Caucasus
European Neighborhood Policies between Eclecticism and Pragmatism, 1991-2021
With a foreword by Nicholas Ross Smith
ISBN 978-3-8382-1735-2

267 Bohdan Harasymiw
Post-Euromaidan Ukraine
Domestic Power Struggles and War of National Survival in 2014–2022
ISBN 978-3-8382-1798-7

268 Nadiia Koval, Denys Tereshchenko (Eds.)
Russian Cultural Diplomacy under Putin
Rossotrudnichestvo, the "Russkiy Mir" Foundation, and the Gorchakov Fund in 2007–2022
ISBN 978-3-8382-1801-4

Contents

Acknowledgements 7

Introduction 9

1. The historical background 17
   1. Jews in Breslau 17
   2. The rise to power of Hitler and its effect on Jews in Breslau 20
   3. Jews in Lwów in 1918 22
   4. Polish Jews and the Second Polish Republic 25
   5. Attitudes towards Jews in the Polish Second Republic .. 29
   6. Emigration of Jews 33
   7. Jews, Ukrainians and Russians 35
   8. Jews in the Soviet Union in the interwar years 38
   9. The Second World War: Poles, Ukrainians and responses to the Holocaust 42

   Conclusion 46

2. Jews in Wrocław and L'viv, 1945-48 49
   1. Shifting of the borders and the exchange of populations 49
   2. Jews and Politics in Poland 52
   3. The transformation of Lwów into L'viv 56
   4. Jewish settlement in Wrocław 60
   5. Finding a job in Wrocław 63
   6. German Jews 66
   7. Jewish educational and cultural organizations in Wrocław 69
   8. Antisemitism in Wrocław 73

		9. The reconstruction of the Jewish community in L'viv ... 76
		10. Antisemitism in L'viv 81
		Conclusion 83

3. Jewish life from 1948 through the 1950s 87
   1. The Soviet Union and the Creation of the State of Israel 88
   2. Polish Jews and the Creation of Israel 92
   3. Jewish Life in Wrocław in the 1950s 97
   4. 1956 as a turning point 103
   5. Jewish Life in L'viv in the 1950s 109

4. The decline of the Jewish communities in the 1960s and 1970s 115
   1. The Closure of the Synagogue in L'viv 117
   2. Jews in Wrocław in the 1960s 122
   3. Schooling for Jews in Wrocław 125
   4. Pressures to Assimilate 129
   5. The Six-Day War of 1967 and the Crisis of 1968 132
   6. Jewish Emigration from Poland 137
   7. Emigration of Jews from the Soviet Union in the 1970s 139

Conclusion 145

Bibliography 159

Acknowledgements

I am very grateful to all the people who have supported me during the work on this topic. I would not have been able to have reached this point without the help and advice of my supervisor in the Department of History and Civilization at the European University Institute (EUI), Professor Steve Smith, who has always commented on my work with great interest and insight. I am also grateful to my former advisor, Professor Philipp Ther, who accepted my project proposal at the EUI and encouraged me to start working on the topic of comparative and transnational history. I would like to express my thanks to Professor Michael Meng, Professor Tarik C. Amar as well as to Professor Kiran Patel for the contribution they have made in helping me. I greatly benefited from the advice given to me by Professor Bożena Szaynok, Professor Krzysztof Ruchniewicz and Professor Arfon E. Rees at an early stage of my doctoral research. I would also like to thank Professor Gangolf Hübinger for kindly preparing a letter of recommendation for me.

I am also grateful to Professor Fritz Stern for the first scholarship that I was awarded. It was as a result of this scholarship, and the practical work that I did with historical records in the archives, that I became interested in doing comparative work on the history of Jews in Wrocław and in L'viv after the end of the Second World War. I was helped greatly by archivists in all the archives in which I worked in Poland and in Ukraine; many thanks to these people also.

I am also grateful to my parents, who supported me when I was writing my dissertation and who visited me in various European cities where I was working towards my PhD. I would also like to thank my sister and her family, who have been very supportive.

Finally, I would like to thank Kathy Wolf-Fabiani, Rita Peero and Anna Coda Nunziate for their administrative help. Especially, I would like to express my warmest thanks to Rita Peero who helped me so much from the administrative and financial point of view in the last stages of my doctoral program.

I would also like to thank all the members of the L'viv Center for Urban History who always welcomed me when I was travelling to L'viv to carry out my research. I am also grateful to the Willy-Brandt Center for European and German Studies in Wrocław for helping me to organise my initial research on the history of Jews in Wrocław in 2006.

Generally, I would not have gone far without the History and Civilization Department at the European University Institute where I was allowed to work on my doctoral thesis with a grant. I would also not have even started without the help of the European University Viadrina in Frankfurt (Oder) and the support from the Faculty for Cultural Studies, where I first became interested in conducting research on this topic.

Introduction

This study examines the attempt to re-establish Jewish communities in two cities that once boasted a substantial Jewish presence, a presence that was utterly destroyed by the Holocaust. The postwar reestablishment of the communities took place in Wrocław, a city that passed after 1945 from Germany to Poland, and in L'viv, a city that passed from Poland to Soviet Ukraine. The process of reestablishment of Jewish life in these two cities was thus overseen by two different communist regimes, and a large part of this investigation is concerned to compare the similarities and differences in the policies of the two regimes. In the end, the attempt to reestablish Jewish life in the two cities largely failed and my study seeks to explain why the effort to create communities that were self-identified as Jewish yet loyal to the communist state did not succeed.

The first chapter looks at the prewar history and wartime destruction of the Jewish communities in Breslau in Germany (or Wrocław, as it became after 1945) and in Lwów in Poland (which was incorporated as L'vov/L'viv into Soviet Ukraine after 1945). The study then goes on to trace the efforts of the postwar regimes, supported by those Jews who had survived the Holocaust and who chose not to leave Eastern Europe, to reconstitute Jewish life. It examines the history of these communities up to 1968 in the case of Wrocław and up to the 1970s in the case of L'viv. Chapter 2 compares how after 1945 Jewish communities were reestablished in two cities that had as a result of the war been moved into new polities, both of which were or soon became in the hands of Communists. There were similar processes of emigration, resettlement and an increase in Zionism in both cities. Chapters 3 and 4 go on to compare the policies of the two regimes that notionally repudiated antisemitism at the municipal level. Analysis of the impact of policy in two cities allows us better to understand how policies on such matters as work, housing, education influenced the attempt to restore Jewish life. The work compares how Jews sought to rebuild their communities but also why they were unable to develop vibrant Jewish communities in both cities, the causes of which lay not only in the policy of the state, but also in the memory and experience of the Holocaust, which manifested itself in political Zionism and emigration, as well as in popular antisemitism. The study concludes by attempting to assess the relative importance of factors such as the small size of the Jewish population, of official policies that were never supportive of Jews and sometimes outright discriminatory, of popular antisemitism, and of the processes of assimilation in determining the relative success of the communities in the two cities. The main research questions thus relate to how similar or different the policy was towards Jews in the Soviet Union and in Poland after 1944 and how it was articulated in the respective cases of the Jewish communities in Wrocław and in L'viv. Secondly, the study asks, how did policy change over time (if at all)? What were the factors that led to the failure to re-establish a vibrant Jewish community in the two cities? What were the factors that led to Jews, by and large, conforming to the values, norms and languages of the surrounding majority. Thirdly, it examines the stereotype of Poles and Ukrainians as antisemites.

In this investigation the micro- and macro-level approaches has very important. This is because I concentrated on state policies and did not confine myself to the policies of the cities. It was important to explain the overall policies of the state and how these policies were implemented in the small scale of two cities. Additionally, because Ukraine was a Soviet republic, the context of the Soviet Union was highly significant in the Ukrainian case. This is due to the fact that the Ukrainian state was not able to introduce its own independent policies towards Jews. The contexts were thus different in the two cases. In the Polish case the context is that of Polish socialism, while in the L'viv context what matters is the Soviet policies towards Jews and their local implementation in Ukrainian cities.

The comparison of the two Jewish communities is explored in relation to five inter- related contexts. The primary context is that of the official policies towards Jews of the government of the Polish People's Republic (this was its official name only from 1952) and of the government of the Ukrainian Soviet Socialist Republic. Chapters 2, 3 and 4 examine the aims and effects of these official policies in some detail, highlighting the many similarities in the policies between the two regimes — similarities that arose not least because Poland, especially in the late-Stalinist era, was required to submit to economic, political and social policies handed down from Moscow. At the most general level the analysis of official policy is concerned to understand the tensions between the desire of the two regimes to integrate Jews as equal members of socialist society and their recognition of some elements of Jewish difference, whether that difference was understood in terms of religion or ethnicity. Soviet Jews, while never having the extensive territorial autonomy awarded to some other national groups, were, for better or worse, recognized as an official nationality. One's Jewishness was a dimension of one's Soviet citizenship in a way that was never true in Poland, where Jews were simply citizens of Poland. Nationality was a key element in individual status in the Soviet Union, recorded in one's internal passport (which was introduced in 1932) and recorded in all official transactions. One's nationality derived from one's parents' nationality, not from one's place of residence, language or subjective identification. There was no possibility of changing one's nationality, except for children of mixed-nationality marriages, who at the age of 16 had to choose one of their parents' nationalities. In some contexts, notably admission to higher education and application for certain types of employment, legal nationality significantly shaped one's life chances, both negatively (especially for Jews) and positively for titular nationalities in non-Russian republics who benefitted from tacit affirmative action. Incidentally, since mixed marriages were common among Jews, this reclassification strategy contributed substantially to the apparently dramatic shrinkage of the Jewish population of the USSR from 2,2m in 1959 to 1,4m in 1989. In Ukraine, according to the 1979 census, only 10.3 percent of children born to a Jewish father and a Russian mother and 9.1 percent of children born to a Jewish father and a Ukrainian mother opted to become Jewish (although even this was higher than in the Russian Federation).[1] As we shall see, then, there

---

1   Rogers Brubaker, *Nationalism Reframed: Nationhood and the National Question in the New Europe* (Cambridge: Cambridge University Press, 1996), http://jwa.org/en

were important differences as well as many similarities in the official policies towards Jews of the two regimes. The focus on official policy requires that we explore how the two regimes viewed the decimated Jewish populations in the two cities after 1945, and how these perceptions shaped policy on the vital matter of emigration, since following the destruction of the war hundreds of thousands of Jews desired only to leave the territory on which the Holocaust had been taken place. The majority of the 270,000 Holocaust survivors registered in Poland, for example, decided to emigrate, so that by 1955 only 75,000 to 80,000 Jews remained in the country. The second context of our enquiry is directly related to the first and concerns how central policies were implemented at the local level of the two cities. Chapter 2 examines official efforts at repatriation and resettlement of Jews in Wrocław and L'viv, while chapters 3 and 4 compare how the local administrations responded to Jewish claims for recognition of cultural and religious rights in areas such as education, language use and the practice of religion. I try throughout to highlight the fact that the Jewish community was not homogeneous, and that there were important divisions between religious and non-religious Jews, between communist, socialist and Zionist Jews, between Jews who were Polonized or Ukrainized and those who were formed in the shtetl.

It is at this point that the contexts relating to official policy and its local implementation intersect with a third context, specifically one that which relates less to communist ideology and policy and more to the particular national contexts of Poland and Soviet Ukraine. As a result of the war, Poland became essentially a mono-ethnic and mono-religious state, whereas the Soviet Union (of which Soviet Ukraine formed a part) remained a multi-ethic and multi-religious state. In Poland, the communist regime was forced to come to terms with a strong Polish nationalism and with a hegemonic Catholic Church, and this had indirect effects on the Jewish population that were not a direct consequence of official policy. Meanwhile in Ukraine, the incorporation of Galicia, which had historically been a bastion of Ukrainian nationalism since the last years

---

cyclopedia/article/demography-soviet-union-russian-federation-and-other-successor-states (accessed 5 February 2012).

of the Austro-Hungarian Empire, strengthened the Ukrainian nationalism that had been gathering pace in Soviet Ukraine since the 1920s. Ukrainian nationalism, combined with the vigorous efforts of the Orthodox Church to assert its dominance in the newly incorporated territories, were factors that had an indirect effect on the policies of the Soviet Ukrainian government towards Jews. As this suggests, despite the massive rupture of the Holocaust and the political revolution that transpired in Poland, both regimes had to contend with the legacies of history (thus the importance of chapter 1). This was nowhere more evident than in respect of the traditions of antisemitism that intersected more or less powerfully with Polish and Ukrainian nationalism.

The fourth context of our enquiry, therefore, explores both popular and official antisemitism and how this shaped the fate of the postwar Jewish communities in Wrocław and L'viv. Both Poland and Ukraine had grim histories of ingrained discrimination and periodic violence against Jews, although the extent and nature of antisemitism is a question that needs to be investigated rather than simply assumed. There is much in this traditional antisemitism that may be characterized as 'anti-modern', with Jews being seen as the cause of the social, political, religious and cultural problems caused by modernity.[2] At the same time, as the Nazis showed only too clearly, antisemitism could be articulated in highly modern terms, and in the case of the two communist regimes it was at various times coupled with 'anti-cosmopolitism', hostility to 'bourgeois' intellectuals, 'anti-speculation' campaigns, anti-religious campaigns and, above all, following the establishment of the state of Israel in 1948, anti-Zionism. Particularly shocking, in view of their purported rejection of any form of racial and ethnic discrimination, was the way in which the two communist regimes in the postwar era succumbed to antisemitism — often under the banner of anti-Zionism. Presiding over Slav populations that had suffered massively during the Second World War, neither the Soviet Ukrainian nor the Polish communist regimes was willing to recognise the specific suffering of their Jewish citizens in the Holocaust. But much worse was the way in which in the late 1940s the Soviet government

---

2   Werner Bergman, *Geschichte des Antisemitismus* (München: Verlag C.H. Beck, 2004), 6.

for the first time engaged in anti-Jewish repression and rhetoric, since in the years prior to the Stalinist terror the Soviet Union had stood out among the interwar regimes of Eastern Europe for its progressive policy towards Jewish self-expression. Ironically, this was an important reason why Jews in Poland joined the Communist Party in significant numbers both before and after the war. Jews who were active Communists were always a small minority among Jews in both Poland and Soviet Ukraine, yet in both countries Jews in general – i.e. that small handful that had miraculously survived the Holocaust – tended to attribute their survival, at least in part, to the Soviet Red Army. We do not have precise figures on the number of Jews in the United Polish Workers' Party, but relative to their number in the population as a whole they were numerous. Jews in the Polish Workers' Party were especially prominent in the Ministry of Foreign Trade, in the Ministry of Public Security and in Military Counterintelligence. These Jews were largely spared the antisemitism unleashed in the Soviet Union (and in Czechoslovakia) in Stalin's final years (although Jewish officers in the Polish army, purged by Soviet officers in 1950 to 1953, were not so lucky). Moreover, in contrast to the anti-cosmopolitan campaign in the Soviet Union, antisemitism in the Polish Workers' Party remained covert until 1956, when the general crisis of the communist regime led to a new wave of Jewish emigration; even then, however, antisemitism did not come to dominate official policy towards Jews until 1968.

The fifth and final context in which we place our comparison of the development of the Jewish communities in Wrocław and L'viv is that of the economic and social modernization that the communist regimes carried out. One of the questions posed is how far the failure of Jewish communities to reestablish themselves as strong vibrant communities in the postwar era had less to do with official policies or with official and popular antisemitism, and more to do with the indirect effects of economic and social processes that led to the assimilation of Jews into the wider society, whether these were Jews 'of the street', i.e. who hailed from traditional, religious, Yiddish-speaking areas, or those who were already more urbanized and Polonized or Russified on the eve of the Second World War.

What is clear is that the majority of Jews in the postwar era lost contact with the religious, cultural and linguistic traditions that were the taproot of Jewish identity, as urbanization, industrialization, education and intermarriage with the dominant populations got underway. In Poland, for instance, from the late 1940s, many Jews took on Christian names and surnames that sounded more Polish.[3]

The aim, so far as sources allow (and they are inevitably uneven for the two cities) is to explore the experience of Jews in Wrocław and L'viv in relation to these five different contexts shaped. By choosing to compare two cities, I hoped to go beyond macro-level generalizations and to explore how Jewish communities re-established themselves at local level after 1945 — from scratch in the case of Wrocław — and also why these communities failed to grow. The two cities had substantial and vibrant Jewish communities prior to 1945, but these were completely decimated in the course of the Nazi occupation. Both briefly experienced an influx of Jews as a result of the forced migrations that took place following the end of the war. From the mid-1950s the Jewish community in Wrocław became the largest of any in Poland — it overtook Łódź at this time — yet it was a community in steady decline, its size falling from 17,747 in 1946 to 3,800 in 1960 (these figures are on the conservative side) or from 9.8 percent of the population to 0.9 percent of the city's population.[4] The Jewish community in L'viv was altogether larger, numbering 25,800 in 1959 and falling slightly to 24,362 in 1970, or from 6.3 percent of the city population (which stood at 410,678 in 1959) to 4.4 percent of the population (which stood at 553,452 in 1979). In 1931 Jews had comprised 24.1 percent of the population of Lwów; in 1989 they comprised just 1.6 percent.[5]

---

3 Ewa Koźmińska-Frejlak, "Polen als Heimat von Juden: Strategien des Heimischwerdens von Juden im Nachkriegspolen 1944-1949," *Jahrbuch zur Geschichte und Wirkung des Holocaust* 2 (1997): 92.
4 http://www.yivoencyclopedia.org/article.aspx/WrocpercentC5percent82aw (last accessed 4 February 2012)
5 http://ru.wikipedia.org/wiki/percentD0percent9BpercentD1percent8Cpercent D0percentB2percentD0percentBEpercentD0percentB2 (last accessed 4 February 2012).

1. The historical background

The chapter offers an overview of the history of Jews in Poland and Ukraine in the interwar years, with particular reference to Breslau and Lwów (L'viv), with a view to providing a benchmark against which the experience of Jews in communist Wrocław and L'viv can be judged. It examines the demography, social profile and political status of these Jews and seeks to trace their changing fortunes over time, particularly by focusing on the extent and nature of antisemitism in the two regions. The first part of the chapter traces the history of Jews in the German territories through to the 1930s, concentrating on Breslau. The second part looks at the life of Jews under the Second Polish Republic, again with a view to providing a point of contrast for the discussion of Jewish life in Lwów after it was incorporated into socialist Ukraine.

1. Jews in Breslau

Between 1800 and 1933, the Jews in Breslau constituted the third largest Jewish community in Germany, after Berlin and Hamburg, at a time when the city was the seventh largest in the Reich.[6] Jews overall made up only 0.95 percent of the Reich population and were concentrated mainly in large cities, although there were those who lived in rural areas and small towns.[7] In 1910 Breslau had a population of 512,000 and a Jewish population of 20,200[8]; Protestants made up 60 percent of the citizens of the city, a further 35 percent were Roman Catholics, and 5 percent were Jewish.[9] Up to 1914 Jews and non-Jews had close contact and interaction in Breslau and it

---

6 Till van Rahden, *Juden und andere Breslauer: die Beziehungen zwischen Juden, Protestanten und Katholiken in einer deutschen Großstadt von 1860 bis 1925* (Göttingen: Vandenhoeck & Ruprecht, 2000), 32.
7 Peter Pulzer, *Jews and the German State: The Political History of a Minority 1848-1933* (Cambridge: Harvard University Press, 1992), 138
8 Martina Steer, *Bertha Badt-Strauss: eine jüdische Publizistin* (Frankfurt/Main: Campus, 2005), 17.
9 Abraham Ascher, *A Community under Siege: The Jews of Breslau under Nazism* (Stanford: Stanford University Press, 2007), 31.

could be said that the Jews were closely integrated into the life of the city. In general Jews in Breslau belonged to the middle-class. A large number were lawyers, businessmen, and teachers. They also held positions in academia, making a major contribution to building the excellent reputation of the universities in Breslau, and were active in the cultural life of the city, for example in the opera and theater. They owned department stores and were active in commerce. Their children mostly attended the best schools in the city.[10] German Jews were thus better integrated into German society than Jews in any other country, some even being German nationalists.[11] German Jews in Breslau were indistinguishable from the rest of the German inhabitants of the city. They spoke German, dressed like the Germans and identified themselves fully with the Germans. They also showed patriotism during the First World War. Nevertheless there was still a kind of barrier between Jews and non-Jews. Jews faced obstacles in achieving positions in the civil service, the army or higher education, and their social relations with Gentiles might be called close but not intimate. The Jews of Breslau were not full 'insiders', but nor were they 'outsiders'.[12]

Defeat in the First World War and the political crisis that ensued caused a deterioration in relations between Jews and non-Jews. Between 1916 and 1923 there were antisemitic campaigns in the city that saw Jews excluded from teaching positions, medical associations, and the boy scouts. By 1919 antisemitic agitation on posters started to appear. In 1920, at the time of the Kapp Putsch, when right-wingers tried to seize power, some Jewish students who removed antisemitic texts from walls were locked in a cellar and roughed up. Half a year later antisemites staged a pogrom: they demolished a Jewish department store and stormed a hotel in which Jews from East Central Europe were accommodated. Although the police arrived in time and an outbreak of violence was prevented, one Jewish student was murdered by a group of Nazis. Another

---

10   Gregor Thum, *Die fremde Stadt: Breslau 1945* (Berlin: Siedler, 2003), 17.
11   Robert Gellately, *Backing Hitler: Consent and Coercion in Nazi Germany* (Oxford: Oxford University Press, 2001), 24.
12   Ascher, *A Community under Siege*, 20-21.

pogrom took place in Breslau on 23 July 1923 during a protest march against unemployment and hyperinflation. About 500 people plundered more than 100 shops, almost all of which were owned by Jews. During the outbreak of violence several Jews were killed and many wounded.[13] Already during the Weimar era Jews were becoming a declining minority in both demographic and economic terms.[14]

The economic situation of the Weimar government was always fragile and the inflation of 1923 followed, after a period of stabilization, by the world economic crisis of 1929/1932 fueled popular hostility against Jews. Jews were suspected of being speculators and swindlers and assumed to be intent on taking over the possessions of the German Volk. Proof of this was, supposedly, the presence of Jewish ministers in the government. Whereas individual savers lost money in 1923 and during the crash, Jewish departments, it seemed, continued to prosper.[15] Economically-based fears of Jews were amplified by fear of being swamped by foreign forces, of being dominated or surrounded by foreign influences [Überfremdung]. Jews coming from East Central Europe—the 'Ostjuden'—were the especial focus of these fears. By the 1920s twenty percent of German Jews were of East Central European descent, of whom approximately one-third had moved to German territories after the First World War. East Central European Jews dressed differently from Germans and their customs appeared strange and even sinister. Germans perceived them as socially and culturally inferior, coarse and loud. There was even a league which called among other things for the expulsion of the East Central European Jews from Germany. Of these East Central European Jews more than a half had Polish passports and some were 'stateless'.[16] There were indeed big differences between East Central European Jews and German Jews, East Central European Jews being reli-

---

13   Ibid., 51-52.
14   Avraham Barkai, *From Boycott to Annihilation: The Economic Struggle of German Jews, 1933-1943* (Hanover: University Press of New England, 1989),1-2.
15   Ascher, *A Community under Siege*, 51-52.
16   Ibid., 56-57.

giously more observant and less educated than their German counterparts. What is more, some of them did not adapt to the 'western' style of clothing and they continued to speak Yiddish. Thirty percent of the East Central European Jews who settled in Breslau came from Austria-Hungary, the rest coming from Upper Silesia and the province of Posen.[17] By the time Hitler came to power there was already a widespread perception that saw Jews as 'international conspirators', able to manipulate inflation, crisis and wars with the aim of achieving control over the stock market, or else as an alien force that threatened the German way of life.

2. The rise to power of Hitler and its effect on Jews in Breslau

Adolf Hitler's rise to power in 1933 and his racial policy on Jews brought an end to German-Jewish coexistence in the Weimar Republic in general and in Breslau in particular. Attempts were now made to exclude Jews from the economy and their property was confiscated. Hitler's obsessive racial antisemitism was actually only partially based on economic motives; for him Jews were to be excluded because of 'blood'. The twenty-five-point program of the NSDAP contained statements and definitions which drew a sharp line between Jews and true Germans: 'Point number four of this program: only a Volksgenosse [member of the folk community] can be a citizen. Only a person who has German blood, apart from any consideration of religion, can be a member of the community. Thus, no Jew can be a Volksgenosse. In particular, the concept of Volksgemeinschaft—the community of the Volk—was of central importance to the integrational capacity of Nazi ideology. This exclusion of Jews from the 'organic folk community' was the basis on which Jews were also excluded from economic and political life.[18] The aim of Nazi policy was at first to encourage Jews to emigrate

---

17 Norman Davies and Roger Moorhouse, *Mikrokosmos: portret miasta środkowoeuropejskiego* (Kraków, Znak, 2004), 336.
18 Barkai, *From Boycott to Annihilation,* 10-11.

and to undermine the material basis of their existence.[19] Some authors, however, claim that the implications of Nazi policy were far more radical, Jews being seen as an anti-race with which the 'Nazi humanity could not coexist [...] on the same planet'.[20]

In Breslau after 1933 the SA and NSDAP organizations gave free rein to their antisemitic hatred. For middle-class Jews the increase of violence and hostility towards them was incomprehensible, Breslau having a reputation for being one of the most liberal German cities. Theater director Paul Barnay was kidnapped by SA men and beaten with rubber and dog whips.[21] In another incident men from the SA came into court and shouted: 'Jews out!' and proceeded to chase and beat the judges and lawyers.[22] The number of Jewish advocates was officially reduced to sixteen. Twenty-eight Jewish doctors at hospitals in Breslau were given notices of dismissal. These actions were a prelude for the Day of Boycott—1 April—when the word JUDE was written on Jewish stores. In 1935 German Jews had their German citizenship revoked and laws were directed towards their total exclusion from the Volk. During the 'Reichskristallnacht' of 9-10 November 1938 Nazis destroyed Jewish property and synagogues throughout Germany and Austria. In Breslau Jews were forced to watch the burning of one of their synagogues and others of the city's nine synagogues were destroyed even earlier.[23] By 1939 Jews were forbidden to enter public spaces such as schools, theaters, cinemas and libraries and were forced to pay a contribution—one milliard German Reichsmarks. The process of 'Arisierung' ('Making it Aryan') of Jewish property followed.[24]

---

19 Ibid., xi.
20 Jehuda Bauer, "Some Introductory Comments," in *Insiders and Outsiders: Dilemmas of East European Jewry*, ed. Jonathan Frankel et al. (Portland: Littman Library of Jewish Civilization, 2010), 6.
21 Michael Wildt, "Violence against Jews in Germany 1933-1939," in *Probing the Depths of German Antisemitism: German Society and the Persecution of the Jews, 1933-1941*, ed. David Bankier (New York: Berghan Books, 2000), 181.
22 Gellately, *Backing Hitler*, 28.
23 Friedrich-Carl Schulze-Rhonhof, "Anstelle eines Vorwortes," in *Geschichte der Juden in Schlesien im 19. und 20. Jahrhundert*, ed. Friedrich-Carl Schulze-Rhonhof (Hannover: Stiftung Schlesien, 1995), 5.
24 Leszek Ziątkowski, *Dzieje Żydów we Wrocławiu* (Wrocław: Wydawnictwo Dolnośląskie, 2000), 103-112.

As a consequence of all these actions taken against the Jews a massive emigration of Jews from Germany followed. The first and the largest wave of Jewish emigration took place in 1933, when almost forty thousand Jews emigrated out of a total Jewish population of 525,000.[25] From 1933 to the end of 1937, between 126,000 and 129,000 German Jews emigrated, and in 1938 between a further 33,000 to 40,000 fled. Finally, in 1939 another 75,000 to 80,000 emigrated. German Jews who stayed behind were robbed, lost their jobs and were reduced to impoverishment. Eventually they were called up for forced labor.[26] So far as Breslau was concerned the Jewish population had already decreased from 20,200 to 18,200 by the time the Nazis came to power.[27] By 1937 there were 16,600 remaining in the city, although 720 left in that year.[28] Over half of the Jews living in Breslau managed to leave the city before the outbreak of the war and therefore survived.[29] Among them was the historian Fritz Stern. By 1938 more than half of Jews who still lived in Breslau were over fifty years old. Mostly it was young people who emigrated. Of those who emigrated in 1937, 18 percent went to Palestine.[30] Almost all the Jewish inhabitants of Breslau who stayed behind perished in the Holocaust. Between November 1941 and April 1944 seven thousand Jews were deported from Breslau and killed in Kaunas, Majdanek, Sobibor, Theresienstadt and Auschwitz.[31]

3. Jews in Lwów in 1918

Lwów, formerly known as Lemberg, was part of the Habsburg Empire from 1772 to 1918, when it was absorbed into the Second Polish Republic. Altogether there were about two million Jews in Austria-Hungary in 1914, roughly five per cent of the population. The majority lived in the small towns of Galicia and in the rural areas of Hungary and Bohemia, although Vienna, Budapest, Prague and

---

25 Barkai, *From Boycott to Annihilation*, 37 and 1-2.
26 Wildt, "Violence against Jews," 208.
27 Ascher, *A Community under Siege*, 92.
28 Ibid., 111.
29 Ibid., ix.
30 Ibid., 145.
31 Thum, *Die fremde Stadt*, 18.

other large cities had sizeable populations. Lemberg was the capital of Galicia, and the two main ethnic groups in the city were Poles and Jews. Its population in 1869 was 87,109, of whom 26,694 were Jews; in 1890 it was 127,943, including 36,130 Jews; in 1900 there were 44,801 Jews in a total population of 159,618. In general Jews in Galicia were socially integrated.[32] Antisemitic parties existed in Austria-Hungary, but the imperial government tended towards a policy of toleration towards Jews: the Austro-Hungarian army, for instance, was almost alone in Europe in promoting Jews to officer ranks.[33] In general, however, antisemitism was an important and integral part of the mentality of the inhabitants of East Central Europe from the middle of the nineteenth century, and this was reflected in the growing nationalist movements. The precariousness of the Jews' position was underlined as Polish and Ukrainian nationalist movements grew within the empire from the late-nineteenth century. Neither movement was sympathetic to Jews. Poles tended to see Jews as exploiters owing to their positions as estate lessees, moneylenders and innkeepers. Jews, for their part, tended to see the peasant population of Galicia—Ukrainians for the most part—as crude and stupid, and Ukrainian nationalist movement resented them for this.[34]

The First World War greatly exacerbated antisemitism in Galicia. On 1 November 1918 the West Ukrainian Republic was proclaimed in Lwów, several days before Poland declared its own independence. A popular uprising took place in Lwów, where most of the population were Polish, and several weeks later the Polish army took control of the city, although it failed in its bid to seize eastern Galicia from the West Ukrainian Republic. The republic

---

32 Philipp Ther, "Chancen und Untergang einer multinationalen Stadt: Die Beziehungen zwischen den Nationalitäten in Lemberg in der ersten Hälfte des 20. Jahrhunderts," in *Nationalitiätenkonflikte im 20. Jahrhundert: Ursachen von interethnischen Gewalt im Vergleich*, ed. Philipp Ther et. al. (Wiesbaden: Harrassowitz, 2003), 123-146.
33 William Macagg, "The Soviet Union and the Habsburg Empire: Problems of Comparision," in *Nationalism and Empire: The Habsburg Monarchy and the Soviet Union*, ed. Richard L. Rudolph et al. (New York: St. Martin's Press, 1992), 49.
34 John-Paul Himka, "Dimensions of a Triangle: Polish-Ukrainian-Jewish Relations in Austrian Galicia," *Polin* 12 (1999): 30.

promised Jews civil equality and national autonomy, but the Jews in Lwów were not certain who would be the ultimate victor in the Polish-Ukrainian war. The local Jewish National Council thus decided to announce its neutrality while the conflict was ongoing, which some Poles regarded as a sign of their support for the Ukrainians. The Ukrainians also condemned Jewish neutrality, interpreting it as a continuation of the traditional pro-Polish attitude of the Jews in the city.[35] Between 18 and 22 November, as Poles and Ukrainians were fighting for control of Lwów, Poles burned and pillaged the Jewish quarter of Lwów and murdered seventy-three Jews. In the eyes of the Poles, this was perceived as vengeance against the exploiting Jews who had never supported the historic claims of the Poles for the city — after all, a majority of the population was Polish.[36] In fact, of the 340 victims of the pogrom two-thirds were Ukrainians — which might suggest that the term 'pogrom' is misleading, and that it was more a military massacre fueled by Polish Anti-Ukrainianism, or even that it was a mindless outburst of brutality on the part of the Polish army against anyone not perceived to be on the 'right' side of the conflict.[37] The violence towards Jews which erupted in 1918 in Lwów was not an isolated example of anti-Jewish violence. For example, in April 1919 during the Polish-Russian war thirty-five Jews were murdered in Pinsk because the Poles saw them as being supporters of communism.[38] The events of these years showed in microcosm the problems that would beset Polish-Ukrainian-Jewish relations in the decades to come.[39] Pogroms against Jews were carried out by both Ukrainian

---

35 Ezra Mendelsohn, *The Jews of East Central Europe between the World Wars* (Bloomington: Indiana University Press, 1983), 52.
36 Ibid., 33.
37 Norman Davies, "Ethnic Diversity in Twentieth Century Poland," *Polin* 4 (1990): 149.
38 Daniel Blatman, "National minority policy, Bundist social organizations, and Jewish women in the interwar period," in *The Emergence of Modern Jewish Politics: Bundism and Zionism in Eastern Europe*, ed. Zvi Gitelman (Pittsburgh: University of Pittsburgh Press, 2003), 58.
39 Norman Davies, "Ethnic Diversity," 149.

and Polish forces, and each side tried to accuse other groups of being provocateurs and perpetrators of these crimes.[40]

4. Polish Jews and the Second Polish Republic

The Polish Second Republic was a parliamentary democracy between 1921 and 1926 and then an authoritarian government under Józef Piłsudski from 1926 to 1935.[41] Among the key problems it faced on coming into office was the issue of national minorities and, not least, the policy towards the Jews.

There were in 1921 2,849,000 Jews in the Polish Second Republic, and by 1931 this number had increased to 3,113,900.[42] They thus made up the second biggest minority group after the Ukrainians, who numbered five million. There were also approximately one million Byelorussians on the eastern territories and one million Germans on the western territories.[43] By 1939, Jews made up nearly 10 percent of the total population.[44] Poland thus had one of the largest Jewish populations in Europe. In 1921 Jews made up one-third of the urban population, and in Polesie and Volhynia they constituted over a half of the urban population.[45] By 1931, 75 percent of Polish Jews lived in cities and Jews now comprised 27 percent of the total urban population. In 1931 Lwów was the third largest city in the Second Polish Republic after Warsaw and Łódź, with a population of around 314,330[46] inhabitants, and it had the third largest Jewish

---

40 Michael Steinlauf, *Pamięć nieprzyswojona* (Warszawa: Cyklady, 2001), 19-20.
41 Jerzy Lukowski and Hubert Zawadzki, *A Concise History of Poland* (Cambridge: Cambridge University Press, 2001), 193.
42 Mendelsohn, *The Jews of East Central Europe*, 23.
43 Ronald Modras, *Kościół Katolicki i antysemityzm w Polsce w latach 1933-1939* (Kraków: Homini,2004), 49-50.
44 Bernard Weinryb, "Poland," in *The Jews in the Soviet Satellites*, ed. Meyer P. Duschinsky et al. (New York: Syracuse University Press, 1953), 210-211.
45 Mendelsohn, *The Jews of East Central Europe*, 23.
46 Wacław Wierzbieniec, "Organizacje żydowskie o charakterze asymilatorskim we Lwowie w okresie II Rzeczypospolitej," in *Żydzi i Judaizm we współczesnych badaniach polskich*, ed. Krzysztof Pisarczyk (Kraków: Antykwa, 2003), 139.

population.[47] In 1931, Jews made up 31.9 percent of the city's inhabitants, 67.76 percent of whom declared their mother tongue to be Yiddish.[48]

In the interwar period Polish Jews were among the most traditional in the whole of Europe yet they were also highly differentiated socially.[49] The typical Jew was active in the retail trade, Jews often working as shoemakers, tailors, bakers, artisans and shopkeepers. The majority lived in poverty and spoke Yiddish. In 1921, more than 60 percent of Poles who worked in commerce and business were Jews. Jewish businessmen were especially active in the textile and food industries. There was also a Jewish middle class. Figures from 1931 show that more than half of medical practitioners in private practices and one third of lawyers were Jews. Generalizing, one might say that Jews in interwar Poland were mainly lower middle class or proletarian, together with an intelligentsia and a wealthy middle class which was socially influential but which made up a rather small percentage of the Jewish population.[50]

Jews were also distributed unevenly across the territory and socially differentiated according to region. In the former German provinces there were not many Jews and they were Europeanized. In Galicia, by contrast, Jews made up almost 10 percent of inhabitants of the region and were strongly traditional, with many Hassidim who spoke Yiddish and wore caftans. The greatest number of Jews lived in central Poland, mostly in Warsaw and in Łódź (territories of the former Kingdom of Poland, commonly known as Congress Poland). They were mostly orthodox Jews (including Hassidim) plus smaller groups who had assimilated to Polish culture.[51] The identities of Jews vacillated between acculturation or Yiddishkeyt, between Zionism and Socialism, between secular identity and religious orthodoxy, between Jewish tenants/leaseholders and

---

47 Grzegorz Siudut, "Pochodzenie wyznaniowo-narodowościowe ludności Małopolski Wschodniej i Lwowa wedle spisu ludności z 1931 r.," w *Lwów: miasto, społeczeństwo, kultura*, ed. Kazimierz Karolczak et al. (Kraków: Wydawnictwo Naukowe WSP, 1995), 274-275.
48 Ibid., 275.
49 Modras, *Kościół Katolicki i antysemityzm*, 194 and 237.
50 Steinlauf, *Pamięć nieprzyswojona*, 28-29.
51 Modras, *Kościół Katolicki i antysemityzm*, 55.

Jews acculturated to a great extent. Between those who were poor and uneducated, and the educated such as lawyers, teachers and journalists there were huge differences in the ways they saw themselves.[52]

Upon independence, Jews in Poland tried to achieve national autonomy within the new state. In 1919 at the Paris Peace Conference Jewish leaders tried to convince the Polish government as well as the great powers that they would benefit from granting national autonomy to the Jews. In June 1919 Poland signed the Minorities' Treaty. Within the Treaty two articles were important for Polish Jews. One of them called upon the Polish government to allow the existence of Jewish schools, controlled by the Jewish authorities and funded by the state. The other article forbade the government from compelling Jews to violate their Sabbath. There was no mention made about the status of the Jewish kehile (kehile meaning in Yiddish an organized Jewish community), of a representative Jewish organization, of proportional Jewish representation in the Polish parliament, or of Jewish officials whose task it would be to look after Jewish interests in the Polish government.[53]

The constitution of 1921 guaranteed equality of rights to all of the Polish citizens without distinction according to their religion, nationality, origins, language or race. Jews benefited from the rights it bestowed and took advantage of the possibility to express themselves culturally and to act politically through the newly granted freedom of the press and freedom of assembly.[54] Nevertheless although Jews enjoyed the same rights as Polish citizens, it would be fair to say that the majority were not integrated into mainstream Polish population.[55] Orientation towards social and political integration, however, varied. Those least traditional believed that the recovery of Polish independence would bring a solution to the so-

---

52 Katrin Steffen, *Jüdische Polonität: Ethnizität und Nation im Spiegel der polnischsprachigen jüdischen Presse 1918-1939* (Göttingen: Vandenhoeck & Ruprecht, 2004), 12-13.
53 Mendelsohn, *The Jews of East Central Europe*, 34-35.
54 Steffen, *Jüdische Polonität*, 23.
55 Ibid.

called 'Jewish question', because it would lead to the fusion of Jewishness and Polishness. Many Jews who had not previously known the Polish language now learned it. For many, Polish became the language of daily communication, publication and education.[56] Some Jews, however, remembered the antisemitism that had surrounded the birth of the Second Republic and feared that increasing Polish nationalism would intensify discrimination against them.[57]

For the majority of Jews in the Second Polish Republic religion remained the essential point of reference for their Jewishness.[58] At the end of 1920s there were approximately 2,000 to 2,500 Jews baptized each year. A minority lost the ties that bound them to the Mosaic Faith, often with a view to smoothing the path to social advancement.[59] For some, political identification with Zionism or socialism served as an alternative to a religiously defined Jewishness.[60] Zionism influenced the educated Jewish population, but did not have much effect on plebeian Jews. The illegal Socialist movement, by contrast, did have influence on Jewish workers. Polish socialists even published in Yiddish, and some of the activists of the movement studied Yiddish to spread Socialist ideas among Jewish workers.[61] The relation of Jews to Zionism defies easy generalization. In Galicia Zionism was not strong, since there had been strong pressures historically for Jews to integrate into Austro-Hungarian society. Where Jews took over the norms and standards of the Polish language and Polish culture some identification with Zionism was not excluded. From this there arose a paradoxical dual feeling of belonging. A similar process had been underway in Germany, where Jews who differed from their fellow Germans only in

---

56   Ibid., 50-51.
57   Ibid., 27.
58   Ibid., 17-18.
59   Jolanta Żyndul, "Z Getta do asymilacji: Żydzi w poszukiwaniu tożsamości," in *Tematy żydowskie: historia, literatura, edukacja*, ed. Robert Traba et al. (Olsztyn: Wspólnota Kulturowa Borussia, 1999), 56-68, 63.
60   Steffen, *Jüdische Polonität*, 16-17.
61   Jerzy Tomaszewski, "The Jews in Poland 1918-1939: An emerging national minority," in *Major Changes within the Jewish People in the Wake of the Holocaust*, ed. Yisrael Gutman (Jerusalem: Yad Vashem, 1996), 117.

their religious confession nevertheless saw no conflict between being German and supporting Zionism.[62] The most nationalist oriented Jewish community on Polish territories was to be found in the borderlands (Volhynia). All these different shades of opinion reflected differing degrees of belonging to Poland and differing forms of Polish Jewishness or the Jewishness of Jews.[63] In Lwów, as in other cities, political differences led to divisions within the Jewish community. The Jews of Lwów were supporters of Orthodoxy, Zionism, Socialism or assimilationism.[64] Assimilationism as an organized movement urging Jews to acculturate to Polish life was very marginal, but social and cultural pressures worked to promote a degree of unconscious acculturation among larger numbers.[65]

5. Attitudes towards Jews in the Polish Second Republic

Jews in the Second Republic were objects of antisemitism, but of an antisemitism that was heterogeneous in character and subject to change over time. At the root of Polish antisemitism lay the historic antipathy of the Catholic Church to Jews as 'Christ killers', their culture seen as a challenge to the values and morality of the Catholic Church.[66] In more recent times, Catholic antisemitism — which was not universal within Church circles — had come to focus on the conviction of the existence of a Jewish-Masonic plot. But in general religious antisemitism was simply a taken-for-granted prejudice rather than a clear-cut theological position.[67] The Gazeta Kościelna, a Catholic newspapers in Lwów, for example, claimed baptism could change a Jew into a Christian but could not make him a Pole. Another newspaper — Mały Dziennik — opined that one could not trust even Jews who were baptized. Nevertheless, the newspaper Nasz

---

62 Steffen, *Jüdische Polonität*, 12-13.
63 Ibid.
64 Wierzbieniec, "Organizacje żydowskie," 139.
65 Ibid., 140.
66 Walter Laqueur, *The Changing Face of Antisemitism: From Ancient Times to the Present Day* (Oxford: Oxford University Press, 2006), 108.
67 Modras, *Kościół Katolicki i antysemityzm*, 194.

Przegląd published articles in which Catholic writers rejected racism as incompatible with Christian belief.[68]

Historically, the visibility of Jews in the retail sector had periodically fuelled bursts of popular resentment against them. But popular antisemitism had never been a constant, rather it had fluctuated in intensity over time, partly in response to the economic situation. The economic crisis of 1929 to 1933 inflamed popular antisemitism. For although the boycott of Jewish shops and firms encouraged by Endecja — see below — had only a limited impact on the shopping habits of Poles, and although the economic crisis affected the great majority of Jews as severely as it affected Poles, middle-class Jews were able to withstand the crisis. And this fed charges that Jews were profiting from the misery of ordinary Poles.[69]

Despite the pogroms that took place during the Polish-Ukrainian and Russo-Polish wars at the time of its birth, the Second Republic initially eschewed antisemitic policies and the outlook appeared to some Jews as promising. As already mentioned, the Constitution of 1921 stated that all minorities within the republic should enjoy 'full and free growth' and also that all religions should be treated equally.[70] Yet from the first there were political movements of an overtly antisemitic kind active in the Republic. According to Narodowa Demokracja (Endecja), the right-wing political movement that had sprung up in the latter part of the nineteenth century, all minorities within the republic had to be Polonised. Jews, in particular, were to be removed from the economic sphere in order to create a space for Poles. Endecja organized several boycotts of Jewish businesses. In 1923, the government introduced a quota system that restricted the number of Jewish students who could study at universities. According to the numerus clausus, the percentage of students from any national minority in the Second Polish Republic could not be larger than the percentage of this group in the overall population. There were even 'ghetto-benches' introduced at universities by right-wing students, where Jews were put at the back

---

68　Steffen, *Jüdische Polonität*, 282-283.
69　Modras, *Kościół Katolicki i antysemityzm*, 222-224.
70　Ibid., 50.

of the classroom.⁷¹ In May 1926 Piłsudski carried out a coup, backed by his Sanacja group (Sanacja meaning a 'Return to political health'), to replace parliamentary government with an authoritarian regime and to promote Polish national interests. To fight the Sanacja movement, Endecja created the Camp of Greater Poland (Obóz Wielkiej Polski) in which exclusion of Jews from economic and political life became a key political demand. Its leader, Roman Dmowski, second only to Piłsudski as a nationalist politician though only briefly in government in 1923, convinced the Polish urban middle classes that Jews were an obstacle to achieving their own social and economic aspirations.⁷² Although the government did not back such measures, it did not do much to stop the anti-Jewish violence and boycotts organized by Endecja.

Jewish political parties in interwar Poland mostly supported Piłsudski because he was perceived as less hostile than Dmowski. Piłsudski's enlargement and reorganization of Jewish communal organizations brought him support among orthodox Jews. And in 1927 his minister for religious matters and public enlightenment had banned the numerus clausus in higher education. The Polish-Jewish press in interwar Poland favored Piłsudski's 'Jagiellonian idea' of Poland, especially in comparison with the 'Piast idea' of Roman Dmowski, with its exclusivist notion of ethnicity.⁷³ Nevertheless, the numerus clausus was implemented despite the ban, and the government refused to support Jewish schools financially. Moreover, it did little to oppose the economic boycott organized by the National Democrats. Yet at the same time Piłsudski's policy towards Jews did little to endear him to certain circles in the Catholic Church that were close to Endecja and that accused him of seeking to create 'a Socialist and Jewish Poland'.⁷⁴

Polish nationalism of all shades tended to be nationally exclusivist. One-third of Polish inhabitants were ethnic minorities—

---

71   Geneviéve Zubrzycki, *The Crosses of Auschwitz: Nationalism and Religion in Post-Communist Poland* (Chicago: The University of Chicago Press, 2006), 57-58.
72   Modras, *Kościół Katolicki i antysemityzm*, 47.
73   Ibid., 52.
74   Ibid., 54-55.

Ukrainian, Jewish, Belorussian, and German — and in the borderlands Poles were a minority. Not only Jews were subjects of partial exclusion from full and equal participation in the social life of Poland. For Endecja, Jews and Germans were presumed to be intrinsically incapable of assimilating into the Polish state, in contrast to Slavic minorities, who could be Polonized.[75] According to the ideas of Endecja, in the best case scenario Poland would have only Catholic Poles as inhabitants.[76] Such attitudes were influential, with many coming to see Jews, in the words of Geneviève Zubrzycki, as 'dangerous chameleons and parasites on the Polish Catholic body'.[77] A new factor aggravating antisemitism in this period was the association made in nationalist propaganda between Jews and Communism. In the eyes of Piłsudski, Soviet Russia's weakness after the Civil War was a chance to try to detach Belarus and Ukraine from Russia and bind them to Poland. He was convinced that this was the best way to achieve and secure Poland's independence. The attempt by Jews in the eastern border-regions (so-called *Kresy*) to remain neutral during the Polish-Soviet war made them suspect.[78] More damningly, Jews were prominent in the communist parties of both the Soviet Union and Poland. In Poland they made up approximately one quarter of party members. Given that there were roughly three and a half million Jews, the 5,000 or so who were Communists constituted a tiny percentage of the Jewish population.[79] Nevertheless as Communists they were publicly visible, and so antisemitism in the interwar period absorbed the stereotype of the 'commie Jew'.[80] The influence of Nazi propaganda also played a part in strengthening this stereotype.

Polish antisemitism, however, in contrast to that of the Nazis, did not tend to perceive Jews in terms of biological difference. Cer-

---

75 Ibid., 55.
76 Ibid., 57.
77 Zubrzycki, *The Crosses of Auschwitz*, 57-58.
78 Antony Polonsky, "Introduction: The Jews of Galicia under the Habsburgs," *Polin* 12 (1999): 3-24.
79 Modras, *Kościół Katolicki i antysemityzm*, 392-393.
80 Steinlauf, *Pamięć nieprzyswojona*, 19-20.

tainly there was racial stereotyping — often going back to the nineteenth century — but race as the rationalization of antisemitism was largely missing.[81] Some authors insist that the right-wing parties did in fact deploy racialist thinking, but that their public influence was limited by mainstream politicians and by the Catholic Church. Others are struck by the almost complete absence of biological arguments in the discourse of antisemitism when compared with Nazi Germany. This conclusion results from the fact that the term 'Jewish race' was not used or was used not very frequently; instead, the use of terms such as 'psyche' and 'spirit' was wide spread.[82] Jews, in other words, were perceived as alien more for their psychological and cultural qualities than for their biological qualities. Nevertheless arguments against the mixing of Polish and Jewish 'psyche' were classically racist.[83]

We thus see a changing and internally contradictory public perception of Jews in the Second Republic. Even to those nationalists opposed to the chauvinism of Endecja, Jews were seen as culturally and racially alien, a view based on a mixture of religious, economic and ideological concerns. The Jew could be seen, depending on context and on the political position of the viewer, as an enemy of Christianity, a speculator and an exploiter, a communist or a spy.[84] Regardless of which label was pinned on Jews, their 'Otherness' not only remained but intensified in the interwar period.

6. Emigration of Jews

The conviction that the presence of Jews in Europe was a problem in the 1930's was widespread among Europeans. It is interesting, as Modras notes, to compare the fact that Jews were considered a problem in Germany where they made up about 1 percent of inhabitants while at the same time in Warsaw they made up 30 percent of inhabitants.[85] Because of the economic crisis and a radicalizing

---

81 Steffen, *Jüdische Polonität*, 279-280.
82 Ibid.
83 Modras, *Kościół Katolicki i antysemityzm*, 280-181.
84 Steffen, *Jüdische Polonität*, 24-25.
85 Modras, *Kościół Katolicki i antysemityzm*, 269.

Polish nationalism, Jews and other ethnic minorities came increasingly to be seen as a problem that required urgent resolution. Unemployment in Poland increased and reached the level of 50 percent in the countryside and 35 percent in cities; and it was commonly believed that the high rate of unemployment was caused by the overpopulation of the country. In 1931 the National Democrats came to see the 'Jewish problem' as the decisive element in the struggle to win power over the country and they forced the issue of emigration of Jews on to the political agenda. In 1936 the Polish government took on board the issue of the emigration of Jews from the country. The problem was to determine the place where Jews should settle. Yet embarrassingly for the government, many Poles too were keen to leave their homeland and settle elsewhere. This was, however, politically unthinkable for a nationalist government so the emigration project was limited to Jews, justified as a measure that would alleviate the economic situation of Poles and resolve the 'Jewish question' once and for all.[86] In the summer of 1937 the Polish Minister for Foreign Affairs prepared a document entitled the 'Colonial Thesis of Poland', in which the importance of emigration as a solution to the problem of unemployment was stressed. According to this, Poland should acquire colonial territories like other European states. In September 1937, on the occasion of the eighteenth annual session of the League of Nations, Poland formally asked for permission for some colonial territories to be granted for herself and for other overpopulated countries. In the same year, Józef Beck, the foreign minister, investigated Madagascar as a potential destination for Jewish migration from Poland.[87] Here parallels to the Birobidzhan project in the Soviet Union can be observed (discussed below). The idea of the settlement of Jews in Madagascar — a French colony at that time — was also considered by Nazi propagandists.[88] The Polish government sent a commission to

---

86 Modras, *Kościół Katolicki i antysemityzm*, 278.
87 Michael R. Marrus, *The Unwanted: European Refugees in the Twentieth Century* (New York: Oxford University Press, 1985), 186-187.
88 Laqueur, *The Changing Face of Antisemitism*, 93.

Madagascar with the aim of assessing the possibilities of establishing a Jewish settlement there. However, Beck did not treat seriously the so-called 'Madagascar plan', which was in his opinion only a political maneoeuvre to draw attention away from the real problems in the country.[89]

Among Jews too, especially among Zionists, the issue of the Jewish presence was also frequently referred to as a 'problem', 'issue', or 'question'. The Polish government supported Zionism. Marshall Piłsudski and other representatives of Sanacja strongly backed plans for the establishment of a state for Jews in Palestine, supporting the proposals of Vladimir Jabotinsky and his New Zionistic Organization. Jabotinsky was convinced that Poland should be privileged above other countries in the emigration programs. He also argued that the establishment of the state of Israel should not only be an issue of consideration for the United Kingdom, but should be in the subject of a discussion forum in which other countries would participate.[90] All in all, between 1921 and 1937 400,000 Jews left Poland, of whom approximately one third settled in Palestine, and by 1937 Polish Jews made up 40 percent of the population in the mandate.[91]

7. Jews, Ukrainians and Russians

The lack of deep Jewish-Ukrainian ties in the twentieth century was a consequence of political history. Ukraine had been alternately part of the Polish-Lithuanian, Austro-Hungarian, Russian, Polish and Soviet states, and Jews in Ukrainian territories had never developed a Ukrainian identity.[92] A Ukrainian identity of any sort only emerged at the end of the nineteenth century as Ukrainians actually began to call themselves Ukrainian. Before that they were called 'Ruthenians' in the Austrian part of the Habsburg Empire, 'Rusnaks' in the Hungarian part, and 'Little Russians' or 'Cossacks' in the Russian Empire. Jews who resided in Ukrainian territories

---

89 Modras, *Kościół Katolicki i antysemityzm*, 278-280.
90 Ibid., 284.
91 Lukowski and Zawadzki, *A Concise History of Poland*, 221.
92 Gitelman, "Native Land," 147.

were actually Russian Jews.[93] Ukrainian hostility towards Jews was based on similar notions to those pervading Europe. These included the teaching of Christian churches about Jewish responsibility for the killing of Christ and the popular view of Jews as heretics and sinners, disrespectful of Christianity, and the economic position of Jews as middlemen between landowners and peasants, perceived by the latter as exploitative agents of the former, and later as direct economic competitors with Ukrainian businesses.[94] Pogroms broke out in the 1880s and in the years 1903-1905.[95] Despite the fact that Jewish culture in Ukraine was influenced by Ukrainian culture, Jews and Ukrainians perceived themselves as totally different from each other. Jews differed with regard to religion, the most important marker of their ethnicity, but also with regard to language, areas of residence, profiles of occupation, life styles, dress, and food. Already at the end of the nineteenth century the migration of Jews from small towns with largely Jewish populations known as shtetlekh to urban centers, with the resulting development of large concentrations of Jews there, was a characteristic trend within the Jewish population. These new patterns of mobility, residence, and population growth were accompanied by shifts in typical Jewish employment and in social stratification.[96]

In order to understand Ukrainian-Jewish relations, the presence of a further nationality, the Russians, has to be taken into account. Most of what became Ukraine was part of the Russian Empire: there were 5,215,805 Jews in the Empire, representing about 4 percent of the population, of whom 30 percent lived in Ukraine. In the eight ethnically Ukrainian provinces almost 8 percent of the population was Jewish, and in urban centers Jews accounted for 27 percent of the population.[97] As a result of war, loss of territory and

---

93   Ibid., 146.
94   Ibid., 147.
95   Ibid., 145.
96   Mordechai Altshuler, *Soviet Jewry Since the Second World War: Population and Social Structure* (New York: Greenwood Press, 1987), 1.
97   Yury Boshyk, "Jewish-Ukrainian relations in Western Ukraine during the Holocaust," in *Ukrainian - Jewish Relationship in Historical Perspective*, ed. Peter Potichnyj et al. (Edmonton: Canadian Institute of Ukrainian Studies Press, 1988), 174.

a certain amount of emigration their number had been reduced to three and a half million by 1917.[98] The Russian population, too, tended to be antisemitic. Russian ethnic identity was defined in terms of the Orthodox faith, and so ipso facto Jews were alien. Dostoyevsky was not untypical in arguing that Jews were a harmful and alien element in the Orthodox community. However, Jews who converted to Christianity, did in fact formally, become free of all legal restrictions and limitations.[99]

There was a certain amount of cooperation between Jewish and Ukrainian political parties in the years up to 1917. Jewish and Ukrainian social democrats shared political and ideological principles and also respected each other's national goals. Nor did they use antisemitism in their agitational work.[100] However, the First World War saw a massive deterioration in the position of Jews, and the civil war between Reds, Whites and Ukrainian nationalists led to massive pogroms carried out mainly by the White and Petliurist forces. The first independent government in Ukraine established a Ministry of Jewish Affairs, and for a brief moment Ukrainians and Jews who had lived in intimate insularity for centuries struggled to forge a mutual rapprochement. But their efforts ended with failure in spring 1919, as pogroms erupted on a massive scale.[101] All in all during the civil war, about 50,000 Jews were killed and 100,000 rendered homeless on Ukrainian territories.[102] It is possible that this figure was even higher, but the exact number is unknown because of the lack of statistics. In Abramson's words the number of killed Jews between 1917 and 1921 'ran in the tens and even hundreds of thousands'.[103] 80 percent of the some thirteen hundred pogroms that were recorded occurred in the right-bank Kyiv, Podolia, and Volhynia, and importantly 80 percent of Jewish population lived

---

[98] Nora Levin, *The Jews in the Soviet Union Since 1917: Paradox of Survival* (New York: New York University Press, 1988), 3.
[99] Leonard Shapiro, "Introduction," in *The Jews in Soviet Russia Since 1917*, ed. Lionel Kochan (Southampton: The Camelot Press, 1978), 1.
[100] Boshyk, "Ukrainian-Jewish Relationship," 193-194.
[101] Henry Abramson, *A Prayer of the Government: Ukrainians and Jews in Revolutionary Times, 1917-1920* (Cambridge: Harvard University Press, 1999), xv.
[102] Gitelman, "Native Land," 137-157, 145.
[103] Abramson, *A Prayer of the Government*, 110.

there at that time. More than half of the Jewish communities came under attack more than once and two of them as many as eleven times.[104] This led to fierce conflict with the Ukrainian national movement, which the Jews viewed as responsible for the pogroms.[105] In the years of the Civil War the state organized the exchange between town and countryside so the Jews lost their position as mediators between the city and the countryside. Jewish traders were convicted of speculating and shot.[106] Shtetls were deserted and many Jews moved to cities.[107] At the beginning of Soviet rule, relations between the Ukrainians and Jews could not have been worse.[108]

8. Jews in the Soviet Union in the interwar years

The February Revolution of 1917 was perceived by the Russian Jews in a positive light, because it abolished the Tsarist regime and brought hope for the establishment of western-type democracy. On 2 April 1917 the Provisional Government issued a decree which lifted all restrictions upon rights of citizens based on race or religion, and so for the first time Russian Jews came to possess equal civil rights.[109] Following the October Revolution, the first years of Soviet power saw many secular Jews enter the state and party apparatus, and generally the construction of a secular Jewish culture, based on Yiddish, was encouraged. The Jewish Communists who were in ranks of the Communist Party built up their own section called Yevsektsia.[110] The Yevsektsia, meaning the Jewish section,

---

104 Ibid., 111.
105 Mordechai Altshuler, "Ukrainian-Jewish relations in the Soviet milieu in the interwar period," in *Ukrainian-Jewish Relations in Historical Perspective*, ed. Peter Potichnyj et al. (Edmonton: Canadian Institute of Ukrainian Studies, 1988), 284-286.
106 Heiko Haumann, *A History of East European Jews* (Budapest: Central European University Press, 2002), 208.
107 Ibid., 283.
108 Altshuler, "Ukrainian-Jewish Relations," 281-305, 286.
109 Joshua Rothenberg, "Jewish religion in the Soviet Union," in *The Jews in Soviet Russia Since 1917*, ed. Lionel Kochan (Southampton: The Camelot Press, 1978), 168-196, 169.
110 Altshuler, "Ukrainian-Jewish Relations," 281-305, 286.

was charged with combating the influence of Bundists and Zionists — significant rivals to the Bolsheviks among the Jewish population — promoting loyalty to the Soviet state among Jews in general and 'enlightening the Jewish masses in the materialistic world outlook'.[111] The problem was that hundreds of thousands of Jews still perceived their identity largely in religious terms and the Bolsheviks had little time for religion. For the first few years there was no attack on synagogues and rabbis similar to that launched against elements of the Orthodox Church who were seen to be sympathetic to the Whites. A lot of Jews were still able to observe the day of rest on Saturdays and not to work on Jewish holidays. Such a contract was possible in those manufacturing co-operatives (artels) and sovkhozes where all or a majority of members were Jews. In the co-operatives, members had official right to make a decision on which day of the week they wanted to have as a day of rest.[112] By the 1920s, however, the Bolsheviks went on a more coordinated offensive against religion. The Yevsektsiya organized agitational 'trials' designed to expose the falsity of the Jewish religion and to discourage religious schools and the observation of Jewish holidays and rituals.[113] Nevertheless until the Stalin years secular Jewish culture was allowed to flourish within parameters set by the regime.

In 1923 the implementation of the so-called *korenizatsiia* (indigenization) policy was launched to promote national languages and national elites.[114] In Ukraine this 'did in fact result in a decline of the Jewish share in various spheres of activity', as Ukrainians were promoted to positions of authority in party, state, education and culture.[115] Before the Soviet annexation of eastern Poland in 1939 there was 1,533,000 Jews in Soviet Ukraine who made up approximately 5 percent of the population.[116] Jews in the countryside, of whom some even became peasants, spoke Ukrainian or Yiddish.

---

111 Rothenberg, "Jewish Religion," 168-196, 172.
112 Ibid., 175.
113 Ibid., 172-173.
114 Terry Martin, *The Affirmative Action Empire: Nations and Nationalism in the Soviet Union, 1923-1939* (London: Cornell University Press, 2001), 10.
115 Altshuler, "Ukrainian-Jewish relations," 294.
116 Karel Berkhoff, *The Harvest of Despair: Life and Death in Ukraine under the Nazi Rule* (Cambridge, MS: Belknap Press, 2004), 60.

In the cities Jews mostly spoke Russian, although there were a few who perceived themselves as Ukrainian.[117] However, the promotion of Ukrainian national identity came about in part at the expense of Jews who had hitherto had influence out of proportion to their numbers in the party and state. Jews who were acculturated to Russian culture often felt negative towards the policy of Ukrainization because it resulted in them being passed over in the party, the bureaucracy, management and even the factory, in favor of Ukrainians, even when the Ukrainians had worse qualifications than them.[118] Nevertheless during the 1920s alliances between Yiddish and Ukrainian national circles served the purpose of countering Russification.[119]

The ethnic groups that benefited from *korenizatsiia* tended to be those that were the titular nationalities of recognized 'autonomous' territories. Jews were recognized as a national group so far as citizenship was concerned; but they lacked the territorial base and geographically concentrated population that many other ethnicities had, and this prevented them developing a national identity in the same way as, notably, the Ukrainians. Soviet Jews experienced a negative policy in respect of the practice of their religion — historically, the key marker of their ethnicity — yet did not have the same scope for the positive development of a secular soviet identity as other 'Soviet nationalities' in that they had no political institutions of their own.[120] According to the prevailing nationalities theory, each nation was supposed to acquire its own territory, and so discussions got underway to provide Jews with their own 'Jewish region'.[121] From 1928 Jews were encouraged to settle in Birobidzhan, along the Transsiberian railway close to the border with China, and from 1934 the region became an autonomous Jewish territory. It was designed, among other things, to be a counter to Jews who wished to settle in Palestine. In general the Birobidzhan project was unsuccessful, because only a very limited number of Soviet

---

117 Ibid.
118 Altshuler, "Ukrainian-Jewish Relations," 294.
119 Ibid., 298.
120 Rothenberg, "Jewish Religion", 171.
121 Haumann, *A History of East European Jews*, 209.

Jews settled there.¹²² This was due to the harsh climate and the unattractiveness to mainly urban Jews of settling in this remote spot.¹²³

The Soviet government first restricted and ultimately eliminated some of the traditional sources of Jewish livelihood but offered possibilities for the integration of Jews into new sectors of the economy in which they had not previously participated. During the 1930s, many Jews found employment in the proliferating industries of the new cities, especially in white-collar jobs.¹²⁴ In Ukraine before 1941 a policy was implemented of encouraging Jews to settle on agricultural land. Jews traditionally had been merchants, craftsmen, shopkeepers and the owners of enterprises, but now in southern Ukraine and Crimea some joined collective farms.¹²⁵

During the worst years of the Stalinist terror, Jews, like a majority of the Soviet people, lived in fear. Having relatives abroad, or relatives who were clerics, being of an 'alien' class background, having done military service in the White army, being in the wrong place during the civil war, having had family members arrested or de-kulakized, having a religious belief, a criminal conviction, prerevolutionary membership in another political party, or having sympathized with the opposition in the 1920s — all were possible reasons why one might be targeted by the state.¹²⁶ Nevertheless antisemitism as such continued to be outlawed. The pejorative word

---

122 Chimen Abramsky, "The Birobidzhan Project, 1927-1959," in *The Jews in Soviet Russia Since 1917*, ed. Lionel Kochan (Southampton: The Camelot Press, 1978), 64-77; Grzegorz Berendt, *Życie żydowskie w Polsce w latach 1950-1956: z dziejów Towarzystwa Społeczno-Kulturalnego Żydów w Polsce* (Gdańsk: Wydawnictwo Uniwersytetu Gdańskiego, 2006), 279-305.
123 Haumann, *A History of East European Jews*, 209.
124 Altshuler, *Soviet Jewry*, 1.
125 Martin, *Affirmative Action Empire*, 44; Artur Patek, "Projekt Birobidżan w teorii i praktyce ZSRR," in *Żydzi a lewica: Zbiór studiów historycznych*, ed. August Grabski (Warszawa: Żydowski Instytut Historyczny, 2007), 66.
126 Sheila Fitzpatrick, "The two faces of Anastasia: Narratives and counter-narratives of identity in Stalinist everyday life," in *Everyday Life in Early Soviet Russia: Taking the Revolution Inside*, ed. Christina Kiaer et al. (Bloomington: Indiana University Press, 2006), 24.

Zhid (Jew) was officially banned, and its use in public formally carried a prison sentence of up to a year. Ukrainians were forced to use the neutral Russian word — *ievrei*.[127]

9. The Second World War: Poles, Ukrainians and responses to the Holocaust

On 1 September 1939, one week after the signing of the Molotov-Ribbentrop pact, the German army invaded Poland and on 17 September the Soviet army entered eastern Galicia. Poles would suffer massively, but for Jews the war would prove catastrophic. The Nazi terror was, in scholar Norman Davies's words, 'much fiercer and more protracted in Poland than anywhere in Europe.'[128] The Nazis strove to destroy Polish culture and 'Germanize' the entire area. They sought to exploit the labour of Polish peasants and workers and prevent the Polish elites from organizing resistance. About two million Poles — about 10 percent of the ethnically Polish population — were killed, and about three million Polish Jews, or 90 percent of the Jewish population of the Second Republic.[129] In part this reflects the fact that the Nazis targeted their reprisals against the Poles — especially on the elites — whereas their policy towards Jews was one of indiscriminate destruction. The issue of relations between Poles and Jews under the Nazi occupation has been enormously divisive. For many years historiography was polarized between Polish historians, who stressed Polish aid given to Jews and pointed out that the passivity of Polish population in the face of the genocide was inevitable given the scale of Nazi terror; and Jewish historians who insisted that widespread antisemitism in Poland had led to Poles becoming secondary collaborators in the Holocaust. In more recent years, there has been more rapprochement, with scholars tending to agree that the Holocaust, though carried out on Polish soil, was the exclusive responsibility of the Nazis and that Poles were in no position to have prevented it. At the same

---

127 Berkhoff, *The Harvest of Despair*, 60.
128 Davies Norman, *God's Playground: A History of Poland in Two Volumes* (Oxford: Clarendon Press, 1981), 193.
129 Steinlauf, *Pamięć nieprzyswojona*, 28.

THE HISTORICAL BACKGROUND   43

time, some point out that as in the rest of Europe, the proportion of the population who offered assistance to Jews was tiny, although how far this was due to a genuine fear of reprisals and how far it reflected indifference on the part of the Polish population remains contentious.[130] There were, moreover, Poles who profited from the elimination of the Jewish population or who denounced Jews or helped the Nazis to kill them, although how far this occurred out of passionate antisemitism, out of situational pressures or out of self-protection and self-interest is difficult to judge.[131] It is probably fair to say that the majority of Poles were 'bystanders' as Jews were put on cattle trucks and sent to extermination in camps on Polish soil; yet what such apparent indifference meant - fear, silent horror, quiet satisfaction? — may never be known. Moreover, there were Poles, such as Zofia Kossak-Szczucka, who showed courage in helping Jews to survive[132] She organized help in the framework of an organization called 'Council for the Help for Jews' or ŻEGOTA. For her, such assistance was an obligation as a Christian, although in some respects her perception of Jews was classically antisemitic.[133] All one can say with any degree of certainty is that it was not possible for Poles to stop the mass killing of Jews, but that signs of solidarity with the persecuted Jews on the part of victimized Poles were few. This is why one may speak of Polish Jews and Poles as 'unequal victims' during the occupation.[134] And bitter memories of what had happened during the Second World War would poison

---

130 Joshua D. Zimmerman, "Introduction: Changing perceptions in the historiography of Polish-Jewish relations during the Second World War," in *Contested Memories: Poles and Jews during the Holocaust and its Aftermath*, ed. Joshua D. Zimmerman (New Brunswick: Rutgers University Press, 2003), 1-18.
131 See generally the publications on the Holocaust in Poland and the behaviour of Poles and on the Polish-Jewish relations; and notably, Jan T. Gross, *Neighbors: The Destruction of the Jewish Community in Jedwabne, Poland* (Princeton: Princeton University Press, 2001).
132 Feliks Tych, "Deutsche, Juden, Polen: Der Holocaust und seine Spätfolgen," 2012, http://library.fes.de/fulltext/historiker/00809002.htm (last accessed 31 January).
133 Zofia Kossak-Szczucka, "Protest!," in *Żegota: Rada Pomocy Żydom: wybór dokumentów*, ed. Andrzej Friszke (Warszawa: Rada Pamięci Walk i Męczeństwa, 2002), 74.
134 Tych, "Deutsche, Juden, Polen".

relations between Poles and the tiny Jewish population in the postwar years.

In Ukraine it has proved equally difficult to come to a common characterization of relations between the Soviets, Nazis, Ukrainians and Jews in the Second World War. The secret protocol to the Molotov-Ribbentrop pact led to the Soviet army entering eastern Galicia on 17 September 1939. Soviet collaboration with the Nazis in the dismemberment of Poland was justified in official propaganda as being motivated by the desire to aid the minorities of Ukrainians and Belorussians who were oppressed by the Polish government.[135] The Soviet aim was to 'Ukrainize' a region that had been a part of Poland since the First World War. The Soviets deported a number of members of the Polish elite and replaced Poles in administrative positions with Ukrainians. Ukrainian became the official language. Additionally, the university in L'viv was given a new Ukrainian patron, Ivan Franko.[136]

Following Operation Barbarossa in June 1941 the Soviets were swept out of eastern Galicia and the area was incorporated into the General Governorship that the Nazis had installed in Poland. Ukrainian nationalists, notably the Organization of Ukrainian Nationalists which had fought since the late 1920s against the Polish government, opted to collaborate with the Nazis. In eastern Galicia, as in Soviet Ukraine, many Ukrainians welcomed the Nazi occupation, something that emphatically was not true in Poland. The attempt of the OUN to establish an independent government in L'viv, however, soon provoked a brutal Nazi clampdown. Initially, the Nazis sought to play off Ukrainians and Poles, but their general aim, as in Poland, was to create 'living space' by reducing the Slav population to forced labour or starvation. With regard to the Jews, of course, the aim was the complete removal of Jews from this territory, although again initially the commandos of the Einsatzgruppen only targeted communist officials and members of the Jewish

---

135 Orest Subtelny, *Ukraine: A History* (Toronto: University of Toronto Press, 1988), 8.
136 Ther, "Chancen und Untergang," 137.

intelligentsia.[137] As in Poland, there is debate about the extent to which ordinary Ukrainians — not members of military units subordinate to the Nazis — participated in the persecution of Jews. Most Ukrainians appear as bystanders to the Holocaust, although how far this was pragmatic adaptation to the realities of power and how far it sprang from antisemitism remains contentious. Again it is important to remind ourselves that while the Nazis targeted Jews for extermination, several million Ukrainians, Poles and Russians died on Ukrainian territory at the hands of the German army.[138]

In L'viv there were 135,000 Jews at this time, a record number (this figure, however, is higher in some other sources, probably because Jews kept coming to the East from occupied Poland so that over time there were more and more people). This was due to the fact that many Jews had fled Poland to come to the city in 1939 and some had come from provincial towns within Galicia.[139] As the Nazis advanced on the city, Jews, in the words of Kahane, 'were overcome with terror'. Yet what actually transpired was beyond their 'wildest imaginings'.[140] Between 22 and 28 June 1941, as the Soviet army retreated, the NKVD executed several thousand inmates of L'viv's prisons, among them Polish, Ukrainian and Jewish intellectuals and political activists. Upon entry into the city, the Einsatzgruppe in retaliation instigated a pogrom in which about 700 Jews were killed by Ukrainians, including elements of the OUN, and perhaps 3,500 by the Einsatzgruppe itself. Later in July, Ukrainian militia were encouraged by the German occupiers to murder several thousand more Jews whose names appeared on prepared lists of supposed Soviet collaborators.[141] It was around this time that Himmler determined that the Jewish population must eventually be annihilated, although the project did not get underway until 1942.

---

137 Kurt Lenin, *Przeżyłem: saga świętego Jura spisana w 1946 przez syna rabina Lwowa* (Ciechanów: Fundacja Zeszytów Literackich, 2006), 78.
138 Kate Brown, *A Biography of No Place: From Soviet Ethnic Borderland to Soviet Heartland* (Cambridge: Harvard University Press, 2005), 212-213.
139 David Kahane, *Lvov Ghetto Dairy* (Amherst: The University of Massachusetts Press, 1993), 6.
140 Kahane, *Lvov Ghetto*, 5.
141 Ibid., 6-7.

Eastern Galicia—with L'viv as the capital of District Galizien—was absorbed into the General Governorship that ruled Poland rather than into the Reichskomissariat Ukraine. In the wake of the pogroms, the Nazis herded all Jews in L'viv into a ghetto that became one of the largest in Europe. It contained some 120,000 Jews most of whom would be deported to the Bełżec extermination camp or be killed locally during the following two years.[142] Jews were forced to wear armbands, close their businesses and form labor battalions. From March 1942 the policy of transporting Jews from the ghetto to the death camps got underway. By 1944 when the Soviet army reached L'viv only 823 Jews remaining in the city.[143]

Conclusion

The Holocaust marked a radical rupture in the history of Jewry in central and eastern Europe, so that it is impossible to see a great deal of historical continuity between the pre-1945 period discussed in this chapter and the postwar history of Jews discussed in the rest of the dissertation. The number of Jews was drastically and violently reduced and survivors of the Holocaust had to rebuild their lives after the war under new regimes, very often in new cities and new states. Many unsurprisingly chose to leave Eastern Europe altogether. The social and economic status of Jews in the regions we have examined was rather varied before 1939. Similarly the policies toward Jews implemented by the Nazi regime, the Second Polish Republic, and the Soviet Union all differed substantially. Even the nature of antisemitism –Catholic and cultural in Poland, racialist and 'scientific' in Germany—differed. Nevertheless the logic of political and economic developments across the region—with the partial exception of the Soviet Union—was essentially similar: toward heightened discrimination against Jews, towards violence in the form of pogroms and boycotts, and towards pressure to emigrate. At the social level a somewhat loveless cohabitation between ethnic

---

142 Eliah Yones, *Smoke in the Sand: Jews of Lvov in the War Years, 1939 - 1944* (Jerusalem: Gafen Publishing House, 2004).
143 Grzegorz Hryciuk, *Polacy we Lwowie 1939 -1944: życie codzienne* (Warszawa: Książka i Wiedza, 2000), 395.

groups gave way to antagonistic competition, with Jews sometimes the indirect victims of competition for dominance between much larger ethnic groups in these archetypical borderlands. Centuries-old antisemitism became politicized and radicalized throughout the region, albeit to different degrees, and this led ultimately, if not inevitably, to the physical annihilation of the Jewish presence from an area of Europe where it had been historically important. Nevertheless, despite the rupture of the Holocaust there were elements of continuity across the Second World War and prewar experiences did shape to some degree official policy and the life-chances of Jews in Soviet L'viv and communist Wrocław. But the radicalization of antisemitism had permanently sharpened popular perceptions of ethnic difference, even if it is hard to prove that it led to an intensification of hostility towards Jews. The tragedy of the Holocaust, moreover, seems to have had little impact in softening popular mistrust of Jews in the ethnically dominant populations of Soviet Ukraine and Communist Poland. Relations between Poles and Jews and between Ukrainian, Poles and Jews, in other words, did not change for the better as a result of the Second World; and in some respects, they may have worsened. Finally, and notwithstanding the formal rejection of nationalism and racism by the postwar Communist regimes, the poisonous legacy of ideologized antisemitism was to leave a dark stain on official policy towards Jews from the late 1940s.

2. Jews in Wrocław and L'viv, 1945-48

'In the postwar period Soviet Jewry represented a disoriented mass of people in search of spiritual and physical rehabilitation.'[144]

East Central Europe was in ruins at the end of the Second World War. War and the Nazi occupation had led to a loss of the Polish population of approximately 6 million. Of this number, 650,000 were combatants who died in battle and more than 5.3 million were civilians who perished at the hands of the Nazi, about 3 million of them Jews.[145] This chapter examines the resettlement of the cities of Wrocław and L'viv as Polish and Ukrainian cities, respectively, with particular attention to the Jewish populations. It compares the situation of Jews in the two cities and explores why so many Jews chose to leave East Central Europe. It also explores how the general destruction caused by the war, the breakdown in law and order, the change in borders, the uncoordinated movements of population, and the tension between the non-Communist majority in Poland and the nascent Communist regime created conditions in which pogroms against Jews flared up once more, although Wrocław and L'viv were spared the worst of this violence.

1. Shifting of the borders and the exchange of populations

The Potsdam Agreements of 1945 placed the new Polish border in the West on the rivers Oder—Odra and Neiße—Nysa. The border in the East was placed on the Curzon line (near Grodno—Brest Litowsk—Przemyśl), as proposed in 1919 at the Paris Peace Conference by the British minister George Curzon. The transformation of

---

[144] Joshua Rothenberg, "Jewish Religion in the Soviet Union," in *The Jews In Soviet Russia Since 1917*, ed. Lionel Kochan (Southampton: The Camelot Press, 1978), 341.
[145] Konrad Zielinski, "To Pacify, Populate and Polonise: Territorial transformations and the displacement of ethnic minorities in Communist Poland, 1944-1949," in *Warlands: Population Resettlement and State Reconstruction in the Soviet East European Borderlands, 1945- 50*, ed. Peter Gatrell and Nick Baron (Basingstoke: Palgrave Macmillan, 2009), 188-89.

the Polish borders was accompanied by an exchange of populations in those territories. The territory of Poland before 1939 covered 390,000 square kilometers. After the Second World War, 181,000 square kilometers of Polish territory in the east consisting of regions such as Podolia and Volhynia, part of Lithuania, and western Belarus, with an estimated population of 11.8 million in 1939, became a part of the Soviet Union. In the west and north, 103,000 square kilometers, comprising the so-called 'Regained Territories' or 'Recovered territories,' were annexed from Germany by Poland. Those territories were western Pomerania, eastern Brandenburg, and the southern part of East Prussia, Lower Silesia and part of Upper Silesia. Their estimated pre-war population numbered 9.1 million. In the new Polish territories in the West, Poles had constituted only a small minority before the outbreak of the Second World War. In Breslau, for example, less than 5 percent of the inhabitants had been Poles.[146] A consequence of the new borders, then, was an essentially forced movement of population. According to the agreements on 'evacuation' between the Polish Committee of National Liberation (Polski Komitet Wyzwolenia Narodowego, PKWN) and the Western republics of the Soviet Union, Poles and Jews with former Polish citizenship were forced to migrate to the new Polish territories. Further agreements changed the citizenship of people living in pre-1939 eastern Polish territories annexed by the Soviet Union after the Second World War. These agreements were signed by the Polish Provisional Government of National Unity (Tymczasowy Rząd Jedności Narodowej, TRJN) and the Soviet government on 6 July 1945.[147] In the 'Recovered Territories' in accordance with the agreement at Potsdam about five million Germans and a lesser number of Ukrainians were 'screened, collected, and expelled' from the newly established Polish territories.[148] Conversely, almost three million people in all returned or were forced to migrate to the newly

---

146 Thum, *Die fremde Stadt*, 15.
147 Włodzimierz Borodziej, Stanisław Ciesielski, and Jerzy Kochanowski, "Wstęp," in *Przesiedlenie ludności polskiej z kresów wschodnich do Polski, 1944-1947*, ed. Stanisław Ciesielski (Warszawa: Neriton, 1999), 6.
148 Zielinski, "To Pacify, Populate and Polonise," 189-90.

established Polish territories; they came mainly from the Soviet Union and Germany.[149] The census carried out in February 1946 shows that the population of Poland was 23,930,000. Of these, 20.5 million declared themselves to be Polish, 2 million to be German and about 400,000 people belonged to other nationalities, including 162,000 Ukrainians and 108,000 Jews. There were a further 400,000 people approximately who were expected to undergo a 'verification and rehabilitation' procedure to establish whether they were Germans or Poles.[150]

In central Asia there were people who had escaped from the Nazis and people who had been deported there during the Soviet occupation of Eastern Poland (1939-1941). The latter included about 325,000 Polish citizens. Among them, 53 percent were by ethnicity Poles, 16 percent Ukrainians and Byelorussians, and 30 percent Jews.[151] Of these Jews, 75 percent were male, 20 percent were women and 5 percent children. 60 percent were males between the age of 18 and 45.[152] Male Jews were in the majority because they had decided earlier than the women to escape to the Soviet Union, and

---

149 Anna Cichopek-Gajraj, *Jews, Poles and Slovaks: A Story of Encounters, 1944-1948*, unpublished PhD thesis, 2008, 94. Michigan University.
150 Zieliński, "To Pacify, Populate and Polonise," 190. In the case of those German citizens who declared themselves to be of Polish origin and who expressed a wish to remain in Poland, but who could not prove their identity, it was necessary, in order to be permitted to stay in Poland, for them to prove that before the war they had lived in Poland itself or in the 'Regained Territories' and that they had showed a 'positive attitude' towards Poles before and during the war. They were also forced to make a declaration of loyalty to the Polish state. These criteria, and their implementation, were not rigid, but the results of the verification / rehabilitation depended mostly on the local authorities who were in charge of applying the procedure. Sometimes it turned out that some ethnic German and Polish minority communities in the 'new' territories in the west, for instance the Silesians, Kashubians, Mazurs and Warmiaks–the so-called autochthons–some of whom were German citizens before the war, could not prove their origin owing to a lack of documents, language skill or witnesses, some of these conditions were relaxed by the authorities.
151 Jan T. Gross, *Und wehe du hoffst... Die Sowjetisierung Ostpolens nach dem Hitler-Stalin-Pakt (1939-1941)* (Freiburg: Herder, 1988), 169.
152 Józef Adelson, "W Polsce zwanej ludową," in *Najnowsze dzieje Żydów w Polsce w zarysie (do 1950)*, ed. Jerzy Tomaszewski (Warszawa: Wydawnictwo Naukowe PWN, 1993), 387-477, 387.

that decision had saved their lives.[153] Many of these returnees, however, did not identify with Jewry any more. [154] And many who returned had acquired a deep antipathy to the Soviet regime. After their arrival in Poland, these Polish Jews seized the chance to acquire Polish citizenship, in the belief that this meant an escape from communist rule. These Jews were more likely to settle in Poland than those who were moved there as a consequence of population transfer.[155]

The national minorities were a problem for the new Polish state. The government perceived the Ukrainian minority in particular as a source of instability. It is estimated that between 1943 and 1944, 60,000 to 70,000 Poles had been murdered by the OUN-UPA on the territories of Podole, Volhynia and Lublin. After the Nazis were driven out, there were still approximately 700,000 Ukrainians (including 150,000 Lemkos) on Polish soil, mostly in the regions of Kraków, Rzeszów, and Lublin. The Polish government unsurprisingly saw Ukrainian nationalism as a threat to the state. It favoured the voluntary relocation of Ukrainians and Byelorussians from the borderlands but in reality supported a 'final removal' of Ukrainians by force out of the southeast Polish territories and into the so-called 'Recovered territories' in the West and North. The plans of the Polish government to remove the Ukrainians were accepted by the Western Allies and the Soviet government.[156]

2. Jews and Politics in Poland

The Polish provisional government, which first resided in Lublin and then in Warsaw, was under Soviet control in military and political terms. Key positions were in the hands of communists. Until

---

153 Szyja Bronsztejn, *Z dziejów ludności żydowskiej na Dolnym Śląsku po drugiej wojnie światowej* (Wrocław: Wydawnicwo Uniwersytetu Wrocławskiego, 1993),24.
154 Irena Hurwic-Nowakowska, *Jeszcze raz o kwestii żydowskiej*, 24.
155 Albin Głowacki "Czy i dokąd wracać? Dylematy repatriacyjne Żydów polskich," in *Świat niepożegnany: Żydzi na dawnych ziemiach wschodnich Rzeczypospolitej w XVIII-XX wieku*, ed. Krzysztof Jasiewicz (Warszawa: Instytut Studiów Politycznych PAN, 2004), 165.
156 Zielinski, "To Pacify, Populate and Polonise," 190-209.

the end of 1947 campaigns were waged against the Polish nationalist, fiercely anti-communist guerillas. The government's policy towards Jews was positive in theory. Zionists such as Emil Sommerstein took over important posts in the Polish Committee for National Liberation (Polski Komitet Wyzwolenia Narodowego, PKWN), the first provisional Polish government, with Sommerstein heading the department for Compensation for Losses caused by the war at the Ministry of Finance. Between 1945 and 1947 the government saw in the Zionist movement an ally in the fight against British imperialism.[157] Even the Communists saw the presence of Zionists in government as a way of legitimizing the new political order in the eyes of Jews.[158] According to the Manifesto of the Communists who belonged to the PKWN, Jews were to be guaranteed full equality with other citizens. In February 1945 the Central Committee of Jews in Poland (Centralny Komitet Żydów w Polsce, CKŻP) was formed in Warsaw. It comprised a shaky coalition of Communists, Bundists, Left and Right Po'ale Tsiyon, Ichud and other smaller Zionist groupings. It was responsible for providing food, shelter, education, medical assistance, cultural activities, and employment for Jews and also for assisting the repatriation of Jews from the Soviet Union and assisting those Jews who wished to emigrate legally. It was funded by the government with the help of JOINT, the American Jewish Joint Distribution Committee.

A range of Jewish parties emerged following the end of the war, with Bundists and Zionists being the most influential. The membership of the socialist Bund had been much reduced during the war: in 1947 there were only 1,500 members of the party on Polish soil.[159] The members of Bund opposed the idea of Jewish settlement in Palestine and struggled to build Jewish autonomy on Polish territories. They desired a secular Jewish culture and the

---

157 Adelson, "W Polsce zwanej ludową," 475.
158 Natalia Aleksiun, *Dokąd dalej? Ruch syjonistyczny w Polsce 1944-1950* (Warszawa: Trio, 2002), 113.
159 Alina Cała and Halina Datner-Śpiewak *Dzieje Żydów w Polsce 1944-1968: Teksty źródłowe* (Warszawa: Żydowski Instytut Historyczny, 1997), 81.

flourishing of the Yiddish language.[160] They were active in helping Jews resettle in Lower Silesia, especially in the creation of production cooperatives. After the pogrom at Kielce they published a statement calling on Jewish workers to avoid panic and stay where they were.[161] The Zionists devoted themselves to helping Jews to go Israel. They opposed both the Bund and the Jewish fraction of the (Communist) Polish Workers' Party because they would not support the project of settling Jews in Palestine. Zionism was very popular for a time, since the Holocaust had convinced many of the need for a Jewish homeland. The sociologist Irena Hurwic-Nowakowska who conducted research on the Polish Jews in the years 1947-1950 came to the conclusion that Zionism and the issue of Palestine were issues that personally and emotionally touched most Jews.[162] Palestine was an issue of intense debate among the Polish Jews. Some convinced Jewish Communists even became Zionists after the Second World War, because having escaped to the Soviet Union during the war they had seen for themselves how the Soviet system worked. The Zionistic organizations and parties in Poland strove for the right of Jews to emigrate to Israel, since they regarded the reestablishment of Jewish life in Poland as impossible. But they were not united, differing in the ways they imagined the future form of a state of Israel, especially with regard to the role of religion and language. In the aftermath of the Second World War Lower Silesia became the center of the Zionist movement.[163] Yet the latter was to exist for only a few years, since the creation of the state of Israel in 1948 led to the banning of the Zionist—and other non-communist—parties.

---

160 Zvi Gitelman, "A Century of Jewish Politics in Eastern Europe: The Legacy of the Bund and the Zionist Movement," in *The Emergence of Modern Jewish Politics: Bundism and Zionism in Eastern Europe*, ed. Zvi Gitelman (Pittsburgh: University of Pittsburgh Press, 2003), 4.

161 Ewa Waszkiewicz, "Program i działalność polityczna Frakcji żydowskiej Polskiej Partii Robotniczej we Wrocławiu w latach 1945-1948," *Sobótka* 3-4 (1994): 302-303.

162 Irena Hurwic-Nowakowska, *Żydzi polscy 1947-1950: analiza więzi społecznej ludności żydowskiej* (Warszawa: Wydawnictwo Instytutu Filozofii i Socjologii PAN, 1996), 63- 64 and 72.

163 Ibid., 270-271.

In general among the Lower Silesian Jews, the most popular political party was the Polish Worker's Party. The latter had an over-representation of Jews in its leadership — Jewish party leaders including Jacub Berman, Boleslaw Bierut, and Hilary Minc. On 30 June 1946 the Communists engineered a referendum. The citizens of Poland were asked three questions. The first was whether the Poles want to abolish the Senat (Upper Chamber of the Parliament); the second was if Poles wished to nationalize the economy; the third asked for confirmation of the new borders of Poland. The Polish Workers' Party urged Poles to answer yes to all three questions.[164] The Jewish fraction of the Worker's Party campaigned hard for a yes vote among Jewish communities in Lower Silesia.[165] In Wrocław the fraction had 400 members in 1947. The following year, in the whole of Lower Silesia the fraction had 4,000 members.[166] Only a minority of Jews were active Communists, of course, but more believed that they were safer from antisemitism under a government controlled by the Communists than one controlled by PSL. The Central Committee of Jews in Poland, for example, allegedly spread rumours that the pogrom at Kielce was provoked by the Polish government in exile.[167] As the outbreaks of antisemitic violence made clear, there were nationalist-minded Poles who continued to see Jews as an anomaly within the Polish state, though how many continued to be contentious.[168] According to the memoirs of Noach Lasman, the interest of Jews in the leftist political movement was an obvious result of the experience of the Second World War and the fact that the Communists promised to treat all ethnic groups equally.[169] Jews were given jobs not only in central government but in local government and in state industries. They were

---

164 Waszkiewicz, "Program i działalność," 302-303.
165 Ibid.
166 Ibid., 308.
167 Magdalena Wajntraub-Busson, *Gesellschaftliche und politische Hintergründe des Judenpogroms in Kielce vom 4. Juli 1946* (M.A. thesis, Europa-Universität Viadrina, Frankfurt/Oder, 2005), 68.
168 Jan T. Gross, *Fear: Antisemitism in Poland after Auschwitz* (New York: Random House, 2006), 62.
169 Noach Lasman, *Wspomnienia z Polski: 1 sierpnia 1944-30 kwietnia 1957* (Warszawa: Żydowski Instytut Historyczny, 1997), 88.

allowed to work in the militia and also in the state security service. This merely fed the perception in the eyes of many Poles of Jews and Communists as being one and the same.

3. The transformation of Lwów into L'viv

The territory of Soviet Ukraine changed as a result of the Second World War, growing by one quarter (64,500 square miles). Its population also increased by an estimated 11 million people. Within the new territories there was a significant number of minorities, the largest being the 1,5 million Poles.[170] The exchange of populations between Poland and the Soviet Union began in the second half of 1944. In a letter to Nikita Khrushchev written by Konstanty Lytwin, Iwan Hrushezky and Mykola Bashan on 14 August 1944, the authors stated that at that moment most of the inhabitants of the city of L'viv – Lwów were Poles. In order to 'give back a Ukrainian character to the city', the writers recommended a mass, 'voluntary' resettlement of Ukrainians out of Poland and into the L'viv region. The authors wrote that the urban Ukrainian population should settle in the city of L'viv, and apartments and workplaces should be prepared for the newcomers. They also proposed that voluntary resettlement of Polish citizens should be encouraged.[171] The new Ukrainian government undertook a propaganda drive to encourage Poles to relocate within a Poland now shorn of its eastern territories. In response, the Polish government in exile, fearful that the exodus of Poles would weaken its claim to the 'lost' territories, tried to discourage Polish citizens from leaving what was now Ukraine.

The policy of exchanging populations was implemented very quickly. All in all, 787,674 Poles left the Ukrainian Soviet Republic. In Lwów as early as autumn 1945, 15,000 – 17,000 Poles were transported to Poland. By the end of the year, three-quarters of the Polish inhabitants of the city were on their way to Poland. For those Poles who tried to stay in the city life was made difficult. According to the diary of Gansiniec, a resident of Lwów, those who hesitated to

---

170 Paul Robert Magocsi, *History of Ukraine* (Seattle: University of Washington Press, 1998), 642.
171 Piotr Mitzner, "Die Säuberung Lembergs," *Karta* 2 (2001): 92.

leave at the request of the General Representative of the Polish Evacuation's Commission were forced by repressions to reconsider the relocation. This repression included confiscation of apartments, forced labour, confiscation of passports, and abolition of free movement.[172] Consequently most Poles had left by July 1946. [173]

In 1944 Lwów-L'viv had less than half its pre-war population. There were 154,000 inhabitants, of whom 66.7 percent were Poles, 26.4 percent Ukrainians, 5.8 percent Russians, and a mere 1.1 percent Jews. Following the redrawing of the borders, only the Ukrainians in L'viv could feel sure of being allowed to stay in the city. During the forced resettlement of Poles between 1944 and 1946 – the so-called 'repatriation' – 78,000 Poles left L'viv for Poland.[174] About 5 percent of the Polish population of Lwów, principally the intelligentsia, was transferred to Wrocław.[175] The term 'repatriation', used at the end of the Second World War to describe the forced settlements, of course literally means to come back to one's own home country. The term was introduced by the Communists and used in propaganda and agitation to persuade people to leave the former Polish eastern territories. But only those deported between 1939-1941 to Siberia who returned to Poland after 1945 could truly be called 'repatriates'. Those who left the eastern territories had never lived within the borders of the new Polish state. And those who chose not to leave were forced to acquire Soviet citizenship, respectively of the Ukrainian, Byelorussian or Lithuanian Soviet Republics.[176]

The settlement movement in L'viv was controlled by the Soviet authorities. The settlers consisted of three groups. The first were people from Galicia who spoke Ukrainian, mostly from small

---

172 Ryszard Gansiniec, "Auf Post für die Stadt: Auszüge aus den Lemberger Notizen 1944-1946," *Karta Historische Zeitschrift* 2 (2001): 122.
173 Ther, "Chancen und Untergang einer multinationalen Stadt," 143-144.
174 Ibid.
175 Archive of the Jewish Historical Institute Central Committee of Jews in Poland, Department of Repatriation, 303 / VI / 63.
176 Zbigniew Kurcz, "Aussiedlungen und Umsiedlungen in den östlichen und westlichen Grenzgebieten Polens," in *Bevölkerungstransfer und Systemwandel: Ostmitteleuropäische Grenzen nach dem Zweiten Weltkrieg*, ed. Helga Schulz (Berlin: Arno Spitz Verlag, 1998), 39-41.

cities and villages near L'viv. The second group came from Eastern Ukraine. This group consisted of skilled workers and labourers, who mostly spoke either Ukrainian or Russian. They can be classified as an urban population who were bound more to the Russian national culture than to the Ukrainian. The third group consisted of newcomers from the Russian Socialist Soviet Republic and other Soviet Socialist Republics. These people were members of the armed forces, engineers and technical experts, members of the Communist Party and employees of the secret service. They were Russian-speakers who did not assimilate the local culture.[177] There were no fewer than 16,000 engineers in L'viv immediately after the war. They were supposed to accelerate the modernization of the economy, but they also assisted in limiting the influence of Western Ukrainian nationalism, since most came from outside Ukraine. During the 1940's and 1950's, there were approximately one million newcomers to Western Ukraine.[178] By 1948, only 10 percent of the inhabitants of L'viv had lived in the city before the war.[179]

Jews in Soviet Ukraine who were not in the category of people allowed to leave for Poland were forced to escape illegally. Many first came to L'viv from other parts of the Soviet Union with the aim of escaping through Poland. They headed mainly for Łódź, the city in central Poland where Zionist organizations were able to help them get out of East Central Europe.[180] There they could obtain false documents and be accompanied to points where they could cross the border. The Zionistic organization 'Brihach' helped Jews leave Poland. They mainly left via the southeast and southern borders where they could arrive in the West. Other organizations that helped Jews in Poland were Pal-Amt (the emigration office of the Jewish Agency), and the HIAS (the Hebrew Sheltering and Immigration Aid Society), which took care of emigration to the United

---

177 Anna Wylęgała, "Die Russen und die russischsprachige Minderheit im gegenwärtigen Lemberg," in *Eine neue Gesellschaft in einer alten Stadt: Erinnerung und Geschichtspolitik in Lemberg anhand der Oral History*, ed. Philipp Ther et al. (Wrocław: Atut, 2007), 218.
178 Ibid.
179 Ther, "Chancen und Untergang," 125.
180 Archive of the State Security Service of the L'viv region, p. 7290.

States of America). The Central Committee of Jews in Poland had an office that took care of emigrants who had official permission to leave.[181] Jews with Polish citizenry were not allowed to take Polish passports with them but only documents that permitted them to travel. To cross the Polish-Czech border one had to pay one's guide 300 zlotych.[182] It is reckoned that between 1945 and December 1946 about 119,000 Jews left Poland illegally with the help of the Zionist organizations. The majority of illegal emigrants left in 1946, especially after the pogrom at Kielce in July of that year. This illegal emigration came to an end in February 1947 when the unofficial agreement on the illegal emigration of Jews came to an end.[183] Most emigrants headed for Palestine, but others ended up in the United States of America, Canada, Australia, and South America. Officially, only about 15,000 Jews left Poland, 11,815 of whom went to Palestine. Though this number leaves out the very much larger number of emigrants who left without official permission, it may give a reliable impression of the overall percentage of émigrés who went to Israel.[184]

The resettlement of L'viv transformed what had been a Polish city into a Ukrainian one. It continued for a long time to be seen by Poles as a symbol of their 'lost' territory. Yet L'viv was situated in a region in which Ukrainians had lived for generations and it was repopulated by Ukrainians from adjacent areas as well as from other parts of Ukraine. For Ukrainians, therefore, the city was a symbol of their long struggle for independence. The resettlement of the 'recovered territories' in the West was a very different affair. Germans had been the overwhelming majority of the population in Lower Silesia before the war and ordinary Poles did not think of these territories as Polish. In the eyes of both Poles and Germans Wrocław was a German city.

---

181 Szaynok, *Ludność żydowska*, 89.
182 Archive of the Polish Institute for National Remembrance, AIPN Wr 053/ 346, 133.
183 Albert Stankowski, "Nowe spojrzenie na statystyki dotyczące emigracji Żydów z Polski po 1944," in *Studia z historii Żydów w Polsce po 1945 roku*, ed. Grzegorz Berendt, August Grabski, and Albert Stankowski (Warszawa: ŻIH, 2000), 107- 111.
184 Ibid., 110-111.

4. Jewish settlement in Wrocław

When the city of Breslau/Wrocław capitulated on 6 May 1945 it was one of the most ruined cities in Europe.[185] With the arrival of the Red Army, the German population was forced to work, mainly in repair of buildings, the reconstruction of factories and burying the dead. Germans were given only half or a third of the food rations supplied to the Poles, and they were forced to vacate their flats and houses to make room for Polish newcomers. The first trains carrying officially 'repatriated' Poles, mainly from central Poland, arrived in Wrocław in January 1946, but people had been going west for months, knowing that Germans were fleeing and abandoning their property. According to a report of November 1945, thefts of public property in Wrocław and bribery were on a grand scale. It noted that people were coming to the city to steal things left behind by the Germans and take them home to central Poland.[186] Given that Poles in general had lost a great deal of property during the Second World War, many did not consider stealing German property a crime.[187]

The settlement of Poles in Lower Silesia began at the end of 1944. There was an immediate drive to Polonise the German city. In 1945 alone 1,500 street names and geographical descriptions were 'Polonized'. Jews participated in this process. A Jew Goldberg submitted an application for the removal of all German inscriptions.[188] In particular there was an attempt to make the city into a new Lwów. Important institutions were transferred there, including the prestigious Jan Kazimierz University and the National Institution of the Ossoliński family. Certain cultural artefacts, including the Racławice battle painting (Panorama Racławicka), the statue of Aleksander Fredro and some items from the churches of Lwów monuments, were also moved to Wrocław. Street names, journal titles,

---

185 Thum, *Die fremde Stadt*, 30.
186 Archive of the Polish Institute of National Remembrance, KGMO 35/922 (Report about the situation in Wrocław between 25 October and 10 November 1945).
187 Ibid.
188 Szaynok, *Ludność żydowska*, 151.

customs, dialect, and sense of humor were also deliberately and consciously transferred to Wrocław. This was all in the name of keeping the 'spirit of the Lwów' alive and transforming Breslau into a genuinely Polish city.[189] In June 1946 among the 23,160 so-called 'repatriates' to Wrocław, only 23 were Jews.[190]

Like all other citizens of Poland, Jews were encouraged to settle in the new Polish territories in the West. Plans for Jewish settlement, especially in Lower Silesia, were developed by the Jewish fraction of the Polish Workers' Party. The aim was to keep Jews in Poland. The Communists and political parties on the left wanted to liquidate antisemitism because it was associated with political parties on the right, their goal being to bind Jews to the new Polish state.[191] The response of Jews to this policy and plans was positive. By 1 July 1946, there were 69,993 Jews in Lower Silesia and 15,057 in Wrocław. The majority of them had lived in southern Poland and in the former eastern territories before the war and had survived the war on Soviet territory. According to a report of the Voivodship Committee of Jews, 49,429 Jews were said to have found work, with 8 percent even settling in the countryside.[192] With 15,057 Jews in 1946, making up 12 percent to 13 percent of the city's population, Wrocław had the second largest population of Jews in Lower Silesia. The first choice of the authorities had been to encourage Jews to settle in the much smaller city of Dzierżoniów.[193] But a report of July 1946 noted that Jews wished to settle in the 'larger Jewish centers', above all in Wrocław. They believed it would be easier to find work and enjoy a community life there. Also there were a lot of furnished apartments left behind by the Germans and help could be

---

189 Padraic Kenney, *Rebuilding Poland: Workers and Communists 1945-1950* (Boulder: Cornell University Press, 1997), 140.
190 Archive of the Jewish Historical Institute Central Committee of Jews in Poland, Department of Repatriation, 303 / VI / 63
191 Szaynok, *Ludność żydowska*, 23.
192 Archiwum Państwowe Wrocław, Wojewódzki Komitet Żydowski, Taśma nr T932 14.
193 Bronsztejn, *Wrocławscy Żydzi*,12.

provided by the Voivodship Committee of Jews.[194] By 1947 Wrocław had a total population of 224,800.[195] The changing number of Jews within that population can be seen in the following table:[196]

	November 1946	December 1946	January 1947	February 1947	February 1948
Wrocław	16,960	15,000	15,000	13,800	6,796

These figures show the number of Jews who were officially registered. Unofficially, according to the archival sources, the number of Jews in Wrocław in 1945 reached 10,000.[197] Some of these, however, may have left the city very quickly. For we must remember that as Jews were coming east to Wrocław many were doing so with the intention of leaving Poland altogether. It is estimated that the total number of Jews who left the Voivodship of Lower Silesia in 1946 was 28,000.[198]

We have rather good data on the social and occupational profile of Jews in the Voivodship of Lower Silesia. In January 1947 there were reckoned to be 56,000, of whom 20 percent were children. Men were more numerous than women, with 120 men for every 100 women, and 140 men for every 100 women in the age-group of 21 to 45, crucial for marriage ability. Those who survived the Holocaust were predominantly young, with only 2.5 percent above the age of 65. Only five percent of the Jewish population in Lower Silesia were traders and merchants, surprising given that so many came from the east where Jews had historically practiced trade. What is more, 80 percent of the people between the ages of 21 and 55 had a vocational-occupational qualification of some kind, and 40 percent of these were women. More than 60 percent of women between 21 and

---

194 Archive of the Jewish Historical Institute, Department of Repatriation (303/ VI / 63) Report summarizing the situation of the incoming migrants for the period of time from January to 1 July 1946.
195 Janusz Albin, *Wrocław: rozwój miasta w Polsce Ludowej* (Warszawa: Państwowy Instytut Wydawniczy, 1971), 77.
196 Szaynok, *Ludność żydowska*, 102.
197 State Archive of Wrocław, WKŻ (Jewish Voivodship Committtee) 17, 111.
198 State Archive of Wrocław, WKŻ Department of Settlement Protocol number 001, 59.

55 years of age were said to be able to work.[199] Data on Wrocław, however, suggest a rather more predictable profile. According to a report of 1946 24 percent of the 15,558 Jews in the city were craftsmen and artisans; 9.4 percent were workers; 5.5 percent were white-collar workers; 5.3 percent were in the free professions; 4.4 percent were traders and 1.6 percent (246 people) were merchants and industrialists. 318 people were manual workers and 119 people were classified as farmers. Students and pupils made up a group of 1,186 people. There were 4,943 people without profession. In the category 'various' there were 1,170 people, including manual workers.[200] Even though the predominance of artisans and traders reflects the social composition of Jews in the eastern territories from which many had moved, the occupational profile at the same time reflects the fact that Jews had been 'modernising' in terms of their economic activities during the interwar years.

5. Finding a job in Wrocław

The process of reestablishing Jewish organizations began quickly. The Jewish Committees, which were tasked with overseeing the settlement of Jews, devoted much of their energy to helping new arrivals find jobs.[201] The Communists wished to see Jews settled in 'productive' work, the hope being that, by proving themselves efficient and useful citizens, Jews would help dispel the antisemitic stereotype of their economic role as speculators and profiteers.[202] In Lower Silesia the Jewish fraction of the Polish Workers' Party thus demanded that even those awaiting emigration from Poland

---

199 State Archive of Wrocław, WKŻ Department of Settlement Protocol number 002, 69.
200 Archive of the Jewish Historical Institute, Documents of the Central Committee of Jews in Poland, Section of Statistics and Records, 303/ V/ 401, Report dated in 1946.
201 Archive of the Jewish Historical Institute, CKŻP Central Committee of Jews in Poland, Department of Statistics and Records, 303 / V/ 401,16. Report for the first half of the year 1946.
202 State Archive of Wrocław, WKŻ 17Jewish City Committee of Wrocław, Report written on 9 July 1948, 186.

should find jobs.²⁰³ Zionists supported the project of placing Jews in 'productive' jobs, since they saw this as a preparation for later work in Palestine. They, however, concentrated their efforts on creating kibbutzim, whereas the Communists favoured industrial and retail cooperatives.²⁰⁴ According to a statute from the head office of the economic organization for consumption and production, the aim of the cooperatives was to provide gainful employment, produce items of daily need and help find their members accommodation.²⁰⁵ In part, official support for cooperatives derived from the fact that they were seen as conducive to the building of socialism, but generally speaking they were seen to be a practical solution to a pressing problem.²⁰⁶ For many Jews arriving in Poland, especially to smaller towns, faced discrimination from employers and local authorities in their attempts to get work.²⁰⁷ In Wrocław many cooperative workshops and retail outlets specialized in clothing and accessories. In the second half of 1946, for example, a cooperative producing leather goods opened. At the start of its operations it employed 25 people, but two years later this number had risen to 269.²⁰⁸ In 1947, on the International Day of the Cooperatives, the cooperatives of Wrocław opened their own department store in the city.²⁰⁹ The formation of cooperatives gave Jews some basic means of survival but it also meant that Jewish workers and craftsmen remained in their own Jewish milieu. This created a community of belonging among the Jews themselves, with Yiddish often the language of communication, but it prevented their integration with

---

203 Andreas R. Hoffmann, *Nachkriegszeit in Schlesien: Gesellschafts- und Bevölkerungspolitik in den polnischen Siedlungsgebieten 1945-1948* (Köln: Böhlau, 2000), 60.
204 August Grabski, "Działalność frakcji PPR w CKŻP (jesień 1944-czerwiec 1946)," in *Między emigracją a trwaniem: komuniści i syjoniści żydowscy w Polsce po Holokauście* (Warszawa: Żydowski Instytut Historyczny, 2003), 15.
205 State Archive in Wrocław, C.S.W. "Solidarność", 2/2,5 / 67.
206 Arnold Goldsztejn, "Produktywizacja ludności żydowskiej na Dolnym Śląsku w latach 1945-1948," *Acta Universitatis Wratislaviensis* 1182 (1991): 128.
207 Adelson, "W Polsce zwanej ludową," 402.
208 Ibid., 94.
209 Michał Grynberg, *Żydowska spółdzielczość pracy w Polsce w latach 1945-1949* (Warszawa: Państwowe Wydawnictwo Naukowe, 1986), 70.

non-Jews in the workplace.²¹⁰ Indeed there were cases where Jewish cooperatives refused to employ Poles.²¹¹ Following the consolidation of the communist regime, Jewish cooperatives ceased to exist. According to an archival source from 23 May 1949, Jewish cooperatives were required to unite with Polish cooperatives.²¹² This undoubtedly reflected intensified suspicion towards Jewish organization in the wake of the creation of the state of Israel, but it was also a reflection of the fact that some Jewish cooperatives had become unsustainable as a result of continuing emigration.

Not all Jews found jobs in the cooperative sector. In April 1946 a branch of the economic center was established in Wrocław, which helped place Jews in industrial jobs. By 1946, for example, 100 Jews were working at Wrocław's 'Pafawag' (Państwowa Fabryka Wagonów), the National Rail Carriage Factory, which was one of the biggest producers of rolling stock in 20th century Europe.²¹³ Ambitious plans were laid to assign thousands of workers to jobs in textile factories, heavy industry, coal mines, and local industry in general. There were also plans for training and retraining those without the necessary skills. The plan even included provision to find work for the intelligentsia in industrial and public administration.²¹⁴ The new regime in Poland favoured the integration of Jews into the working class and the opening of avenues of upward mobility for loyal and hardworking Jews, especially young men. In April 1948 the First Meeting of Jewish Worker Leaders of Production (Pierwszy Zlot Żydowskich Robotników Przodowników Pracy) took place in Wrocław. It was a demonstration of the new kind of Jewish worker favoured by the Polish Workers' Party. This meeting opened with the following statement:

---

210 Ibid., 69.
211 Kazimierz Pudło, "Wybrane problemy z organizacji życia zbiorowego ludności żydowskiej na Dolnym Śląsku (1950-1967)," *Acta Universitatis Wratislaviensis* 1182 (1991): 156.
212 State Archive of Wrocław, WKŻ, Jewish Voivodship Committee for Lower Silesia of 23 May 1949
213 Ibid., 359.
214 Archive of the Jewish Historical Institute, CKŻP Central Committee of Jews in Poland, Department of Statistics and Records, 303 / V / 401, Report on conducted local briefings.

'We meet today in Wrocław, a very old Polish city, that returned to the Motherland after centuries of being outside the native country. We meet in this city with the aim of reporting to the whole country, to the government and to the whole organized community, the achievements of Jewish workers in the mines, factories and cooperatives of the Polish Republic.'[215]

As this testifies, Jews who identified with the working class and, not least, with the Poland of the so-called recovered territories were encouraged to play a role in building a communist society. They did so, in this period at least, as Jews: but primarily their identifications were to be as citizens of Poland and as workers making a productive contribution to the new order

6. German Jews

Polish Jews arriving in Wrocław were determined to exact revenge on local Germans. Jakub Egit, an active member of the city's Jewish organizations, recalled in his memoirs:

'The former victims of the Nazis extracted their vengeance on the spot. The homes, clothes and food left behind by the Nazis were distributed to the survivors. Factories, farms and businesses that were intact became their property. Yesterday's victims who were only 'numbers' now dressed in clothes left by the Germans and became masters not only of their own lives but also of the material possessions of those who had wished to exterminate them. Though emerging from the camps three-quarters dead, starved, frightened and exhausted, the survivors were consumed by the overwhelming desire for vengeance, vengeance, vengeance for what they had suffered, vengeance for the murder of their mothers, fathers and brothers, for the deaths of their violated sisters. The Nazis had good reason to fear their victims.'[216]

Such sentiment made life very difficult for the handful of German Jews in the city. Szaynok puts the number of these at 400 in Wrocław, although other authors believe the number was as low as

---

215 *Solidarność* 5-6 (1948): 6.
216 Egit, *Grand Illusion*, 43.

135.²¹⁷ It is estimated in one archival source that the number of German Jews registered in Wrocław was 963 people.²¹⁸ German Jews were far more assimilated and secular than the mass of Jews who came from the East. Carla Wolf, who witnessed the post-war situation in Wrocław, described how Poles coming to the city perceived German Jews as Germans, and were understandably hostile to them. She explains how difficult it was to persuade people that she was not really German, but only spoke German.²¹⁹ There was a considerable amount of friction between Polish and German Jews in Lower Silesia. When the German Jews of Hirschberg (Jelenia Góra) organized their own Jewish Committee and contacted the Jewish Committee of Polish Jews in Wrocław, they were told by Egit, the president of the Jewish Voivodship Committee of Lower Silesia, that there was only one Jewish Committee in Rychbach (Dzierżoniów) and that was the organization of Polish Jews.²²⁰ The City Committee of Jews in Wrocław even wrote letters to German Jews in Wrocław, saying they must vacate their apartments, and it even participated in transporting German Jews out of Wrocław.²²¹

This in part arose because the authorities in Wrocław had difficulty deciding whether to treat German Jews as Jews or as Germans. In the immediate aftermath of the war, there were German Jews in Wrocław who had been liberated from the concentration camps of Auschwitz–Birkenau and Mauthausen and to whom the authorities refused food.²²² Although German Jews were never forced to work as other Germans were, many were subject to forci-

---

217 The number of 135 Jews with German citizenship is given in Szyja Bronsztejn, *Z dziejów ludności*, 8, Andreas Hofmann, *Die Nachkriegszeit in Schlesien*, 371, Leszek Ziątkowski, *Die Geschichte der Juden in Breslau*, 113.The number of 400 German Jews is given in Bożena Szaynok, *Ludność żydowska*, 28.
218 Archive of the Jewish Historical Institute, Central Committee of Jews in Poland, Department of Statistics and Records, 303/ V/ 683.
219 Szaynok, *Ludność żydowska*, 43.
220 State Archive of Wrocław, Jewish Voivodship Committee, Protocols of the Jewish Committee of the Wrocław Voivodship, 8 August 1945 (number of the Zespół 415).
221 State Archive of Wrocław, WKŻ 17 (Jewish Voivodship Committee) Protocol from 4 December 1945 from the meeting of the City Committee of Jews.
222 Hofmann, *Die Nachkriegszeit in Schlesien*, 375-376.

ble resettlement. Not surprisingly, some chose to leave the city rather than suffer discrimination. However, the Voivodship Committee of Jews received letters from Polish as well as German Jews complaining about discrimination. There were claims that some Germans were working for the local authorities when Jews were unable to find jobs, claims that Germans were living in huge apartments with four or five rooms while Jews were living in cabins. Former prisoners of the Ludwigsdorf camp were, apparently, forcibly relocated. There were also complaints about clearly antisemitic behavior on the part of local authorities.[223]

Alongside the division between German and Polish Jews there was the usual division between religious and secular Jews. Irena Hurwic-Nowakowska, who studied survivors of the Holocaust immediately after the war, came to the conclusion that some Jews 'returned' to Judaism and established a new relation to Judaism on the basis of ethics. Some of this reconnection, however, may have been entirely practical, with Jews registering at synagogues and other Jewish institutions in the hope that this would facilitate making contact with lost relatives. At the same time, there was evidence that some Jews were anxious to 'escape from the Jewish group' in the aftermath of the Holocaust.[224] In 1946 the Jewish religious community in Wrocław was reestablished around the historic White Stork Synagogue, situated in Włodkowica Street, which had functioned as Breslau's main synagogue between 1829 and 1943.[225] There was a mikvah (a ritual bath), a kosher kitchen, a Talmud-Thora school, and a set of offices for the Congregation.[226] The more conservative elements of Jewry appear to have controlled it. Zygmunt Dzieganowski, who witnessed the aftermath of the Second

---

[223] State Archive of Wrocław, Department of Settlement, 4, Reporting about controlling the districts of Rychbach (Dzierżoniów), Wałbrzych, and Kłodzko. (...)Dopiero w ostatnich dniach zagrożono wysiedleniem byłym więźniom obozu pracy w Ludwigsdofie (...).
[224] Irena Hurwic-Nowakowska, "Jeszcze raz o kwestii żydowskiej," *Więź* 7-8 (1986): 98-99.
[225] Jerzy Kos, "Synagoga pod Białym Bocianem we Wrocławiu," *Sobótka* 2 (1991): 191-203.
[226] Waszkiewicz, *Kongregacja Wyznania Mojżeszowego*, 81-87.

World War in Wrocław, noted the predominance of Hasidim in the synagogue.[227]

7. Jewish educational and cultural organizations in Wrocław

The communist authorities in Poland, unlike their counterparts in Soviet Ukraine, initially allowed the creation of a system of schools and nurseries for Jewish children. The school in Wrocław, which was financed by the Central Committee of Jews in Warsaw, opened its doors on 10 January 1946. There were only three teachers at first and four pupils. By June 1946 there were six teachers and 150 children attending lessons.[228] The growth in numbers forced the school to move from Włodkowica Street to Zbożowy Square.[229] The number of pupils who attended the school was never constant. The highest number of children was 220 between 1 January 1946 and the end of June 1946. By the end of the second year only 21 pupils remained. This prompted the so-called 'school action' in 1948, which aimed to recruit more Jewish children. The action was intended to convince the parents of the children that the level of teaching at the school was better than at the standard Polish school.[230] The bulk of children who attended the school had spent the war years on Soviet territory. They made up 96 percent of the school children; the remaining 4 percent had spent the war on Polish territory.[231] Many had been in hiding during the war and were in a bad psychological and physical state.[232]

---

227 Zygmunt Dzieganowski, *Wrocławska szansa*, ZNiO, Akc. 46/ 2004/ 1. Zakład Narodowy im. Ossolińskich, Dział Rękopisów. (Unpublished manuscript of diary of Zygmunt Dzieganowski, a citizen of Wrocław after 1945).
228 State Archive of Wrocław, WKŻ-Jewish Voivodship Committet, Report written on 21 May 1948,222.
229 Archive of the Jewish Historical Institute in Warsaw (ŻIH), Documents produced by the Social and Cultural Association of Jews in Poland, Department of Organization, 61- 62, Correspondence (Korespondencja)
230 State Archive of Wrocław, WKŻ-Jewish Voivodship Committet, Report written on 21 May 1948,222.
231 Bronsztejn, *Z dziejów ludności*, 32.
232 Szaynok, *Ludność żydowska*, 74.

The main problem in these years was that most of the pupils knew Russian and were unfamiliar with Yiddish, the language of instruction, and with Polish.[233] According to a report on Jewish schools in Lower Silesia in 1946, while 30 percent of pupils knew Polish, only 20 percent could understand Yiddish and only 15 percent had an active knowledge of the language.[234] Similarly, at the nursery school in Wrocław in 1947 70 percent of pupils could not speak Yiddish. We should note the attempt to resurrect Yiddish at this time. According to some, the aim should be to make Yiddish the sole language of instruction, since the purpose of the schools was to promote the national Jewish 'spirit'.[235] In addition to Yiddish, the formal language of tuition, the syllabus of the Jewish school included Hebrew and Jewish history. At the nursery school the language of instruction was Polish but the Yiddish language was gradually introduced via songs and poems.[236] Teachers at the nursery were not enthusiastic about the idea of promoting Yiddish, since they felt that it was harder for children to learn two languages and, practically speaking, Polish was of more use to them. Yet many in the Jewish community at this time opposed the full assimilation of Jews into Polish society and argued that children would pick up Polish soon enough, and that within the Jewish educational institutions the promotion of Yiddish was vital to preserve Jewish identity. The compromise solution was that Yiddish remained the official language of instruction within the Jewish schools but Polish was also used.[237] The Jewish school began the school year in August

---

[233] Archive of the Jewish Historical Institute, Department of Statistics and Records, 303 / V / 401, 44. Report on the work of the schools with Yiddish language as a language of instruction at the Jewish Committee of the Lower Silesian Voivodship for the period of time: 1 January-1 June 1946.
[234] Archive of the Jewish Historical Institute, 303/ 2/ 130 Central Committee of Jews in Poland, Department of Controlling and Organization, Report on the activities of this department written in 1946, 16.
[235] State Archive in Wrocław, AP WKŻ 17, Information concerning the Yiddish language at the kindergarten, from 22 April 1947.
[236] State Archive of Wrocław, WKŻ (Jewish Voivodship Committtee) 17, Protocol of the meeting of the City Jewish Committee on 11 December 1946.
[237] State Archive in Wrocław, AP WKŻ 17 Protocol of the meeting of the City Jewish Committee on 23 January 1947.

1946, a month earlier than the official school year, so that the children could be given intensive tuition in Polish. In the first period, the pupils were taught using newspapers because textbooks were lacking.[238] The teachers very often had to use different languages in lessons. A reason for the decline in numbers at the school may have been that as pupils acquired facility in Polish they were transferred by their parents into Polish school.[239]

In 1946 a branch of the Association for Health Care was established in Wrocław, staffed by fifteen Jewish doctors. It was responsible for overseeing the general health of Jewish patients, for maintaining hygiene and preventing disease, for establishing medical centres and for organizing holidays in health resorts.[240] It also organized child-nurseries and holidays for children in health resorts.[241] The branch in Wrocław coordinated the work of a Jewish nursery, which in 1949 had 35 children.[242] In addition, there was another kindergarten which in 1947 had 231 children.[243] According to archival sources, there were also six orphanages in the city which nursed 25 to 100 children each.[244] The Zionist party 'Ichud' was in charge of the orphanage in Wrocław in which 52 children lived until January 1948, when they departed for Palestine.[245]

During the academic year of 1948-49 there were 255 Jewish students at Wrocław university. They made up 3 percent of the total number of university students in Wrocław at that time.[246] The total number of Jewish students and professors seems to have been

---

238 Archive of the Jewish Historical Institute in Warsaw (ŻIH), Documents produced by the Social and Cultural Association of Jews in Poland, Department of Organization, 61-62, Correspondence (Korespondencja).
239 Bronsztejn, Z dziejów ludności, 33.
240 Archive of the Jewish Historical Institute 324 / 1184 Society for Health Care, Reports (TOZ Sprawozdania).
241 Archive of the Jewish Historical Institute, 324 / 1180, Society for Health Care, Reports (Sprawozdania TOZ).
242 Archive of the Jewish Historical Institute 324 / 1190 Society for Health Care, Reports (TOZ Sprawozdania).
243 Szaynok, Ludność żydowska, 127.
244 Archive of the Jewish Historical Institute, 324/ 1172 (TOZ Sprawozdania) Society for the Healthcare, 54.
245 Szaynok, Ludność żydowska, 133.
246 Ibid., 45.

350.²⁴⁷ Jewish students had their own association and were involved in different political organizations. Yet the Jewish Committee of the Wrocław Voivodship regretted the fact that so many Jewish students did not speak Yiddish and were not interested in actively participating in Jewish organizations. The contact of students with the Committee consisted mainly of requests for financial help.²⁴⁸ The tendency of Jewish students towards assimilation was strong. The periodical "Głos Akademika ('Academic Voice')" noted in 1947:

> 'My friend P., who is an active member of the academic milieu in Wrocław and one of the leaders of the local organization Ichud, has made sufficient progress to feel that being Jewish and a member of Ichud has now become a disadvantage. He has changed his surname into P- ski and justifies this on utilitarian grounds. It is interesting to note that his father ...was not embarrassed to use his Jewish surname before the war. But his son suddenly feels the need to change his surname to P-ski, because it sounds better.'²⁴⁹

In order to resist trends to assimilation, the Voivodship Committee made strenuous efforts to promote Jewish culture, but a culture that was 'national' rather than one of the ghetto and 'street'.²⁵⁰ A Jewish theatre was established in Wrocław by the Jewish Association for Culture (ŻTK, Żydowskie Towarzystwo Kultury), which in 1950 was transferred to the charge of the Social and Cultural Association of Jews. It put on plays and shows in Yiddish such as 'Der Goldfaden-Traum' (The dream of Goldfaden") and 'Hershele Ostpoler'. It featured well-known actors such as Jakub Rotbaum and Ida Kamińska. It continued to be based in Wrocław until 1955, when it moved to Warsaw.²⁵¹ There was also a Jewish Music School in the

---

247 Archive of the Jewish Historical Insitute, Central Committee of Jews in Poland, Department of Organization and Controling, 303/ II/ 133, 8 Report of the Jewish Voivodship Committee in Wrocław.
248 Szaynok, *Ludność żydowska*, 136.
249 Ewa Koźmińska-Frejlak, "Polen als Heimat von Juden: Strategien des Heimischwerdens von Juden im Nachkriegspolen 1944-1949," *Jahrbuch zur Geschichte und Wirkung des Holocaust* 2 (1997), 92.
250 Archive of the Jewish Historiacal Institute, 303/ II/ 127 Report from 25 October 1949 of the Jewish Voivodship Committee and the Jewish Association of Culture, 21.
251 Ziątkowski, *Geschichte der Juden in Breslau*, 122.

city. In 1947 there were 100 children at the school and 160 in 1948. There was also a Ballet school for Jewish children.[252]

A key aim of the Organization for Creative Development (ORT, Organizacja Rozwoju Twórczości) was educational — to combat illiteracy and to create libraries and choirs. Significantly, in these years the use of Yiddish was not discouraged by the authorities, and the Organization played a key role in the promotion of the Yiddish press.[253] There was a publishing house called Yiddish-Buch (Yiddish-book), but it ran into difficulties, as with time fewer and fewer people were able to read the language. By 1951, only 111 people subscribed to the Yiddish-language press in Wrocław. Nevertheless, efforts were made to boost this number and by 1952 the number of subscribers in the city rose to 360.[254]

8. Antisemitism in Wrocław

Among the Polish citizens who were 'repatriated' from the newly enlarged Ukraine, Poles made up 94.5 percent but 4.3 percent were Jewish. It is likely that the Polish category included some who were ethnically Ukrainian, Byelorussian or Jewish. Between February and June 1946 some 136,000 Jews returned from the USSR to Poland, many of whom had lived in the pre-1939 eastern Polish voivodships. In July 1946, the Central Jewish Committee in Poland estimated the number of Jews in Poland at 243,000, although this was soon to fall sharply.

Given the hatred against Jews propagated by Nazi ideology, and amplified by elements in the Polish and Ukrainian nationalist movement, it is hardly surprising that anti-semitic violence broke out in Poland in the aftermath of the war. Ethnic divisions had sharpened in the interwar period, not least as a result of the concern of nationalizing states to categorise their populations, but it was violence and war that firmed up fierce sentiments of ethnic division

---

252 Bronsztejn, *Z dziejów ludności żydowskiej*, 267.
253 Grynberg, *Żydowska spółdzielczość pracy w Polsce*, 137-139.
254 Archive of the Jewish Historical Institute, 73 Social and Cultural Association of Jews, Protokół narady aktywu z udziałem Egita, analiza przeprowadzonej kampanii Idisz Buch na rok 1952 i wytyczne na rok 1953.

and competition. And the aftermath of the war, the redrawing of borders and population exchange further 'revised ethnic images of victims and perpetrators'.[255] However, the triggers for outbreaks of antisemitic violence were more conjunctural: the general misery caused by war, the breakdown of law and order, and the presence of the Soviet troops on Polish soil. Some of the violence against Jews was precipitated when Jews returned to claim property that had been seized by Polish neighbours in the course of the war.[256] Some anti-Jewish activity was purely opportunistic. During the transport of Jews to the new areas of settlement, some were robbed and sometimes killed. Meanwhile the nationalist underground systematically accused Jews of being allies of the new communist rulers and enemies of true Poles. The National Armed Forces (Narodowe Siły Zbrojne, NSZ) initiated the so-called 'railway action', murdering Jews who traveled in trains. Of the 2,000 Jews murdered in Poland by 1947, approximately 200 were victims of the 'railway action'. In some cases, the local militia did not search for the perpetrators even though enough evidence and witnesses could have been found.[257] But it was in the pogroms such as those in Kraków, Kielce, Kiev, and Topol'čany that violence toward Jews was manifested most dramatically.[258]

In the so-called 'recovered territories' there were no pogroms. This was due mainly to the absence of right-wing nationalist groups such as the Narodowe Siły Zbrojne — National Armed Forces — in the area and also because Lower Silesia lacked a numerous lower middle class.[259] This did not, however, mean that the authorities did not fear pogroms. The Poles who came to Wrocław generally regarded Jews negatively, as speculators.[260] A report produced by the political and pedagogical section of the Militia in Wrocław Voi-

---

255 Cichopek, *Jews, Poles and Slovaks*, 277-278.
256 Gross, *Fear*, 29.
257 Joanna Michlic-Coren, "Anti-Jewish Violence in Poland, 1918-1939 and 1945-1947," *Polin* 13 (2004): 35-61.
258 Archive of the Jewish Historical Institute (ŻIH), Central Committee of Jews in Poland, Department of Repatriation.
259 Adelson, "W Polsce zwanej ludową," 387-477.
260 Thum, *Die Fremde Stadt*, 127.

vodship between 15 April and 15 May 1946 (shortly before the pogrom at Kielce in July 1946) concluded that there were no signs of antisemitism in Wrocław. However, according to 'confidential' information, antisemitic remarks had been heard in Rychbach, Lignica, and Wrocław. These were blamed on 'reactionary elements' who thought it was wrong for Jews to participate in the rebuilding of the local industry and economy.[261] The adjective 'reactionary' may indicate that those accused were members of the Polish Home Army, which strongly opposed the new political system and the dependence of Poland on Moscow. Furthermore, between 15 July and 15 August 1946, shortly after the pogrom at Kielce, 15 members of the militia were dismissed for 'active carrying on of antisemitism' in the Wrocław Voivodship. Eight more people were arrested for their participation in antisemitic riots. In fact, there were some riots in Wrocław, but not pogroms. Attempts were made to combat antisemitism in the militia by giving seminars and presentations on the 'lack of enlightenment' among officials.[262]

The pogrom at Kielce, which is in central Poland, aggravated already bad relations between Poles and Jews. After the pogrom attempts were made to provoke riots by circulating rumors about a ritual murder in Wrocław, but the rumors were suppressed.[263] A special commission was quickly set up to prevent violent forms of antisemitism in Lower Silesia, with guards being set up at key points.[264] In the wake of the pogrom in Wrocław, as in Poland as a whole, the Central Committee of Jews organized Jewish self-defense committees.[265] Jews were given carbines, machine guns, and other weapons to protect the building housing the Jewish Committee on Włodkowica Street and the nearby synagogue.[266] There were

---

261 Archive of the Institute for National Remembrance, AIPN KGMO 35/ 922. Report of the Militia of the Wrocław Voivodship for the period from 15 April to 15 May 1946.
262 Ibid.
263 Szaynok, *Ludność żydowska*, 82.
264 Archive of the Jewish Historical Institute, Central Committee of Jews, Department of controlling and organization, 303-2-130,43.
265 Danuta Blus-Węgrowska, "Pogromstimmung," *Karta: Zeitzeugnisse aus Ostmitteleuropa* 3 (2002):161-162.
266 Davies and Moorhouse, *Mikrokosmos*, 546.

guards at every building that belonged to the Jewish organizations organized by the Voivodship Committee of Jews. There were also people charged with informing the militia and other people about the occurrence of antisemitic and anti-state intrigues.[267] The Jewish Committee of the Lower Silesian Voivodship did its best to calm feelings among local Jews and to discourage emigration.[268] The Committee opined that the new government was one of the most democratic in the whole of Polish history and expressed confidence that it would destroy the remnants of fascism in Poland. However, the Committee noted that most Poles were in an antisemitic mood (antysemicko nastrojona) and that many Jews would emigrate if they had the chance.[269] In the wake of the pogrom it is reckoned that around 90,000 Jews emigrated from Poland, 35,346 in August 1946 alone.[270]

9. The reconstruction of the Jewish community in L'viv

In 1944, with the arrival of the Red Army in L'viv, the Jewish community in the city began to rebuild itself. Those who came to the city often did not have any connection to it. L'viv was a 'station' for people previously deported to the Soviet East who with the end of the war were returning to Poland or intending to emigrate.[271] On 18 May 1944 the Jewish Antifascist Committee wrote to Molotov,

---

267 Archive of the Jewish Historical Institute, Central Committee of Jews, Department of controlling and organization, 303-2-130, 43; State Archive of Wrocław, WKŻ Jewish Voivodship Committee, Protocols of the main body of the Jewish Voivodship Committtee and other meetings number 415, Protocol of 17 March 1946 (Następnie w Milicji Obywatelskiej w miastach, w których mieszkają Żydzi, większy będą stanowili Żydzi. Czynna jest również milicja przemysłowa, która ma za zadanie pilnowanie obiektów fabrycznych. Do tej milicji będą przyjmowani Żydzi. W sprawie żołnierzy zdemobilizowanych, to przedstawiciele tychże zasiadają w komitetach i czynnie współpracują dla dobra wszystkich Żydów).
268 State Archive of Wrocław, WKŻ Jewish Committee of Lower Silesian Voivodship, 12th Protocol 27 July 1946.
269 Ibid.
270 Zieliński, "To Pacify, Populate and Polonise," 190.
271 Katrin Boeckh, "Fallstudie: Lemberg in Galizien. Jüdisches Gemeindeleben in der Ukraine zwischen 1945 und 1953," *Glaube in der 2. Welt* 4 (2002): 23.

drawing his attention to the material and moral condition of Jews and requesting he help the Jews on the liberated territories of the Soviet Union to find accommodation or transportation to return to their places of origin.[272] The local Soviet authorities in L'viv did their best to help, but it was the Jewish community of the city, defined, as we shall see below, as a 'national-cultural organization', which did most to provide financial assistance to survivors of concentration camps, Red Army soldiers, orphans, pensioners, and Jews who wanted to move to Poland.[273] Whereas in Poland Jewish political parties revived at this time, Soviet Jews did not have the opportunity to do the same and Zionist organizations in particular were the object of deep suspicion by the regime. However, illegal Zionist organizations, often based in Poland, did help Jews to emigrate from the Soviet Union following the end of the war.[274]

Given the constraints on political self-expression, much of Jewish community life in L'viv was built around the synagogue. In the wake of the Holocaust, Soviet Jews appear to have rallied around the synagogue not only in order to express their religious feelings, but also to experience 'a Jewish unity of belonging'. They needed to discuss their experiences with those who had suffered the same 'fate' and 'destiny'.[275] In that sense, attending the synagogue was an act and expression of Jewish identity. According to a decree of the Council of People's Commissars of 19 November 1944, a minimum of twenty Jews (a dvadtsatka) was necessary plus a potential location for a house of prayer for a group to register as a religious congregation. However, the authorities denied Jews the right to publish religious literature and refused them facilities for training rabbis and ritual slaughterers. In many places with only small Jewish communities, moreover, the authorities withheld permission to re-open synagogues. Non-authorised minyans — i.e.

---

272 Central State Archive of Public Organizations of Ukraine, TsDAGO, 1/ 23/ 3851.
273 Ibid., 34.
274 Archive of the State Security Sernice, L'viv, p-7290.
275 Frank Grüner, "Jüdischer Glaube und religiöse Praxis unter dem stalinistischen Regime in der Sowjetunion während der Kriegs-und Nachkriegsjahre," *Jahrbücher für die Geschichte Osteuropas* 52 (2004): 541-542, 550.

groups of ten males who came together to pray — were closely monitored by the secret police and sometimes closed down. The first chairman of the Jewish community in L'viv, Dr. D.B. Sobol', a Hassidic Jew, was accused by the security organs of complicity with US intelligence. In October 1945 he left for Poland with a group of Hassidim destined for Palestine. His successor was Lev Izrailevich Serebriannyi who was the chief signatory of a petition calling for the reopening of the synagogue. Other signatories included Ivan Arnol'dovich Rukh, who had been director of the Polish-Hungarian Chamber of Commerce from 1932 to 1939 and director of the Zhovkovskii works from 1939 to 1941 and at this time was a technical inspector in L'viv; and Aleksandr Iur'evich Shtakel'berg, a member of the Communist Party, a decorated military captain and deputy director of nutrition in L'viv.[276] The first rabbi of the synagogue, Yankel' Samoilovich Guragi, and the first cantor, Shmul' Moshkovich Zil'berfarb, do not appear to have arrived until 1947.

In Soviet Ukraine prior to 1940 there had been 657 synagogues. In 1947 there were 78 Jewish communities and 59 rabbis.[277] By April 1948 there were only 55 with 54 rabbis, reflecting the emigration of Jews from Soviet Ukraine.[278] In 1945 it was reckoned that approximately 5,000 Jews attended the city's synagogue. At the beginning of 1946 there were approximately 6,000 'Polish Jews' in L'viv but this was a transient population, with many intending to leave for Poland or further afield. By the end of 1946, there were about 1,500 Jews registered as members of the L'viv synagogue.[279] Yet while Polish Jews were leaving for Poland, Jews from the Eastern part of the Soviet Union were coming to the city. They were less religious than 'Polish Jews' and by the end of 1946 already constituted 95 percent of the community. Only 100-120 of them attended

---

276 TsDAHO, Report on the work of the UKSSR Commissioner of the council for the affairs of religious cults.
277 Central State Archive of Public Organizations of Ukraine, TsDAGO, 1/ 23/ 4556, 109. Documents produced by the Plenipotentiary for Religious Cults.
278 Central State Archive of Public Organizations of Ukraine, 1/ 70/ 1281, 7.
279 State Archive of the L'viv Region, Documents produced by the Plenipotentiary of Religious Cults, p- 1332-2-6-57.

synagogue regularly. But on important religious festivals and holidays approximately 1,500 Jews were present in the synagogue.[280] This was an ageing congregation, as the younger and more active Jews had left to start new lives. Data for 1950 show that 80 percent of regular attenders at the synagogue were aged 50 or over. Only 18 percent of attenders were between the ages of 30 and 50, those younger than 30 making up only 2 percent. Women comprised 60 percent of the regular worshippers.[281]

Lev I. Serebriannyi, head of the Jewish community in L'viv, from October 1945, who was chief signatory to the petition for a synagogue, told the authorities that he was essentially not a religious person and that his main interest was in extending material aid to Jews, especially by organizing workers cooperatives.[282] Perhaps under some pressure to make itself acceptable to the authorities by downplaying the importance of its religious raison d'etre, the Jewish community defined its aims as being: a) the national-cultural and religious unification of the Jewish population of L'viv city and oblast'; b) raising the political, national, and cultural consciousness of the Jewish population; and c) implementing various measures to improve the material living conditions of the Jewish population of L'viv and L'viv Oblast.[283] It is interesting to note that Serebriannyi requested that the Jewish community should not be called a religious community. This term was to be avoided, above all on the community's seal.[284] To expedite its aims various commissions were set up, such as those for cultural-religious matters, orphans, finance, and the search for family members.[285] In the first years the community spent much time trying to facilitate the legal exit of Polish Jews out of Soviet Ukraine. The evidence of its activity in food distribution is also plentiful. Until 1946 the community was

---

280 State Archive of the L'viv Region, Documents produced by the Plenipotentiary of Religious Cults, p- 1332-2-15.
281 Amar, "Yom Kippur in L'viv," 93.
282 TsDAHO F.1, OP 23. D. 1640, LL 155A, 176-180, Report on the work of the UKSSR Commissioner of the council for the affairs of religious cults for 1945, reprinted in Khanin, *Documents*, 68-72.
283 Ibid.
284 Ibid.
285 Ibid.

permitted to acquire goods and food packages from JOINT, the Jewish Joint Distribution Committee, via Iran[286] In 1946, among others, it gave food parcels to 232 students and provided scholarships for some of them.[287]

In contrast to the Polish authorities, who allowed Jewish organizations considerable latitude, the Soviet authorities were extremely nervous that the Jewish community organization in L'viv was a cover for a 'Jewish nationalist underground', i.e. for Zionist activity. Jewish leaders, including rabbis and leaders of minyans, as well as the committee members of the community organization, were all carefully monitored by the secret police. JOINT, as an organization that was based in the United States and with operations in Palestine was particularly suspect. All letters coming from abroad to the Jewish communities were intercepted.[288] The Soviet authorities believed that the Jewish community organization in L'viv was especially involved in liaison with Zionist organizations in America, the United Kingdom, and Palestine. It was accused of sending slanderous information about the apparently desperate situation of Jews in the Soviet Union to foreign organizations.[289] The same accusation was made against the Jewish Antifascist Committee in the Soviet Union. In March 1947 Lev Serebriannyi was arrested, the security organs having gathered evidence that he was organizing illegal border crossings of Zionist Hasidim from his base in the L'viv synagogue. At the same time, it is fairly clear that Serebriannyi was giving information to the security organs about the networks that had been set up to enable Jews to leave the Soviet Union and to funnel money from the USA. He had been an agent of the security services, the Cheka, from 1919 to 1926 and was recruited at the end of the war. A report from an agent of the Ministry of State Security states that 'citizen X' — almost certainly Serebri-

---

286 Memorandum of Colonel Meistruk. L'viv, 5 January 1950, reprinted in Khanin, *Documents,* 90-92.
287 Central State Archive of Public Organizations of Ukraine, TsDAGO, 1/ 23/ 5070, 17. Documents produced by the Plenipotentiary for Religious Cults.
288 State Security Service Archive of Ukraine, Kiev, n—105, 23, April 1946.
289 State Security Service Archive of Ukraine, Kiev, ф—16, o-7/ 4, 1948, vol. 6.

annyi—had warned Mordechai Dubin, a Zionist activist from Moscow, of his imminent arrest and advised him to leave Moscow. At the same time, information provided by 'agent X' seems to have been vital in enabling the security organs to arrest 25 Hassidim who were discovered crossing the border with false passports in January 1945. After his arrest in March 1947, Serebriannyi admitted to 'double-dealing' and was sentenced to five years in prison. [290]

10. Antisemitism in L'viv

As in Poland, the postwar years saw outbreaks of popular antisemitism in Ukraine. High-ranking leaders of the CPU CC received detailed information in the second half of 1944 about antisemitic activities that were perceived to be becoming more common. They included attacks by citizens on Jewish soldiers, beatings of people who had returned from evacuation and sought to acquire their property and homes, and refusals to employ Jews. On 7 September 1945 a pogrom erupted in Kiev, in which about one hundred Jews were severely beaten. Of those 36 were hospitalized and five died. This particular pogrom took place after similar though not equally violent episodes happened in eastern Ukraine in the summer of 1944. Although the authorities took steps to quell such antisemitism they were reluctant to confront the scale of it. Ukrainian leaders preferred to categorize these events as isolated incidents.[291]

A nasty pogrom was narrowly averted in L'viv by the swift action of the authorities. On the afternoon 14 June 1945 a crowd of Ukrainians and Poles, which soon grew to 400 people, gathered close to the synagogue in Krakow Market and began shouting that there were eighteen murdered children buried in the basement of the synagogue. The secretary of the Komsomol, Shuman, who happened to be on the scene was accused by the mob of supervising the killings. He tried to calm things down by taking Mikhailo Badak,

---

290 I.I. Osipova, 'Presledovaniia Khasidov vo L'vove v 40-kh godov', Khasidus po-russki, http://chassidus.ru/history_of_chassidism/osipova/7.htm (accessed 22 January 2012).
291 Vladimir Khanin, "Introduction" in *Documents on Ukrainian Jewish identity and emigration 1944 -1990* (London: Cass, 2003), 8.

an illiterate 34-year-old Polish porter at the railway station, into the synagogue to see if they could find any corpses. A Jewish woman who complained to a policeman about the antisemitic abuse to which she had been subjected by a 38-year-old peasant woman was attacked by the crowd, who yelled: 'The Polish people hid her from the Germans but now she kills Polish children and must be killed herself.' A 25-year-old Ukrainian metalworker, Ivan Fedak, grabbed an old Jewish man and started to beat him, calling on the crowd to set fire to the synagogue. He and four others were arrested. The police, accompanied by Rabbi Kopolovich, carried out a search of the synagogue but discovered nothing more sinister than a shed where chickens were slaughtered. The five were charged with incitement of bigotry against Jewish people under statue 156 of the Ukrainian Criminal Code. In addition, Fedak was accused of having been a police officer under the Wehrmacht from 1943, responsible for guarding Red Army prisoners of war and Jews on their way to the camps. Various people testified to the ways he had abused his power, seizing merchandise and demanding bribes. A Jewish survivor, Leonid Langman, testified that thefts from Jews by usually drunken Ukrainian police were an everyday occurrence. Fedak denied the charges and said that he had served in the police only to avoid service in the Ukrainian SS Galicia. The NKVD, which had taken control of the case, was discomfited when Fedak announced to the military tribunal that he was an informer for the Major Bilichenko of the NKVD. This stalled the judicial proceedings for months, while four of the five arrested were kept in custody. In May 1946, after intervention from the higher organs of the secret police, the case against Fedak was dropped. [292]

This near pogrom had similarities to the far more terrifying pogrom that took place in Kielce in Poland. Both incidents testify to the ways in which the blood libel, revived as a consequence of the war, had become a prime cause of violence against Jews. Typically,

---

292 State Archive of L'viv Region, Documents produced by the Plenipotentiary of Religious Cults.p-1332; Ilya Eli Luvish, 'Post World War 2 Pogroms,' http://www.ilyaluvish.com/post-world-war-2-pogroms/#_ftn40 (accessed 24 November 2011).

rumours would spread that Jews had murdered a Christian child and crowds would gather in the center of the town and threaten or carry out violence against Jews and Jewish property. Although the blood libel was centuries old, the conditions that triggered its reemergence were very much connected to contemporary fears: fears that the Jews would reclaim property belonging to them, fears that the Soviets were a Jewish regime that would exact revenge on Ukrainians or Poles. Moreover, although in the L'viv case the authorities prevented violence, the fact that the case was referred up the chain of command and was eventually dropped points to the fact that there was considerable antisemitism within the Communist Party itself. Just as many Poles and Ukrainians had no wish to see the return of Jews into their communities, so the Soviet authorities had no enthusiasm for dealing with the problem of returning Jews, in many cases viewing them with deep antipathy.

Conclusion

It is reckoned that 150,000 Jews left Poland legally and illegally between 1944 and 1948, often with help from religious and secular Zionist organizations.[293] Huge migrations of Jews from Poland took place after the war, many being Jews who came to Poland en route from Ukraine. Most did not wish to live on the territory where the Holocaust had taken place. And many who contemplated staying were induced to leave following renewed pogroms. Those who chose to remain in Poland concluded that life would be better for them under the emerging communist system. In Lower Silesia Jewish organizations strove to resurrect and preserve Jewish identity in the newly implanted communities. As we shall see, however, pressures towards assimilation were strong, especially among the more educated ranks of the population and this, combined with continuing emigration, made the task an uphill battle.

After the shifting of Polish borders, the expulsion of Germans, and the incorporation of eastern territories into the Soviet Union, the majority of the inhabitants of the Polish People's Republic were

---

293 Berendt, *Życie żydowskie w Polsce*, 7.

ethnic Poles. By 1946, Catholics made up 96.6 percent of the inhabitants of Poland. Because the new state lacked popular support and a mandate that was doubtful, political legitimacy was symbolically transferred to the church, which served as a rallying point for opposition to the communist regime. Religion and the Catholic Church became sites of moral and political resistance to the regime.[294] Cardinal Stefan Wyszyński would author a version of Polish nationalism in which the nation would be seen as a 'chosen people', a religious vision reinforced by nineteenth-century ideas of Polish messianism. According to Wyszyński, the Polish nation was 'a living organism constituted of families and common land, with a common faith and tradition, a common language, culture and spirit'. This was a highly ethnic vision of the national community, heavily influenced by the ideas of Roman Dmowski.[295] Clearly this was a conception of the nation at odds with the official conception of the communist regime. It was a conception in which Jews were doubly excluded from the Polish nation not only because they did not share the religion of the overwhelming majority but also because they were widely perceived as supporters of the communist regime. This conception did not go unquestioned, and in the course of the 1950s and 1960s official discourse and secular symbols of the state would influence the dominant conception of nationhood through the media, the school system, the workplace, the military, and other cultural and social institutions.[296] It was to this more secular vision of Polish nationhood that Jews would struggle to assimilate in the course of the 1950s and 1960s.

It was much harder for Jews to leave the Soviet Union, unless they were Polish citizens. However, many did so. In addition to a desire to escape the memory of the Holocaust, Soviet Jews were induced to try to leave because of the difficulties of practicing their faith of educating their children in Judaism. Some were also keen

---

294 Geneviève Zubrzycki, *The Crosses of Auschwitz: Nationalism and Religion in Postcommunist Poland* (Chicago: University of Chicago Press, 2006), 63.
295 Ibid.
296 Ibid.

to pursue their own business ventures, an impossibility in the Soviet Union.[297] As we shall see in the next chapter, the principal problem faced by Jews in Soviet Ukraine was that they were seen as covert Zionists, and thus objects of official suspicion even after the death of Stalin in 1953. In Ukraine, as in Poland, there was a strengthening of the idea that Ukraine belonged to Ukrainians, with Jews under pressure to abandon Yiddish in favour of Ukrainian. The religious landscape was more complex there than in Poland, however, and religion was less hegemonic in shaping conceptions of nationhood. After 1944, the Uniate Church, with a relatively organized membership of four million people in the western part of Ukraine, proved a thorn in the side of the Soviet authorities. Accused of having sided with Ukrainian nationalists and having welcomed the Nazi aggressors, the authorities, with cooperation from the Russian Orthodox Church, sought to liquidate it.[298] Yet the Russian Orthodox Church did not succeed in making western Ukraine Orthodox: they only achieved formal recognition of the Moscow Patriarchate and an administrative ban on the Uniate Church.[299] These conflicts within Christendom lessened the extent to which the religious affiliation of Jews was seen as a problematic, compared with Catholic Poland.

---

297 Archive of the State Security Service of the L'viv region, p-7290.
298 Markus Vasyl, *Religion and Nationalism in Soviet Ukraine after 1945* (Cambridge: Harvard University Press, 1985), 104-106.
299 Ibid., 112-113.

3. Jewish life from 1948 through the 1950s

> 'The core of the message of the anti-cosmopolitan campaign in the late 1940s was that the Jew remained a Jew, an eternal alien to the body national despite the circumstances. The term cosmopolitan appeared in public already during the war and with unmistakable reference to the Soviet Jews.'
>
> Amir Weiner, *Making sense of war*

This chapter explores the recreation of Jewish communities in the two cities from 1948 through to the late 1950s. It explores how in the Soviet Union the limited toleration of Jewish activity during the war was brought to a halt with the anti-cosmopolitan campaign that commenced in 1946, a campaign that in Ukraine was, to some degree, instrumentalised by Ukrainian national interests. It goes on to show how Poland was fortunate to be spared the official antisemitism that raged in the last years of Stalin in the Soviet Union and in Czechoslovakia. However, in both countries the creation of Israel led to the linking of official policies towards Jews with 'Zionism', seen in the context of the Cold War as a policy designed by the USA to destabilize communist regimes. The heaviest emigration was over by this time and these were years that saw in both cities an attempt by Jews to recreate Jewish life around institutions acceptable to the communist regimes. The range of acceptable activity was considerably broader in Wrocław than in L'viv, extending to education and cultural facilities that were no longer tolerated in the Soviet Union. In L'viv the synagogue was the only Jewish organization that remained and, always subject to close surveillance by the secret police, it was threatened with closure by 1960. In Poland the political crisis in 1956 saw renewed signs of popular (and some official) antisemitism although there was some liberalization of policy thereafter, including renewed immigration of Jews from the Soviet Union to Lower Silesia.

1. The Soviet Union and the Creation of the State of Israel

In April 1942 Stalin had authorized the formation of the Jewish Anti-Fascist Committee and in the course of the war there had been a strong assertion of Jewish identity within the Soviet Union. In 1947 the Soviet Union joined with the United States in endorsing the partition of Palestine into Jewish and Arab states and it supported Israel in the Arab-Israeli war of 1948. By this time, however, the political atmosphere within the Soviet Union was becoming toxic. In 1946 Zhdanov, Stalin's cultural commissar, launched a campaign against intellectuals accused of 'groveling before and slavish imitation of liberalism, formalism, and cosmopolitanism.'[300] This campaign quickly took on an antisemitic tone. At this time the Anti-Fascist Committee was starting to document the Holocaust. Members of the committee were travelling around the world with the aim of informing about the crimes of Nazis committed on Jews. Though formally supporting the creation of Israel, Stalin was unhappy with the vocal expression of support for Israel in Jewish circles.[301] In January 1948 Solomon Mikhoels, chair of the Jewish Anti-Fascist Committee and one of the loudest supporters of a state of Israel, was murdered by the secret police on Stalin's orders. Stalin's unhappiness was compounded following the promulgation of the state of Israel in May 1948, when Golda Meir arrived as first Israel ambassador to the Soviet Union. The sight of thousands on the streets applauding her visit to a Moscow synagogue on Yom Kippur on 13 October stiffened Stalin's determination to crush 'Zionism'. In October the members of the Anti-Fascist Committee were arrested, charged with bourgeois nationalism and with planning to set up a Jewish republic in Crimea with US backing. In L'viv the Union of Jewish Youth (Soiuz evreiskoi molodezhi), an informal group of high-school students pledged to fight antisemitism and to

---

300 Konstantin Azadovskii and Boris Egorov, "From Anti-Westernism to Anti-Semitism," *Journal of Cold War Studies* 4:1 (2002): 66.
301 Mirosław Czech, "Antysemityzm w ZSRR: rozjechani ciężarówką," *Gazeta Wyborcza*, February 8, 2010, http://wyborcza.pl/1,97737,7533270,Antysemity zm_w_ZSRR__rozjechani_ciezarowka.html (accessed 2 February 2012).

study Yiddish and Jewish history, was arrested in 1949 and most of its members sentenced to ten years imprisonment.[302] In Birobidzhan the Jewish cultural institutions that had been established under Stalin's earlier policy of support for 'proletarian Jewish culture' were closed down between late 1948 and early 1949, as were Yiddish theatres throughout the Soviet Union.[303] The wave of repression against leading Jews culminated in 1952 with the 'unmasking' of a plot by a group of prominent Moscow doctors, predominantly Jews, accused of conspiring to assassinate Soviet leaders.[304] Their lives were spared only because of the death of Stalin. From 1951, articles started to appear in which Zionism was construed as a 'reactionary national movement', associated with 'fascist methods of government and discrimination against the Arab population in Israel.'[305] The late-Stalinist period, then, which corresponded with the onset of the Cold War, saw two million Soviet Jews, who had hitherto been loyal to the Soviet system, recast as a potential fifth column.

Meanwhile in Czechoslovakia, Rudolf Slánský, General Secretary of the Czechoslovak Communist Party, and 13 other communist leaders, 11 of them Jewish, were arrested on 20 November 1952, accused of participating in a 'Trotskyite-Titoite-Zionist conspiracy'. Eleven were shot and three sentenced to life imprisonment. The trial arose as the result of a split within the communist leadership about the extent to which the Czech state should follow the Soviet model and was part of Stalin's purge of 'disloyal' elements in the national communist parties of Eastern Europe. As we shall see below, the Polish Communist Party, with its relatively large Jewish element, was relatively lucky to escape this ugly outbreak of antisemitism in the international communist movement.

---

302 Yaakov Ro'i, *The Struggle for Soviet Jewish Emigration* (Cambridge: Cambridge University Press, 1991), 47.
303 Alfred Skerpan, "Aspects of Soviet Antisemitism," *The Antioch Review* 3:12 (1953): 317.
304 Benjamin Pinkus, *The Jews of the Soviet Union: the History of National Minority* (Cambridge: Cambridge University Press, 1988), 219.
305 Ibid., 171.

The creation of the state of Israel posed problems for Jews. The idea of Jews as a 'nation' had always been problematic within the Soviet context. Whereas Birobidzhan had had the potential to become a republic that was 'national in form but socialist in content', the creation of a 'bourgeois' state of Israel infused the idea of a Jewish 'national form' with 'bourgeois' content. This potentially made Soviet Jews a diaspora nationality analogous to those nationalities that had been subjected to deportation during the purges and the Second World War, i.e. ethnic groups whose loyalties were seen to lie beyond Soviet borders. In addition, during the anti-cosmopolitan campaign Jews came to symbolize people without roots, bowing and scraping to all things foreign, passport-less wanderers. It was no longer enough to seek to integrate into Soviet society. In February 1949 some Jews who were discovered to be using Russian pseudonyms — e.g. Yakovlev instead of Klotsman — were denounced to the authorities and calls were made for the 'removal of the mask from the true faces of the cosmopolitans'.[306]

In Ukraine the anti-cosmopolitan campaign was used by the local intelligentsia to deepen the process of Ukrainization. Given that it was not possible to attack Russians openly, an attack on prominent Jews served as a means to promote Ukrainian interests both practically and ideologically.[307] In February 1948, the number of Jewish students allowed into medical and law schools in the university was restricted (as it had been in the RSFSR). In 1950 the department of Jewish language, literature and folklore at the Ukrainian Academy of Sciences was closed. The linguist I. Spivak, the head of department, had already been arrested in January 1949.[308] During the 1920s a vigorous network of schools for Jewish children using Yiddish as the language of instruction had existed, although these had tended to decline during the 1930s. Following the Second World War, the Yiddish schools were extended to the territories annexed by the Soviet Union, including western Ukraine, but during

---

306 Pinkus, *The Jews of the Soviet Union*, 159.
307 Ibid., 161.
308 The Case of the Jewish Antifascist Committee that was liquidated in November 1948, after having been established in 1942, is described in the Journal *From Archives* №3/4(8/9) ВУЧК-ГПУ-НКВД-КГБ" (1998).

the antisemitic campaign of 1949 they came under attack. By 1951 the last remaining Yiddish schools in the Soviet Union—in Birobidzhan—had been shut down.[309] So in contrast to Poland, where instruction in Yiddish was possible, Jewish children in Ukraine were taught either in Ukrainian or in Russian.

In L'viv the anticosmopolitan campaign, exacerbated by the declaration of the state of Israel in 1948, made life very tough for the Jewish community. The local council for religious affairs described the community as 'more like a community of trader-dealers than a religious one'. The local celebration of the establishment of Israel was said to have been marked by 'exclusivist pomposity'.[310] In 1949 the denunciatory rhetoric was stepped up. The principal charge now made against the local Jewish community was one of 'speculation' and 'embezzlement of socialist property', a charge that echoed the centuries-old antisemitic theme that associated Jews with greed and financial exploitation. In a report to the Ukrainian Central Committee from late 1949, the synagogue in L'viv was said to be a place where trade, speculation, and even crime were rife. It was proposed that the synagogue be removed from the centre of the city to a more acceptable location.[311] There were in fact two synagogues that had survived the Second World War, one in the center of L'viv and the other on the outskirts of the city. The report stated that 'all kinds of crooks from non-religious elements' gathered where the graves were situated to make money and to promote 'nationalist tendencies'.[312] As yet, however, the authorities took no steps to close the synagogue.

---

309 http://www.yivoencyclopedia.org/article.aspx/Soviet_Yiddish-Language_Schools (accessed 28 January 2012).
310 Amar, "Yom Kippur in L'viv," 95.
311 Ibid.
312 Ibid., 96.

2. Polish Jews and the Creation of Israel

Polish historians estimate the number of Jewish people living on Polish territories in March 1947 to have been about 124,000 people.[313] By this time, the phase of mass emigration was over, although many Jews were still eager to leave Poland and did so, following the creation of the state of Israel in 1948. In Wrocław there were reckoned to be 12,300 Jews in August 1950, yet 5,599 were said to have applied to emigrate.[314]

We saw in the previous chapter that the Polish government pursued a relatively liberal policy towards Jews in the immediate aftermath of the war. Jewish Committees functioned at different levels: the Central Committee of Jews in Warsaw, the Voivodship Committee of Jews, and the Jewish Committees in cities. And until 1948 Jews were allowed to express themselves politically in the Zionist movement. The aim at this time was 'national autonomy'. Indeed in comparison with other minorities, Jews in Poland after 1945 had relative freedom to express their culture and religion, being allowed to rebuild their institutions and associations, whereas Germans, Ukrainians and Byelorussians were allowed to do so only after 1956.[315] In this respect the new political system contrasted with the exclusivist nationalism of the Second Republic. It sought to include Jews in the Polish mainstream while recognizing their distinctive cultural and religious needs.

A turning point in the history of Jews in Poland came with the establishment of the state of Israel on 14 May 1948. This led to the banning of Zionist parties and a tougher policy towards any Jewish activity that smacked of Zionism. The Central Committee of Polish Jews, which had played such a central role in reestablishing Jewish life in Poland, was dissolved. Nevertheless, Polish anti-Zionist pol-

---

313 Stankowski, "Nowe spojrzenie na statystyki," 107-111.
314 Szaynok, *Ludność żydowska*, 194; Stankowski, "Nowe spojrzenie na statystyki," 114.
315 August Grabski, "Kształtowanie się pierwotnego programu żydowskich komunistów w Polsce po Holocauście," in *Studia z historii Żydów w Polsce po 1945 roku*, ed. Grzegorz Berendt, August Grabski, and Albert Stankowski (Warszawa: Żydowski Instytut Historyczny, 2000), 67.

icy continued to differ in many respects from that executed by Moscow. Whereas in Czechoslovakia and the Soviet Union there was outright antisemitism, the Polish government succeeded in resisting this, not least because Jews were well represented in the leadership of the party. Nevertheless because the popularity of the Polish United Workers' Party (Polska Zjednoczona Partia Robotnicza, PZPR) was so low and the visibility of Jewish activists so high, the general secretary of the party, Władysław Gomułka, took steps to decrease Jewish visibility in the higher levels of the party and state. At the June 1948 plenum he blamed the 'erroneous national policy' of the interwar years for the fact that Jewish representation in the party was so high. In December 1948 he wrote a letter to Stalin stating that he intended to reduce the number of Jews in the higher ranks of the party and complained that his plans were being thwarted by 'political opponents'.[316]

> '[...] On the basis of my numerous observations, I can confirm with complete responsibility that some of the Jewish comrades do not feel tied by any bonds to the Polish nation and therefore to the Polish working class. They take a position that can be designated by the label of national nihilism. Attitudes like this, however, are not taken into consideration at all when candidates for various high positions are selected. [...] I actually consider it necessary to discontinue any further increase in the percentage of the Jewish element within the state as well as the party apparatus, but also to decrease progressively this percentage, especially within the higher echelons of that apparatus. On the basis of the experience I gained during the period when I occupied the post of Party General Secretary, I am convinced that given the situation in which I find myself, I could not take the smallest step in that direction without risking various kinds of open or surreptitious campaigns targeted to ultimately 'finish me off' within the Party. As a Politburo member, I would not be able to treat passively the matter under discussion.'[317]

Stalin was not impressed and urged the Polish president, the hardline Stalinist Bolesław Bierut, who some claim was himself Jewish, to pursue the case against Gomułka.

Some historians think that in the early 1950s there may have been a move to organize the Polish equivalent of the Slánský trial,

---

[316] Andre Gerrits, *The Myth of Jewish Communism: A Historical Interpretation* (Brussels: Peter Lang, 2009), 161.
[317] Lech Gołuchowski, "Gomułka Writes to Stalin," *Polin,* 17 (2004): 365-381.

with Jakub Berman in the starring role.[318] Berman was one of the most powerful figures in the communist regime, second only to Bolesław Bierut. He was responsible for culture and ideology, but crucially controlled the security apparatus (Urząd Bezpieczeństwa). The fact the he escaped the fate of Slánský may have been due only to Bierut's protection. Following Stalin's death, the security apparatus was removed from Berman's control. And when Bierut died in Moscow in 1956, shortly after Khrushchev's 'secret speech', Berman submitted his resignation from the Politburo, which was accepted. In the following year, the Central Committee of the Polish Workers' Party revoked his party card, accusing him of being responsible for 'Stalinist-era errors and distortions', i.e. gross repression.

The growing concern with Zionism led to the targeting of individuals, although not to the same extent as in the Soviet Union. On 26 November 1952 Arie Lerner who worked in the Israeli Embassy in Warsaw was arrested.[319] In 1953 Jakub Egit, vice-president of the Jewish Committee of the Wrocław Voivodship, was arrested on trumped-up charges. He was accused of trying to detach Lower Silesia from the Polish People's Republic with the help of the Jewish JOINT Distribution Committee and some other Jewish American organizations, in order to hand over the territory to Israel so that a Jewish national state could be established there.[320] This suggests that the government, having encouraged Jewish settlement in the area after 1945, had begun to perceive the territorial concentration of Jews as a problem in the wake of the creation of Israel. Later, however, Egit was permitted to emigrate, which again suggests that those accused of Zionism were not treated as badly as in the Soviet Union. Egit did not find it an easy decision to leave Poland:

> 'For me such a decision was hard to make. Before the war, I had been involved with the movement that dreamt of a new Poland where the Jews

---

318 Bożena Szaynok, "Sprawa Arie Lernera - nieznany fragment walki z syjonizmem w Polsce pierwszej połowie lat 1950," in *Polska w podzielonym świecie po II wojnie światowej do 1989 roku*, ed. Mieczysław Wojciechowski (Toruń: Wydawnictwo Adam Marszałek, 2002), 270.
319 Szaynok "Sprawa Arie Lernera," 265.
320 Egit,*Grand Illusion*, 100.

would benefit from the concept of justice and equality for all, with no nationalistic or social oppression because of race or religion. I had fought and suffered for this new Poland and could not easy relinquish it'.[321]

Following an order of the Ministry of Public Administration, all the Zionist political parties were ordered to suspend their activities before February 1950.[322] At the same time the Zionists were slowly pushed out of the Central Committee of Jews. In January 1949 during a Party Congress the Bund in Wrocław united with the Polish United Workers' Party with the aim of building socialism among the Jewish working class.[323] In April 1949 the Congress of Jewish Committees took place. This was a meeting of all Jewish Committees that existed in Poland at that time. It soon became clear that the members of the Polish United Workers' Party were the majority of delegates. So those decisions that were in accord with the official line of the Polish United Workers' Party were taken. Very similar processes took place in the local committees in Lower Silesia. The policy was to mobilize Jews in secular organizations that would work harmoniously with the regime.[324]

Those who wished to leave Poland in order to go to Israel were allowed to do so. They were told that they had until April 1951 to leave. Between 1945 and 1949, it is reckoned that 96,000 emigrants went to Palestine.[325] Between 1 November 1949 and 15 July 1951, a further 27,915 Polish Jews left for Israel. Emigration continued on a small scale thereafter. According to official estimates, there were in January 1952 about 70,600 Jews in Poland.[326] The majority were workers in industry, 20 percent worked in commerce, administration or communal enterprises, 12.8 percent worked in the professions and 8 percent was divided into further subgroups.[327] According to Stankowski, the people who left were overwhelmingly unskilled (although in the case of legal emigration it was easier to get

---

321 Ibid., 37.
322 Aleksiun, *Dokąd dalej*, 219.
323 Szaynok, *Ludność żydowska*, 90.
324 Ibid., 172.
325 Stankowski, *Nowe spojrzenie na statystyki*, 104.
326 Ibid., 116-117.
327 Szydzisz, *Społeczność żydowska*, 84.

permission if one could establish that one did not have any special qualifications). Other emigrants were civil servants, merchants, and artisans and 9 percent were intelligentsia. This broadly corresponded with the social profile of Polish Jewry.[328]

The pluralism of Jewish institutions that had existed since the Second World War thus came to an end. Some institutions were shut down, some amalgamated and some nationalized. Many Jewish nursery schools, hospitals, and schools, for example, were absorbed into the state educational and healthcare systems.[329] The Association for Health Care and the center of the cooperatives *Solidarity* were shut down. The Commission for Research on the Holocaust and the projects to build monuments and memorials where Jews had been exterminated ceased.[330] In Wrocław an exhibition on the part played by Jews in the 'recovered territories' was planned for summer 1948. The thematic approach of this exhibition was, in the words of the organizers, intended to stress 'technical progress, Polish-Soviet friendship and the achievements in rebuilding the western territories'. The preparation of this exhibition was accompanied by a huge propaganda effort. The main aim was to prove Polish rights to the western territories and it was hoped to strengthen feelings of unity among the inhabitants of Wrocław.[331] The Jewish Committee of the Voivodship of Wrocław was charged with preparing two pavilions about the role of Jews in the 'recovered territories' and in establishing cooperatives. Two weeks before the exhibition was due to open, a government official, a Soviet officer, and the head of the Security Service in Wrocław ordered the closure of the Jewish part of the exhibition. They considered that it highlighted the autonomy of the Jews too much. Despite protests from local Jews, the exhibits were integrated into the main exhibition[332] Jews insisted that the pavilions were intended to show Jews

---

328 Stankowski, *Nowe spojrzenie na statystyki*, 117.
329 Szydzisz, *Społeczność żydowska*, 103.
330 Steinlauf, *Pamięć nieprzyswojona*, 87- 88.
331 Jakub Tyszkiewicz, *Sto wielkich dni Wrocławia: wystawa Ziem Odzyskanych we Wrocławiu a propaganda polityczna Ziem Zachodnich i Północnych w latach 1945-48* (Wrocław: Wydawnictwo Arboretum, 1997), 117.
332 Szaynok, *Ludność żydowska*, 169-170; Davies and Moorhouse, *Die Blume Europas*, 553; Tyszkiewicz, *Sto wielkich dni Wrocławia*, 112-117.

as people committed to the rebuilding of Poland through their work and creative life in Lower Silesia.[333] But the government was annoyed that it had not been consulted, and insisted that separate pavilions were equivalent to Jews separating themselves from the citizenry of Poland and creating a ghetto.[334] There was, in other words, no room for negotiation. The terms on which Jews were allowed to organize and represent themselves were to be set by the government. The overriding aim was to transmit the will of the Party into the Jewish milieu.

3. Jewish Life in Wrocław in the 1950s

In 1950 CKŻP, which had to date overseen the organization of Jewish life, was merged with the Jewish Association for Culture. A new organization, the Social and Cultural Association of Jews in Poland, came into being, the brainchild of Grzegorz Smolar. The Association had branches in all cities where there was a concentration of Jews.[335] So far as the government was concerned, the prime task of the Association was to raise support among Jews and Poles of Jewish descent for official goals. As the only institution officially recognized as serving the needs of the Jewish population, the activists of the Association hoped that they could indeed mobilize support for the regime and at the same time provide a social space in which Jews could come together as Jews without any taint of 'Zionism'. The Association was strictly secular and campaigned against religious observance. But at the same time it organized Jewish cultural events under the banner of 'culture performed in the so-called Socialist manner or style'. Here Jews could learn Yiddish and study Jewish history, so long as this was done in a way that accorded with

---

333 Archive of the Jewish Historical Institute, 303 / II / 126 Report from 25 June 1948 written during the meeting of the Jewish Voivodship Committee "Przekona on zwiedzających (pawilon), że również Żydzi mogą być produktywnymi współobywatelami,tworząc takie żywe i twórcze życie na Dolnym Śląsku."
334 Ibid.
335 See the Statute of the Social and Cultural Association of Jews in Poland, in Szaynok, *Ludność żydowska*, 195.

the ideology and norms of the regime. It organized meetings on Friday evenings of a broadly educational character on topics such as the situation in Israel.[336] The Wrocław branch was responsible to the Warsaw main office of this Social and Cultural Association of Jews. During a so-called 'home action' in Wrocław, 86 agitators visited 950 apartments belonging to Jews and tried to persuade them to join the organization.[337] Similarly, the Wrocław Association campaigned to inform the Jewish population about the Nationality Councils and their role in local politics. In 1954 it visited 72 apartments to tell Jews about its activities.[338]

In 1950, the year of its foundation, the Wrocław branch of the Social and Cultural Association of Jews had 700 members. Two years later, this had risen to 1,658 members. Since the city was reckoned to have a Jewish population of around 8,000 in 1952, this represented about one-fifth of the entire population. Of these 1,658 members, 782 worked in cooperatives, 45 in industry, 32 in heavy industry, 30 were artisans, and 95 were employed in other sectors (these figures appear to relate to men). In addition, there were 139 working women, 421 women who were not in employment, 102 women who were students and 12 young female workers who belonged to the city branch. As this suggests, the membership was predominantly working class. It is possible that those who worked in the cooperatives may have come under pressure to join the Association, which may account for the heavy worker representation.[339] At first there were no intellectuals in the association. According to one author, this was because the Association was seen to be involved in spreading primitive propaganda; there were some

---

336 Archive of the Jewish Historical Institute, Social and Cultural Association of Jews.
337 Archive of the Jewish Historical Institute, 324 / 1190, Letter of the Social and Cultural Association of Jews in Wrocław to the Main Executive Committee in Warsaw, March 31, 1954.
338 Archive of the Jewish Historical Institute, Social and Cultural Association of Jew, 77, Notatka informacyjna o udziale TSKŻ w akcji wyborczej do Rad Narodowych.
339 Archive of the Jewish Historical Institute TSKŻ, 817.

who charged the Association with 'leftist fundamentalism'.[340] According to other scholars, distrust of the Association among some intellectuals arose from the fact that it was seen as betraying the Jewish tradition.[341]

One of the aims of the Social and Cultural Association of Jews was to campaign against the Jewish faith. The so-called 'Friday evenings' were an alternative to celebration of the Sabbath and were designed to bring Jews together in a secular environment rather than at the White Stork synagogue.[342] This was a policy in line with the anti-Sabbath policies practiced in the Soviet Union before the Second World War.[343] It is not possible to estimate whether or not this policy succeeded in diverting Jews in Wrocław from going to the synagogue. What we do know is that not all members of the Association signed up to its secular, leftist ideology. Some members continued to attend the synagogue and refused to work on days of Jewish festivities. Some even expressed a desire to emigrate to Palestine.[344]

The popularity of the Association appears to have derived from its program of cultural and educational activities. Although the Association broadly followed the political line of the government, it sought to meet the interests and concerns of the Jewish population. Some of its activities were completely in line with government policy for the entire population. The association, for example, organized outings to the Festival of Soviet Cinema that was held in the city in 1954. And the Association put on talks for housewives urging them to play their part in the construction of socialism. Yet the prime function of the Association was to promote the interests of Jews. So the Wrocław branch complained for instance that there were no dramas in Yiddish on the radio and it provided a range of

---

340 Bronsztejn, *Z dziejów ludności żydowskiej*, 18.
341 Szyja Bronsztejn, "Ludność żydowska na Dolnym Śląsku po II wojnie światowej," *Sobótka* 2 (1991): 269-270.
342 Archive of the Jewish Historical Institute, 324/1190. The letter written by the Wrocław Social and Cultural Association of Jews to the main board of the Social and Cultural Association of Jews in Warsaw, written on 31 March 1954.
343 Walter Kolarz, *Religion in the Soviet Union* (London: Macmillan, 1962), 375.
344 Marcin Szydzisz, *Społeczność żydowska*, 116-117, Szaynok, "Walka z syjonizmem," 270.

Yiddish classes.[345] This was not at odds with official policy, of course, which allowed the teaching of Yiddish both by the Association and in Jewish schools, but it did represent the assertion of a Jewish identity that the authorities might see as problematic.[346] Sometimes, moreover, the activities of the Association quite clearly ran the risk of government disapproval. It put on talks, for example, on the situation in the Middle East and the policy of the new state of Israel—sensitive topics so far as the government was concerned.[347] It may thus claim to have been a genuine attempt to create a culture that was Jewish in content and socialist in form.

In 1953 the authorities took the step of forbidding the use of Yiddish as the language of instruction in Jewish schools. Exactly why this decision was made is not clear. The language of instruction was henceforward to be Polish, but the teaching of Yiddish remained obligatory. (These schools were later called by the authorities 'schools with the additional teaching of Yiddish'). The decision may simply have been a response to the processes of the assimilation of Jews that were visible by this stage. The number of children who attended the school for Jews in Wrocław was never very high. In the school year 1953 / 1954 there were 338 children in the school, in 1954/1955 370 children, and in 1955/1956 the same number.[348] These figures, though not insignificant, do reflect the fact that not all children of Jewish descent attended Jewish school. Following the nationalization of schools in 1948/1949, many parents had opted to send their children to standard Polish schools. This was also due in part to the fact that Jewish teachers were leaving the country following the disbanding of the Zionist organizations.[349] But pressure

---

345 Archive of the Jewish Historical Institute, Department of Education, 303 / IX/ 1584.
346 Archive of the Jewish Historical Institute, Department of Organization, 77, Protokoły z odbytego w dniu 12 October 1954 zebrania Zydow - pracowników Wrocławskiego Zjednoczenia Elektormontażowego.
347 Archive of the Jewish Historical Institute, Department of Organization, 77, Notatka informacyjna o udziale TSKŻ w akcji wyborczej do Rad Narodowych.
348 Archive of the National Institute of National Remembrance, IPN BU MSW II 7148.
349 Arnold Goldsztejn, "Produktywizacja ludności żydowskiej," 132.

from the government was also a factor at work. In mid-1951 Bergman, the director of the Jewish school in Wrocław, was dismissed because he refused to cooperate with the Social and Cultural Association of Jews and was accused of undermining respect for the Association among his pupils. The Association threatened to withdraw all cooperation with the school unless Bergman were replaced with someone who had the backing of the Association.[350] The decision reflected government support for secular Jewish organizations over those whose orientation was more religious or Zionist.

One cannot say that the Association promoted a programme of assimilation per se, since its raison d'etre was to articulate a Jewish identity within parameters set by the government. Yet the fact that significant numbers of Jewish parents chose to send their children to mainstream schools suggests that social pressures to assimilate into the wider Polish society were making themselves felt. The younger generation was growing up not knowing Yiddish and far comfortable in the Polish language than their parents. Success in education depended on being able to function confidently in Polish. The pressure to assimilate was thus particularly evident with respect to the intelligentsia. The eminent biologist, Ludwik Hirszfeld, who had discovered blood groups and who was the director of the Institute for Medical Microbiology in Wrocław until his death in 1954, had this to say on the question of Jewish assimilation:

> 'The Jews have the choice, either to pray differently, to talk differently, to eat differently from their surroundings and to feel themselves always as others, or they can decide to become the children of this country, to become fully equal with the citizens of this country. If they want to preserve their own character and to take away from future generations the stigma of one-sided love, then they should build a motherland [i.e. in Israel, IK].'[351]

Another area in which pressure to assimilate was evident was that of marriage. The Jewish community in Wrocław was small and the chances of young people meeting marriage partners outside that

---

350 Archive of the Jewish Historical Institute, Social and Cultural Association of Jews, Department of Organization, 61-62, Wyciąg z protokolu posiedzenia Prezydium Wojewodzkiego TSKZ z dnia 22 sierpnia 1951.
351 Ludwik Hirszfeld, *Historia jednego życia* (Warszawa: PAX, 1989), 353.

community strong. According to statistical data produced by the Congregation of the Mosaic Faith, between 1947 and 1948 122 marriages took place in Wrocław.[352] Before the war, 94 percent of local Jews (in Poland) had married Jews. In 1947 and 1948, in only 57.7 percent of marriages were both spouses Jewish.[353] Such mixed marriages took place in the registry office rather than in the White Stork synagogue. The tendency to marry outside the faith was not only an effect of the much diminished size of the Jewish community in the city, it also reflected the fact that 75 percent of Jews who survived the Holocaust were men. How far this shows a positive desire to assimilate, then, and how far it was a response to circumstances is hard to gauge. We may, though, assume that those who chose to stay in Poland rather than emigrate to Israel were more likely than emigrants to wish to assimilate into Polish society.

Further evidence of assimilationist tendencies included the tendency to give children Polish names. This was a trend both in families where both parents were Jewish and in families where only one parent was Jewish. The practice of circumcision also declined. During the Nazi occupation circumcision had been a way whereby the Nazis identified Jewish males for extermination. The memory of this, plus the fact that circumcision was not practiced in Catholic Poland, seems to have discouraged Jewish parents from circumcising boys eight days after birth: in Wrocław only 366 boys were circumcised between 1947 and 1955.[354] There was also a tendency for Jews to celebrate Soviet festivals. In 1953 even the Social and Cultural Association of Jews organized a New Year's party with a Christmas tree.[355] In 1955 the Association had a Christmas tree as well as presents and games.[356] It was not, however, a Christmas celebration, but a Soviet way of celebrating a New Year by dressing

---

352 Ziątkowski, *Die Geschichte der Juden in Breslau*, 116.
353 Bronsztejn, *Z dziejów ludności żydowskiej*, 29.
354 Ziątkowski, *Die Geschichte der Juden*, 116.
355 Archive of the Jewish Historical Institute, Section: The Social and Cultural Organization of Jews, No. 65, Correspondence.
356 Archive of the Jewish Historical Institute, Department of Organization, Social and Cultural Association of Jews, TSKŻ 67 documents written on 23 and 19 December 1955.

up a tree.[357] At the same time, we must be cautious about reading such evidence as proof that Jews were ceasing to think of themselves as Jews. In 1947–1950 73 percent of Jews who were interviewed saw themselves as Jews, compared with 22 percent who saw themselves as Poles. 2 percent saw themselves as Poles and Jews, and 1.7 percent said they belonged to no national group.[358]

4. 1956 as a turning point

In February 1956 the Twentieth Party Congress of the Soviet Communist Party, at which Khrushchev denounced the crimes of Stalin, which was closely followed by the death of the arch-Stalinist Bolesław Bierut, significantly weakened the hardliners within the Polish Workers' Party. Protests in Poznań revealed the extent of popular opposition to the regime. In June workers rose up in Poznań to protest food shortages, falling wages and bad housing. Dozens of people were killed as the disturbances were quelled. Street protests grew apace, culminating around the time of the VIII plenum of the Central Committee on 19-21 October and assuming an explicit nationalist and anti-Soviet character. A reformist faction led by Władysław Gomułka seized control of the party and, after tense negotiations with the Soviets (already alarmed at events in Hungary), began to introduce liberalizing reforms.[359] Ironically, if Gomułka's reforms led—at least for a period—to an easing of the plight of ordinary Poles, they led to a worsening of the situation of Polish Jews. The crisis within the Polish Workers' Party necessarily shone a light on the visibility of Jews within the leadership. The Central Committee discussed the need to regulate the party's structures according to nationality.[360] Many Jewish members of the party and the Security Service were dismissed from their posts at this time. Such signals from the top were one contributing factor to

---

357 Serhy Yekelchyk, *Ukraina: Narodziny nowoczesnego narodu*, (Kraków: Wydawnictwo Uniwersytetu Jagiellońskiego, 2009), 168.
358 Hurwic-Nowakowska, *Żydzi polscy*, 112-113, 179.
359 Paweł Machcewicz, *Polski rok 1956* (Warszawa: Mówią Wieki, 1993), 217; see also Szydzisz, *Społeczność żydowska*, 144.
360 Machcewicz, *Polski rok 1956*, 217-219.

the flare-up of antisemitism at the popular level.³⁶¹ Khrushchev's revelations had intensified antisemitism, since Jews such as Berman and Bierut, who had led the Polish Workers' Party since the war, were held responsible for the crimes committed in the name of Communism. Jakub Berman, as head of the Polish State Security Service, was particularly despised and the Service he led was widely seen as a bastion of Jews.³⁶² The strikes and attacks on official bodies often took on an antisemitic character. In Wrocław flyers with antisemitic slogans such as 'Jews out!' circulated, individual Jews received anonymous threats, others lost their jobs. At the peak of the antisemitic outburst, while the VIII plenum of the Central Committee was in session, slogans appeared on 22 October on the walls of the Jewish People's Club at the Social and Cultural Association saying: 'Down with Perec and Lewartowski — the Władysław Gomułka Polish club'. Here the Communist Gomułka was counterposed, as a true Pole, to the Yiddish writer, Iccak Lejb Perec (1852 - 1915), and to Józef Lewartowski, 1895-1942, leader of the Polish Socialist Party. Over the next few nights windows at the Jewish People's Club were smashed. On 28 October a group of Jews leaving the club was attacked by a shower of bricks. The following night sulphur was thrown into the toilet of the club and so on.³⁶³ Although the director of the club went to the militia station and asked for help, the police did not intervene until 3 November.³⁶⁴ There was even a case of a murder of a Jew in Wrocław in 1956. The culprit, who was sentenced to death, explained that he wanted to take revenge on the Jews. Predictably his action spurred the desire of many to Jews to leave the Polish People's Republic.³⁶⁵

---

361 Andrzej Paczkowski, "Żydzi w UB: próba weryfikacji stereotypu," in *Komunizm: ideologia, system, ludzie*, ed. Tomasz Szarota (Warszawa: Neriton, 2001), 204.
362 Jerzy Eisler, *Polski rok 1968* (Warszawa: IPN, 2006), 101.
363 Archive of the Jewish Historical Institute, Social and Cultural Association of Jews, Department of Organization 115, page 3. Letter to the Communal Police Station (Militia) written by the Social and Cultural Association of Jews in Wrocław on 3 November 1956.
364 Ibid.
365 Stankowski, "Nowe spojrzenie na statystyki," 123.

JEWISH LIFE FROM 1948 THROUGH THE 1950S   105

Gomułka's reforms made it easier for Jews to leave Poland. The number of Jews in Poland at this time is imprecise. The figure of 50,000 was generally given, but this may have discounted 20,000 to 30,000 who hid their ethnicity. Between 1951 and 1955 only 1,200 Jews had been allowed to emigrate from Poland. In the course of 1956 this increased to 5,700. A Polish-Israeli agreement signed in early July 1956 stipulated that 20,000 Jews would be permitted to emigrate to Israel, of whom 9,000 were to leave by January 1957, a quota which was not met.[366] Grzegorz Smolar reckons that as many as 80 percent of Jews sought to leave Poland, in the face of more overt antisemitism and perceived government indifference.[367] Between 1956 and 1960 it has been estimated that 51,000 Jews left Poland of whom 57 to 60 percent were from Lower Silesia.[368] In 1956 there were about 13,000 Jews in Wrocław, which made it by far the largest concentration of Jews in Silesia (Legnica had 6,000; Wałbrzych 5,000; Dzierżoniów 3,150; Świdnica 1,800; Kłodzko 1,500; and Bielawa 900).[369] After the outbreak of antisemitism, about 70 percent of the Jewish population left the region and went abroad.[370]

Yet as Jews left Wrocław, others entered the city. These were the so-called 'repatriates' who arrived in Poland in the framework of an agreement of April 1957 between the Polish People's Republic and the Soviet government. Some 18,000 Polish Jews were reckoned to be still living in the Soviet Union at the end of the Second World War.[371] Jews were included in the agreement to allow for the repatriation of Polish citizens from the USSR, although the Soviet gov-

---

366 Open Society Archives. Radio Free Europe News & Information Service, 'Emigration of Polish Jews,' 6 June 1957, http://www.osaarchivum.org/files/holdings/300/8/3/text/39-1-175.shtml (accessed 22 January 2012).
367 Notes of Grzegorz Smolar for the Central Committee of the Polish United Worker's Party, February 1957 with the title Kwestia żydowska w chwili obecnej (The Jewish question at the moment), in August Grabski, "Sytuacja Żydów w Polsce w latach 1950-1957," *Biuletyn ŻIH* 4 (2000): 515-519.
368 Bronsztejn, *Z dziejów ludności*, 18.
369 Szydzisz, *Społeczność żydowska*, 30.
370 State Archive of Wrocław, 74/ 04 / 76, 228.
371 Bronsztejn, *Z dziejów ludności*, 18.

ernment may have been unenthusiastic about this. Jews who applied to emigrate in L'viv and Vilnius, however, faced fewer bureaucratic obstacles than elsewhere since the discontented Jewish communities of these cities were perceived to be impeding the process of Sovietizing these territories. Given the difficult economic situation in Poland at this time, we infer that Polish government assumed that most Jews who applied to leave the Soviet Union were intent on going to Israel and would leave Poland, just as they had done in the late 1940s. Initially, they were granted exit visas almost as soon as they arrived in Warsaw. It was only in March 1957, three weeks before the repatriation agreement was signed, that the Polish government insisted that repatriated Polish Jews must apply for emigration 'in the normal way', i.e. after at least a year's residence in Poland. This appears to have been a concession to a complaint from Khrushchev that Soviet citizens were taking advantage of the repatriation agreement in order to get to Israel. In 1957 Jews comprised 15 percent of all repatriates to Poland, but the percentage declined to five percent in 1958 and 1959.[372]

In the framework of the repatriation agreement, 1,500 Jewish families came from the Soviet Union to the Wrocław Voivodship. They settled in a few cities: 300 families — another source says 500 — settled in Wrocław, 150 families in Dzierżoniow, 200 families in Wałbrzych, 600 families in Legnica and 30 families in Świdnica. The incomers came mostly from urban centers such as L'viv and Vilnius and were thus called 'an urban element'. They were often people with occupational qualifications that the city of Wrocław needed. Nevertheless it was not easy to find them jobs and housing. In particular, the city administration was reluctant to give flats to incoming Jews, despite a government order of 12 April 1957. Soon the authorities were accused of dealing very slowly with applications for housing.[373] Some families occupied flats without authorization and the Wrocław city administration then undertook a few evictions, which were far from peaceable. In other cities of southwest Poland

---

372 Ro'i, *The Struggle for Jewish Emigration*, 256-257.
373 Ibid.

there were not such huge problems with housing, there the problems related more to employment.[374] Problems also arose in Wrocław in employing repatriates in industry and in cooperatives. Many skilled workers lacked the necessary competence in Polish — especially to take written examinations — and many lacked certificates attesting to their job qualifications. There were few openings in administration for those who had worked previously in administrative jobs. This is why general cooperatives were set up for the repatriates to provide job training.[375] Of those in Wrocław and the surrounding area about 70 percent were employed in about 100 cooperatives and 20 percent in mines and in factories such as PAFAWAG.[376] The atmosphere changed for better after several meetings of prosecutors and judges in Wrocław, following the creation of Nationality Councils attached to party committees and after several press articles and a speech by the prime minister Józef Cyrankiewicz in the Sejm, the Lower Chamber of the Polish Parliament.[377]

As the reference to the role of Nationality Councils hints, one of Gomułka's reforms entailed a liberalization of policy towards national minorities, with ethnicities such as Belarussians and Lithuanians being allowed for the first time to establish associations and broaden the use of their languages as the medium of instruction in schools. In this context the Social and Cultural Association of Jews evolved ideologically, and tried more and more to achieve the aim of cultivating a Jewish national identity.[378] Although it was a state-financed body whose first aim was to spread socialism, it became after 1956 primarily an institution where the secular manifestation of Jewish culture and identity was cultivated.[379] Because of the emigration of Jews from the city of Wrocław and the incoming Jews

---

374 State Archive of Wrocław, 74/ 04 / 76, 229.
375 Bronsztejn, *Z dziejów ludności*, 18.
376 State Archive of Wrocław, 74/ 04 / 76, 227.
377 State Archive of Wrocław, 74/ 04 / 76, 228.
378 Grzegorz Berendt, *Życie żydowskie w Polsce w latach 1950-1956: Z dziejów Towarzystwa Społeczno-Kulturalnego Żydów w Polsce* (Gdańsk: Wydawnictwo Uniwersytetu Gdańskiego, 2006), 9.
379 Ibid.

from the USSR the cultural work of the Social and Cultural Association was forced to change. The 'Friday evenings' still took place, along with evenings of questions and answers, courses in the Polish and Yiddish languages and photography, but the amount of people who were reading the Jewish press was falling and the drama group and the mandolin orchestra and the dancing group were wound up.[380] The 'repatriates', however, showed an interest in the cultural work of the Association and the number coming to its events increased. A musical group was organized to give concerts. About 100 children from the 500 families that came to Wrocław in 1957 were sent to the Jewish school, although this was far from representing the total number of children who arrived from the Soviet Union, not least because the school was situated rather far from the centre. (For four years the school attempt to change premises but failed).[381] In 1962, 35.3 percent of members of the Wrocław Association were aged fourteen or under; 45.8 percent were aged between 15 and 49; and 18.9 percent were fifty or over.[382] So although all age-groups were represented in the Association, there was a heavy representation of children. 63 percent of the members were male.[383]

The Social and Cultural Association of Jews was also active in pressing the claims of Jews with the authorities. It met the City Committee of the Polish United Worker's Party to discuss problems with housing, with the general cooperatives, with the Jewish school and with antisemitism. The Association made clear that it was by no means satisfied with the response of the City Committee.[384] After the antisemitic disturbances in Wrocław the Voivodship Committee met with some members of the Social and Cultural Association of Jews on 24 August 1956. Nearly all participants in the discussion accepted that there was 'growing antisemitism' in the acute political crisis but the Party was criticized for failing to publicise the issue of popular antisemitism.[385] On 14 August 1957 the Social and

---

380 Bronsztejn, *Z dziejów ludności*, 18.
381 Ibid., 25.
382 Ibid., 27.
383 Ibid., 25.
384 State Archive of Wrocław, 74/ 04 / 76, 229.
385 State Archive of Wrocław, 74 / 04/ 72, 81.

Cultural Association sent a letter to the prime minister, Józef Cyrankiewicz, informing him about instances of local antisemitism and problems with the allocation of flats. The letter described a disturbance that had taken place on 5 August when a group of drunken hooligans had gone to a flat where Jewish families were living, screaming antisemitic slogans, and had thrown dishes around and destroyed furniture. Only the swift intervention of the police had prevented this developing into a bigger anti-Jewish disturbances. This incident seems to have been provoked by the allocation of accommodation to the families by the city administration. Even though dozens of Jewish families were leaving the city at this time, local people felt that they had greater claims for accommodation than recent incomers.[386] The letter, however, did concede that as a result of heightened propaganda against antisemitism in the press and on the radio the situation had improved on the previous year.[387]

5. Jewish Life in L'viv in the 1950s

The death of Stalin in 1953 led to a certain easing of restrictions on Jewish life. In that year the plenipotentiary for religious affairs asked Yakov Samoilovich Makhnovetskii, the leader of the Jewish community in L'viv, why as many as 1,600 people had attended the synagogue on the eight day of Passover. Makhnovetskii explained: 'Many non-believing Jews come to the synagogue out of curiosity, not least because this year people were in a good mood because of the government statement 'In the Ministry of Internal Affairs' which exonerated the group of (Jewish) doctors. This statement removed the oppression we felt.'[388]

---

386 Archive of the Jewish Historical Institute, Social and Cultural Association of Jews No. 118, Letter to the Prime Minister Józef Cyrankiewicz.
387 Archive of the Jewish Historical Institute, Social and Cultural Association of Jews in Wrocław, AZIH TSKZ 118, document dated: 31 July 1957.
388 "L'vovskaia sinagoga na ulitse Ugol'noi" http://clubs.ya.ru/461168601842742 5093/replies.xml?item_no=421 (accessed 22 January 2012).

Although there was some easing of the situation following the death of Stalin, the rapid onset of Khrushchev's anti-religious campaign from 1956 meant that the Jewish community was constrained and under intense surveillance for much of the 1950s. The Jewish community and the synagogue—the two organizations tolerated by the authorities in L'viv—were the objects of great suspicion on the part of the security organs. Following the creation of the state of Israel, it seems that educated Jews began to take a new pride in their heritage, to study Jewish history and to learn Hebrew. Such study groups existed in all major Soviet cities. But in the toxic atmosphere of the anti-cosmopolitan campaign, which was compounded by the onset of the Cold War, such expressions of Jewish pride were seen as 'Zionism' of a most dangerous kind. When in May 1948 the Jewish religious community in L'viv organised a 'celebration' to mark the founding of the state of Israel this was still seen as tolerable though worrying. By 4 November 1949, when the council for religious affairs sent a report to Khrushchev, then first secretary of the Ukrainian Communist Party, in which it mentioned that Shmul' Zil'berfarb, the rabbi of the L'viv synagogue, had called on members to raise funds to help their brothers in Israel, this was seen as outrightly anti-Soviet.[389] By the 1950s, any expression of support for Israel was viewed by the security organs as equivalent to support for US imperialism. In this context, the many Jews who identified with Israel and hoped to emigrate—and some Polish Jews in Ukraine were able to do so following the 1957 agreement on the "repatriation"—were now regarded as ipso facto enemies of the Soviet state, consciously or unconsciously manipulated by the USA to undermine the regime. In 1956 the L'viv oblast' security organs therefore set up a 'fourth department' to disrupt the 'hostile activity of Jewish bourgeois nationalists'. It employed 48 operatives, of whom seven had higher education, five incomplete higher education and the rest secondary education.[390]

---

389 Archive of the State Security Service of Ukraine, 13/ 535. Instruction about Zionism and the so-called Jewish nationalists written for the purposes of the KGB in Moscow in 1956.
390 "L'vovskaia sinagoga na ulitse Ugol'noi,"

Visits to the L'viv synagogue by representatives of the Israel embassy in Moscow were watched with particular suspicion by the security organs, who reported in detail on how many matzos or lemons were distributed. The attempts by the synagogue to raise funds to help its poorer members also aroused suspicion. Needless to say the organs looked hard for any evidence of espionage on behalf of Israel.[391] What is particularly striking in their reports is the complete absence of any reference to the Holocaust or to the particular suffering experienced by Jews. In the eyes of the regime, Jews were simply some of the millions of Soviet citizens who had perished at the hands of the Nazis. Their fate was nothing special.[392] Later in 1956, when fear that Jews were a fifth column within the Soviet Union was particularly acute, the security organs reported that religious leaders were expressing support for anti-communist rebellions in Poland and Hungary.[393]

There was in L'viv no organization comparable to the Social and Cultural Association in Wrocław. The Jewish theatre had returned to L'viv from wartime exile in Alma-Ata at the end of the war, but by 1948 it had been shut down. Jewish activity revolved exclusively around the officially recognised community and the closely monitored synagogue. Lev Serebriannyi, whose arrests for 'double dealing' in March 1947 was discussed in the last chapter, was succeeded by Yakov Samoilovich Makhnovetskii as leader of the Jewish community in L'viv, and he served in that capacity until 1960.

The Council of Religious Affairs was prepared to tolerate only the most limited forms of religious practice and subjected requests to set up prayer houses, organise religious instruction and so on to the strictest control. It allowed, for example, for ritual slaughter of animals but would not allow the opening of a kosher restaurant. In 1954 the synagogue was allowed to build a ritual bath (mikvah) but this was not completed until 1959 (when the women's gallery of the

---

391 A pamphlet written by the KGB in 1956. State Security Service Archive in Kiev: 13/ 535.
392 Altshuler, "Jewish Holocaust Activity," 271-296.
393 TsDAHO 1/ 24/ 4265/ Document concerning the mass political work among the population of L'viv oblast, reprinted in Khanin, *Documents*, 149.

synagogue was also restored). A sign of just how much the council for religious affairs interfered was evident in its plan to discourage—and then ban within three years—the practice whereby the congregation shouts 'Next year in Jerusalem' at the end of the Passover Seder.[394] In 1957 the plenipotentiary for religious cults, embarrassed at the fact that Israel had been sending matzos to the community, asked the higher authorities for permission to bake matzos at one of the bakeries in L'viv, because he was afraid that foreign visitors would learn of the ban and see in it an expression of the oppression of the Jewish religion. [395]

The number of Jews who participated in the religious life of the synagogue was small. By 1959 it is reckoned that there 25,800 Jews in L'viv. However, the average attendance at the synagogue on the Sabbath was 100 in 1955, 160 in 1956 and 186 in 1957. Attendance on holidays was much higher: in 1953 there were 1,400 and 1,900 visitors on two days of Yom Kippur; in 1955 the congregation at Yom Kippur was 3,660 and donated 45,000 rubles; in 1956 the attendance for Yom Kippur was 2,800 and in 1957 3,800. In 1958 it reached a peak of 4,000 and the collection totaled 47,000 rubles.[396] Given the intense discouragement of religion in the Soviet Union—and in particular, the difficulties of taking time off work for Jewish festivals—this was not a bad attendance. The activists in the synagogue—the rabbi and other officials—were said to be Hassidim, of whom in 1954 there were reckoned to be 200 in L'viv. A report from the security organs opined:

> 'The Jewish clerics and Hassidim are hostile towards Soviet rule, and find a common language and organization around the synagogue. They play on the national feelings of the Jewish population, inculcating worshippers with a nationalistic spirit and trying to imbue them with traitorous intentions, agitating for emigration from the USSR.'[397]

---

394 State Archive of the L'viv Region, p - 3/ 8/ 120, 81-88.
395 Ibid.
396 "L'vovskaia sinagoga na ulitse Ugol'noi."
397 Memorandum on the background of Church and Sectarian activities in L'viv oblast: 5 February 1954, reprinted in Khanin, *Documents*, 116.

Notwithstanding the fact that the council of religious affairs and the security organs were able to monitor—and even regulate—the activities of the synagogue, they felt in 1956 they were losing control of the situation. A so-called 'Hassidic opposition' was said to be seeking to take over leadership of the synagogue and this appears almost to have ended in success.[398] Makhnovetskii, chair of the community, was said to be aware of the 'disorder in the synagogue' and conscious that it was 'reaching the infringement of Soviet laws' but he was accused of doing little to prevent the 'Hassids seizing power'.[399] In the eyes of some in the community, however—apparently more traditional elements (i.e. Hassids)—Makhnovetskii was accused of financial irregularities, links to the 'organs' and general 'dictatorship'. In 1957 a new community council and chairman were elected. However, the plenipotentiary for religious affairs did not want to register the new council of the synagogue, and that is why Makhnovetskii was still officially the leader of the religious congregation in 1960.[400]

---

[398] State Archive of the L'viv Region, p-1332/2/25: 96f, in Amar, *The Making of Soviet L'viv* (PhD diss. Princeton University, 2005).

[399] State Archive of the L'viv Region, p-1332/2/25: 76. The Hassidim were according to some authors, for instance Walter Kolarz, the heart and soul of Jewish religious resistance to communist atheism. The movement historically developed from the eighteenth century onwards in what to-day is the Western Ukraine and Western Byelorussia. It is a mystical brand of Judaism which puts the main emphasis on a personal ecstatic contact with God. Hassidim lived mainly in Jewish Byelorussian and Ukrainian townships such as Braslav, Medzhibozh, Lyubavichi and others where their rabbis, called 'Tsadikim' ('the righteous ones') lived and taught. By the end of the 19th century Hassidim had about 250, 000 active adherents in Russia and comprised between one-fifteenth and one-twentieth of Russian Jewry, but the spiritual and moral importance of Hassidim was greater than this figure suggests, and this is particularly true for the Soviet era. See Kolarz, *Religion in the Soviet Union*, 380.

[400] State Archive of the L'viv Region, p-1332/2/25: 76, 96f, in Amar, *The Making of Soviet L'viv*.

4. The decline of the Jewish communities in the 1960s and 1970s

'During Khrushchev's antireligious campaign, 1959-1964, large numbers of synagogues were closed, and the practice of Judaism has become all but impossible in the USSR. As in the case of the Uniates, the strong linkage of Judaism with non-Russian nationalism (in this case identification with Israel) has marked out Soviet Jews for special repression.'[401]

Although the era that followed Stalin's death is commonly called the 'thaw', the period that ran from the late 1940s through to 1964 was one in which official policy towards religion became much tougher than it had been during the Second World War and its immediate aftermath. Yet within this period, anti-religious policy was tougher at some times than at others. Upon reaching the pinnacle of power, Nikita Khrushchev had favoured a return to the militant anti-religious policies of the 1930s, yet he tried and failed in 1954 to launch an anti-religious campaign. However, from 1959, he succeeded with a vengeance, and a fierce policy of suppressing public manifestations of religion continued until his political demise in 1964. The aim of this campaign was nothing less than the 'final and complete uprooting of religious prejudices' among the Soviet people. By 1965 the number of religious congregations registered on the territory of the Soviet Union had been cut to half the number registered in 1954. In 1960, for example, the government closed 11 monasteries and 1437 churches, many of which were confiscated or destroyed. In 1962, it closed 1,423 more churches as well as more monasteries and seminaries, and in 1963 1,700 more Orthodox parishes were shut down.[402]

So far as Judaism was concerned, the period up to 1959 saw a certain relaxation of policy, compared with the rigours of Stalin's last years. Delegations of American rabbis began to visit the Soviet

---

401 Bohdan R. Bociurkiw, *Ukrainian Churches under Soviet rule: Two Case Studies* (Cambridge: Harvard University Press, 1984), 15.
402 Ibid., 48.

Union and some even met with Khrushchev. In 1957 the Soviet government permitted the publication of a new prayer book (*siddur*) in five thousand copies. For the first time since the 1920s, it also permitted the establishment of a yeshiva for the training of religious personnel. This was the Kol Ya'akov yeshiva in the precinct of the Moscow choral synagogue, which opened with just ten students. At the synagogue in L'viv a ritual mikvah and a women's gallery were inaugurated in 1959. The authorities may well have hoped by these measures to convey a more positive impression of Soviet policy to Israel and to world Jewry. If so, the calculation ceased to be relevant in 1959 once Judaism, like Christianity and Islam, became a target of the anti-religious campaign. By 1962, the number of functioning synagogues had been drastically cut (see below) and the Kol Ya'akov yeshiva had only five students; with time, it ceased to function.

Official anti-religious discourse was tailored to meet the specific characteristics of each of the major religions. Between 1960 and 1964 over 300 articles attacking Judaism appeared in the Soviet press. As we saw in the last chapter the campaign against 'Zionism' had been in progress since 1948, and was more political than religious in nature, inspired by the belief that any expression of sympathy for Israel or desire to emigrate to Israel was a reactionary, pro-imperialist and anti-Soviet movement. With the Khrushchev clampdown on religion, specifically anti-religious arguments were mobilized to justify the antipathy to Zionism, claiming, for example, that it derived from the theological belief that Jews were the 'chosen people', and accusing rabbis of providing the theological justification for Zionism. Zionism, so anti-religious tracts alleged, inspired hatred of other groups of peoples and religions. This anti-religious discourse propagated banal clichés from secular antisemitic discourse, such as that money was the Jews' god, and that synagogues were not places of worship, but markets where business deals were struck and illegal trading done.[403] Yet it seems that so far as the Soviet government was concerned, hostility to Zionism

---

403 Joshua Rothenberg, "Jewish Religion in the Soviet Union," in *The Jews in Soviet Russia Since 1917*, ed. Lionel Kochan (Southampton: The Camelot Press, 1978), 348.

as a dangerous political movement was always stronger than hostility to the Jewish religion per se. Nevertheless, determining how far the campaign against the Judaism was a specific manifestation of political ideology, including the more general struggle against religion, and how far it was motivated by antisemitism is not straightforward.

During the antireligious campaign Jews lost most of their legal facilities for worship.[404] The following numbers show how many synagogues and minyans there were in Soviet Ukraine between 1949 and 1976: [405]

Year	1949	1951	1959	1961	1968	1972	1973	1974	1975	1976
Synagogues	79	41	41	15	12	14	14	14	14	14
Minyans[406]	n/d	33+	n/d	n/d	52	76	58	56	58	54

Official data often confused synagogues, minyans and prayer groups, so these figures may not be completely accurate. But it is noteworthy that as the number of synagogues decreased, the number of illegal minyans increased. This suggests that although the Jewish synagogues were closed down, Jews still met to pray outside of synagogues.

1. The Closure of the Synagogue in L'viv

According to official figures, in L'viv there were 25,800 Jews in 1959. Other estimates put the figure as high as 40,000 (see below).[407] The numbers attending the synagogue on important holidays were:
    1957 – 3,800 people at the synagogue
    1958 – 4,000 people at the synagogue
    1959 – 4,300 people at the synagogue

---

404 Bociurkiw, *Ukrainian Churches*, 48.
405 Vladimir Khanin, "Judaism and Organized Jewish Movements in the USSR / CIS after the World War II: The Ukrainian Case," in *Jewish Political Studies Review* 11 (1999): 75.
406 Minyans are groups of at least ten Jews who come together to pray. There have to be at least ten male Jews at the same time in one place in order to pray.
407 http://www.eleven.co.il/article/12523 (last accessed on 3 February 2012).

1960 – 4,000 people at the synagogue

This suggests that between 10 percent and 15 percent of the Jewish population attended the synagogue on holidays. Of these, 60 percent were male and 40 percent were female. They appear to have been mainly older members of the community. It was said that only 1 percent of those attending were younger than 25; 34 percent were between 25 and 45; and 65 percent were aged 45 or over. The plenipotentiary for religious affairs investigated whether Jews in L'viv were breaking labour discipline by celebrating Jewish holidays, but reported that this was not the case.[408] The anti-religious campaign – and the events reported below – seem to have deterred many in L'viv from attending synagogue. In 1960 on the eve of Passover there were only 2,200 in attendance and in 1961 only 2,000.[409]

In 1962 the synagogue in L'viv was shut down, an astonishing move, given the size of the Jewish population. On the eve of Passover, just 190 people attended synagogue and 200 on the final day of the feast.[410] Although 26 synagogues had been closed down in Ukraine between 1959 and 1961, there were particular reasons why the synagogue in L'viv was closed. Officially, the reason had nothing to do with the anti-religious campaign but was part of the campaign against 'speculation'.[411] According to a memorandum of the plenipotentiary of religious affairs, the attaché of the Israeli consulate in Kiev had come to L'viv on 26 March 1960 to visit the synagogue with his wife. He had brought presents, participated in prayers and also asked questions about the wellbeing of the local Jews. For instance, he had asked about the possibility to bake matzos, to which the head of the synagogue had replied that local Jews, like all Soviet citizens, were doing well and that the state did not prohibit the baking of matzos. A few days later, the head of the community received 4 kilograms of matzos from Paris, France. He

---

[408] State Archive of the L'viv Region, p-3/ 8/ 120, 91.
[409] State Archive of the L'viv Region, Documents produced by the Plenipotentiary for Religious Cults in L'viv. p-3/8/446/ 86.
[410] Ibid.
[411] Amar, "Yom Kippur in L'viv".

THE DECLINE OF THE JEWISH COMMUNITIES 119

claimed not to know who had sent them. The plenipotentiary actually complained in his report that the fact that state bakeries were not making matzos allowed local 'speculators' to bake matzos and sell them for 20 rubles a kilogram — much higher than the state price.[412]

The plenipotentiary continued his memorandum as follows:

> With the help of foreign 'tourists', synagogues are very often turned into havens of hard currency speculation and other shady dealings. Thus, for example, over the course of several years, a band of speculators in hard currency and gold was active in the L'viv synagogue. The leaders of the communities — Kantorovych, Shaposhnykov, Belebets'kyi, Senders'kyi and others — were the ringleaders of this group. One of them — Kantorovych — alone performed currency operations between 1947 and 1960 exceeding one million rubles in value [...], smuggling valuables abroad. In one such 'operation', for example, he gave Senders'kyi 120,000 rubles with which the latter 'acquired' 900 American dollars in cash and about fifteen gold English pounds. The total sum [of the deal] amounted to 300,000 rubles. Kantorovych not only bought hard currency but gold coins minted by the tsars. Thus in 1957-1959, he acquired 200 tsarist chervintsi [10 ruble gold coins] in exchange for 200 thousand rubles. M. Chernobyl'skii, a senior engineer at the technological construction bureau of the L'viv oblast (region) administration of small industry, was also a member of the gang of speculators that used the synagogue as an operational base. Between 1959 and 1960 Chernobyl'skii himself made a two million ruble 'deal', 'leaving' Kantorovych almost three hundred gold chervintsi. The L'viv synagogue was turned into 'black market', a place of criminal machinations aimed at undermining the economy of our state. It is a building of commerce and small peddling. In their search for profit and [personal] enrichment, the criminals have even systematically acquired state bonds, reselling them at speculative prices.[413]

A million rubles was a huge sum in the Soviet Union at this time, when the minimum wage was 400–450 rubles (1959). The average salary in the state economy in 1960s was close to 100 rubles per month. After the monetary reform of 1961, old rubles were replaced by new ones in a proportion of 10 to 1. The minimum wage was

---

412 State Archive of the L'viv Region, p - 3/ 8/ 120, 87-88.
413 Memorandum on the so-called Jewish Question in the UdSSR, in reprinted Vladimir Khanin, *Documents on Ukrainian Jewish Identity and Emigration, 1944-1990* (London: Frank Cass, 2003), 171.

then increased to 80 rubles.[414] Thus, these transactions were impressive.

On 16 February 1962 *L'vovskaia Pravda* published an article 'Prayer and Speculation' which accused leaders of the Jewish community of holding a 'black market' in the synagogue. The head of the community, Makhnovetskii, the cantor Shmuel' Zil'berfarb and other members of the community board resigned. The press published a letter from 26 Jewish garment workers accusing community leaders of turning the synagogue from a 'house of God into a centre of shady deals and foreign currency operations' and calling for the synagogue to be closed down. In March three members of the board of the synagogue were arrested. The prosecution claimed that a raid on the house of Kantorovich had uncovered 2,563 US dollars and 12 pounds sterling—hardly very much—and that the search of Sapozhnikov had unearthed 500,000 old-style rubles, a much more considerable sum. On 27 March the local Soviet declared that the synagogue would be closed and be offered as a sports centre to the L'viv printing institute. A few were still praying at the synagogue in April when things took a turn for the worse. In that month the synagogue was allegedly visited by the secretary of the US embassy and the secretary of the Japanese embassy, who asked the elder of the synagogue, Brodskii, various questions (it was he who said that he thought there were between 30,000 and 40,000 Jews in the city). He explained that the rabbi had recently died and had been buried in the Jewish cemetery. The envoys asked why they had no matzos, to which Brodskii said they were able to bake them when needed. Hemingway, the US official, then told him that the US ambassador had spoken with President Kennedy and he had promised to supply Soviet Jews with matzos. It is possible that the two envoys were in reality agents provocateurs from the fourth department, but assuming they were not, this visit seems to have been the final straw so far as the authorities were concerned. On 14 April the closure of the synagogue was confirmed and the synagogue elders were accused of 'allowing on the territory of the synagogue political activity by Israeli diplomats and turning the

---

414 This information I was given from Nazar Kholod, PhD in economic history.

synagogue into a place where criminal elements gather'.[415] Jews in L'viv would not succeed in reopening the synagogue until 1989.

Khanin has proved that the shutting down of the synagogue in L'viv was a joint operation organized by the Ukrainian Communist Party Central Committee's Division of Propaganda and Agitation, the CPU's L'viv Obkom, the UkSSR KGB, and the Council for Religious Affairs of the USSR Council of Ministers. At a meeting in L'viv on 23 March 1962, representative of these bodies decided to 'organize' statements in the press and radio by religious Jews to demand the closing of the synagogue. It was also decided to 'organize' one or two articles by academics (who had to be Jews) that would disclose the reactionary essence of Judaism' and 'with the help of children—Communists and Komsomol members—arrange for their parents to write letters about leaving the religious community', letters intended to highlight the wicked deeds of the synagogue leaders.[416]

What is striking about official discourse around the closure of the synagogue in L'viv is the absence of the rhetoric associated with the ongoing anti-religious campaign. Charges that Jews engaged in speculation had been rife since 1949 and were nothing new. Indeed they were a staple of antisemitism at both the popular and official levels. Just how much 'speculation' was actually taking place at the synagogue is unclear, but for the authorities 'speculation', already a serious offence, became intolerable when 'interference' by foreign diplomats was added to it. Indeed it may have been less the embarrassment at the fact that foreign diplomats were seeking to alleviate the plight of Jews in L'viv that was the trigger for closing the synagogue. Base antisemitic prejudice plus hostility to 'speculation'— whether real or imagined—were probably constant factors: it was the fear that the US and Israel were using the problems faced by Jews in L'viv to undermine the security of the Soviet state that was all-important. The official excuse of 'speculation' served more to tie

---

415   State Archive of the L'viv Region, p- 3 / 8/ 446, 85-86.
416   TsDAHO, f.1. op. 24. d. 5488, ll. 57- 9, reprinted in Khanin, *Documents,* 172.

the charge of profiteering, one traditionally ascribed to Jews, to foreign-backed efforts to undermine the economic and political stability of the Soviet Union.

2. Jews in Wrocław in the 1960s

By 1960, the Jewish population of Wrocław stood at between 3,800[417] and 4,500.[418] The Social and Cultural Association estimated that there were about 7,500 Jews living in Lower Silesia as a whole, principally in the cities of Wrocław, Wałbrzych, Legnica, Dzierżoniów, and Świdnica.[419] Wrocław now had the largest Jewish population of any Polish city, having overtaken Łódź in the mid-1950s. [420] In Lower Silesia the majority (56.5 percent) of the Jewish population was male. Concretely, there were 77 Jewish women for every 100 Jewish males. As we saw in the previous chapter, despite continuing emigration, the Jewish population of the area had been boosted by the influx of Jews who had come to Poland under the 'repatriation' agreement with the Soviet Union. Those who emigrated from the Soviet Union to Lower Silesia were mainly married couples in which both spouses were Jewish, rather than people in mixed marriages. Fifty-five percent of these 'repatriates' were male, a figure that broadly accorded with that of the Jewish population of Lower Silesia in 1960. According to research by Bronsztejn on the social profile of members of the Social and Cultural Association, Jewish women on average married at the age of 28.9 years, whereas men married at the age of 36.5. In around 60 percent of cases people married fellow Jews; but one quarter of marriages were between Jews and Poles; and 14 percent were with Ukrainian or Russian partners. 93.2 percent of those who entered mixed marriages were males. The relatively high proportion—around 40 percent—of Jews who entered into mixed marriages was one index of the growing assimilation of the Jewish population into

---

417 http://www.yivoencyclopedia.org/article.aspx/WrocpercentC5percent82aw (accessed 27 January 2012).
418 Szydzisz, *Towarzystwo*, p.43.
419 Archive of the Polish Institute of National Remembrance, IPN BU MSW II 829.
420 Berendt, *Życie żydowskie w Polsce*, 343.

THE DECLINE OF THE JEWISH COMMUNITIES 123

Polish society. Another demographic reason for the relative decline of the Jewish community was a low birth rate. Among Bronsztejn's sample, family size was small, with an average of just 2.24 people. Another reason for the larger proportion of males in the population was that 98 girls were born for every 100 boys in Wrocław.[421]

Another sign of growing assimilation was the falling number of Jews attending the White Stork synagogue. At the end of 1966, there were 19 Congregations of the Mosaic Faith in Poland, 11 synagogues and 19 houses of prayer, and 67 Jewish cemeteries. This number decreased in the wake of the campaign of official antisemitism in 1968, and by 1974 there were 16 Congregations, and 24 synagogues and houses of prayer.[422] The twin processes of assimilation and increased emigration were already weakening the synagogues before 1968, but the burst of emigration spurred by the 1968 crisis dealt them a harsh blow. There are no reliable figures for the number of Jews who were registered members of the White Stork synagogue, but these were clearly a small minority of Wrocław's Jewish population. One source says that there were 165 families registered with the Congregation of the Mosaic Faith in 1963 but that as many as 2,000 visited the synagogue occasionally.[423] Through the 1960s, as many as 2,000 attended the synagogue on holidays, but many of these came into the city from surrounding towns and villages.[424] In 1959 a Talmud-Thora school still functioned under the Congregation of Mosaic Faith, but it is not clear how many pupils studied there or even whether there was a teacher. Two years later there were said to be ten children at the school plus one teacher, but the report said that teaching did not take place regularly. On 12 April 1962, the Talmud-Thora school closed its doors owing to the fact that there were only a few pupils and no teacher. Most Jewish children by this time were enrolled in state schools.

---

421 Bronsztejn, *Z dziejów ludności*, 29-30.
422 August Grabski and Albert Stankowski, "Życie religijne społeczności żydowskiej," in *Następstwa zagłady Żydów, Polska 1944- 2000* (Lublin: Wydawnictwo Uniwersytetu Marii Curie-Skłodowskiej ŻIH, 2011), 230-232.
423 Waszkiewicz, *Kongregacja*, 141.
424 Ibid., 144.

Usher Ziebes, who became rabbi in 1959, arrived in the city in 1957 under the repatriation agreement with the Soviet Union. He served as rabbi of the White Stork synagogue and also as Chief Rabbi for Poland until 1966.[425] In that year he left Poland for the USA. His replacement held the post for less than two years, however, before passing away in 1968. In addition to its religious function the synagogue provided various social functions. At the beginning of 1958, the kosher kitchen of the Congregation of Mosaic Faith gave out food to 300 people every day, and it seems that Jews had access to kosher facilities in the slaughterhouse in Wrocław.[426] In 1967, the synagogue provided 140 free lunches each day, although this changed from 1 January 1968 when those receiving lunch had to pay.[427] By this stage the fabric of the White Stork synagogue was in a poor condition and this was the reason eventually given by the authorities for closing it down. In 1965 the Congregation had had to pay ten men to build a place where a minyan could meet, which suggests that it could no longer rely on volunteer labour.[428]

In 1964, an official clampdown on a 'black market' at the Wrocław synagogue took place, which was very similar to that which had taken place in L'viv a few years earlier. Estimates of the number of people arrested range from 30 to 150. One person, allegedly, was discovered to have 20,000 dollars in his possession, but less money was found on those accused of speculation than in L'viv. The official documents claim that those arrested were widely known to be 'speculators'. The detailed evidence for 'speculation' is unclear: there is some suggestion that the activities around the synagogue may have been connected with the organization of emigration.[429] There is evidence, although it is not conclusive, that foreign currency exchange was taking place on the synagogue premises as a way of helping Jews to emigrate. Certainly, US dollars

---

425 Ibid., 126.
426 Ibid., 130, 137, 138-139.
427 Archive of the Polish Institute of National Remembrance, AIPN Wrocław, 372, 348.
428 State Archive in Wrocław, Komitet Wojewódzki PZPR, 74/ XIV/ 17, 47.
429 Archive of the Polish Institute of National Remembrance, AIPN Wrocław, 258, 261.

seem to have been found. Since foreign currency exchange outside of official channels was illegal, this 'speculation' was used as a way of discrediting the synagogue. It was only in 1968, however, when the officially-backed antisemitic campaign was in full spate that the White Stork synagogue was closed. The rabbi had recently died, which meant that only a cantor remained. And although the synagogue shut its doors, the Congregation of the Mosaic Faith continued to exist and prayers were permitted in the prayer room of the offices of the Congregation. The kosher kitchen also continued, and it remained possible to use the mikvah. By this time, however, the Congregation had ceased to play a significant part in the life of the depleted Jewish population in Wrocław. Insofar as the latter had an organized centre it remained the Social and Cultural Association of Jews, which itself was now threatened by the heavy emigration provoked by the official campaign.[430]

3. Schooling for Jews in Wrocław

On 8 October 1956 the Ministry of Education agreed to a request from the Social and Cultural Association that the history of Jews be once again taught as a subject in Jewish schools.[431] As mentioned in the previous chapter, the continuance of Jewish schools that were permitted to teach Yiddish marked out the relatively greater liberalism of Polish communist policy compared with Soviet policy, since the last Yiddish schools in the Soviet Union had disappeared in 1951. In 1959, there were seven such schools in Poland, with an enrolment of 2,350 pupils. [432] From the administrative point of view, the schools were subordinate to the Ministry of Education and Higher Education, although the Social and Cultural Association of Jews in Wrocław attempted to influence their operation, intervening on such matters as the appointment of the school director. The schools aimed to uphold the Jewish tradition, to teach the

---

430 Waszkiewicz, *Kongregacja*, 144-145.
431 Archive of the Jewish Historical Institute in Warsaw, Social and Cultural Association of Jews, AŻIH, TSKŻ 2, letter written on 8 October 1956.
432 Archive of the Jewish Historical Institute in Warsaw, AŻIH TSKŻ 4, Uwagi i wnioski o szkolnictwie żydowskim.

Yiddish language and to maintain Jewish culture. Yet it was not easy to steer a course that was acceptable to the authorities. The authorities, for example, were ever vigilant to ensure that the syllabus was not favourable to Jewish separatism and Zionism. For their part, the local Jewish community wanted to see the schools preserve Jewish identity and not merely serve as a means to enable Jewish children to move into the mainstream of secular Polish society. The kind of compromise that this produced is evident with respect to the teaching of Jewish history. After 1956, Jewish history played a significant part in the syllabus of the schools, but only limited mention was made of the creation of the state of Israel. Indeed the word 'Israel' only appeared in textbooks discussing Jewish literature.[433] Added to the difficulties of having to work within the regulations of the Ministry of Education and Higher Education was the fact that the schools were plagued by a shortage of suitably qualified teachers, especially teachers who could teach Yiddish and Jewish history. The Social and Cultural Association blamed this on the lack of a department for Jewish history, culture and languages in any Polish university. [434]

Jewish schools in Poland increasingly faced the problem that the Yiddish schools in the Soviet Union had faced in earlier decades, namely, that Jewish parents were increasingly reluctant to send their children to Jewish schools since they feared this would damage their chances of advancing through the educational system and into good jobs within mainstream society. In the academic year 1963/ 64, no children enrolled for the first class in the Jewish primary school in Wrocław, the first time this had happened. Already in 1960 enrolment at the secondary school was said to have reached a critical level. In response, the Social and Cultural Association of Jews campaigned to encourage local parents to register their children at the Jewish schools. In the short term this seems to have paid

---

[433] Archive of the Polish Institute for National Remembrance, AIPN BU MSW II 7148, Information about projects of organizing primary and secondary schools with the additional teaching of the Yiddish language for the academic year 1967/ 68.
[434] Archive of the Jewish Historical Institute in Warsaw, AŻIH TSKŻ 4, Uwagi i wnioski o szkolnictwie żydowskim.

off. In 1964/65, twenty children enrolled in the first year of the Jewish primary school.[435] By this time, too, action by the Association had turned around the fortunes of the secondary school. Between 1960 and 1961 enrolment at that school almost doubled, reaching a peak of 123 in 1963-64: [436]

	Number of schoolchildren at the secondary school for Jewish children in Wrocław
1957/ 58	42
1958/ 59	38
1959/ 1960	40
1960/ 1961	76
1961/ 62	107
1962/ 63	113
1963/ 64	123
1964/ 65	109
1965/ 66	97
1966/ 67	53
1967/ 68	29

The Social and Cultural Association of Jews, as well as lobbying parents to send their children to the secondary school, covered the costs of transporting children to the school from all corners of the city.[437] Children who came from outside Wrocław were housed in a dormitory. As an extra incentive, the Association outlined the possibility of scholarships for students who qualified for higher education. For instance, they advertised the fact that a student who came from Legnica to study at the Polytechnic in Wrocław had won a scholarship of 600 złotych from the Polytechnic and one of 250 złotych per month from the Central Committee of Jews in Poland.[438]

---

435 Archive of the Polish Institute for National Remembrance, AIPN BU MSW II 7161, Information about the meeting of women who were members at the Social and Cultural Association of Jews. This took place on 15 June 1963 in Łódź at the Social and Cultural Association of Jews.
436 Bronsztejn, *Z dziejów ludności*, 35-36.
437 Archive of the Polish Institute for National Remembrance, AIPN BU MSW II 7148, Information about projects of organization of primary and secondary schools with the additional teaching of the Yiddish language for the academic year 1967/ 68.
438 Archive of the Polish Institute for National Remembrance, AIPN BU MSW II 7268, Information on the expulsion of JOINT.

In addition to the efforts made by the Social and Cultural Association of Jews to encourage parents to send their children to the Jewish secondary school, another factor that explains increased enrolment at the school in the first half of the 1960s may have been that some families decided to send their children to the school in readiness to emigrate. Certainly the fall-off in enrolments after 1965 was due mainly to emigration. And we know that in 1965-66, students from the school contacted the Israeli embassy in Warsaw and formed a group pressing for improved rights to emigrate. Needless to say, this put the school in a difficult position with the authorities.[439] By this date, too, the shortage of qualified teachers was exacerbated by the fact that Jewish teachers were leaving Poland.[440]

By 1965 the problems faced by the secondary school served as a further discouragement to parents to consider sending their children to Jewish schools. Some children attended Jewish primary school but then transferred to a Polish secondary school.[441] A survey of children attending Jewish school found that only a minority spoke Yiddish at home. In homes where one of the parents was not Jewish the language of communication was Polish or Russian, and Jewish traditions in general were not cultivated.[442] The extent to which a Jewish parent might wish his or her child to go to Jewish school in order to learn Yiddish, therefore, was limited. Certainly, Yiddish was valued by some as a badge of identity, but even they might doubt the value of studying the language for any length of time. In the academic year 1967/ 68, out of nine children in the eighth class of the Jewish school in Wrocław, four had studied Yiddish for only one year; two for two years; two for three years and

---

439 Archive of the Polish Institute for National Remembrance, AIPN BU MSW II 7148, Information about the education for Jews in the Polish People's Republic.
440 Archive of the Polish Institute for National Remembrance, Letter written on 8 August 1965, to the Ministry of Education by the Social and Cultural Association of Jews, IPN BU MSW II 7148.
441 Archive of the Polish Institute for National Remembrance, AIPN BU MSW II 7161, Information about the meeting of women who were members at the Social and Cultural Association of Jews. This took place on 15 June 1963 in Lodz at the Social and Cultural Association of Jews.
442 Archive of the Polish Institute for National Remembrance, AIPN BU MSW II 7148. Letter written on 17 May 1968 about the situation of schooling for Jewish children in the Polish People's Republic.

only one for seven years. This made for huge problems for the teacher charged with teaching the Yiddish class.[443] Even for those families thinking of emigrating, Hebrew or a West European language would prove more useful than Yiddish.

After the academic year 1965/66, the number of pupils at the Wrocław secondary school decreased drastically. By academic year 1968/69 there were only five pupils registered in the first three classes. With the explosion of antisemitism in 1968, the school closed its doors.

4. Pressures to Assimilate

Before going on to examine the 1968 crisis that convinced so many Jews that they should leave Poland, it is worth pausing to look at the extent of assimilation of Jews into Polish society. An interesting research project carried out by Julian Ilicki on Polish-Jewish immigrants who moved to Sweden between 1968 and 1972, following the 1968 crisis, gives us insight into the extent to which assimilation of Jews had taken place in Poland since 1945. For our purposes the sample is somewhat skewed, since almost half the emigrants to Sweden came from Warsaw and had a higher social status than those who came from Lower Silesia or Łódź. Many were senior officials, professionals and members of the intelligentsia, whereas those who came to Sweden from Lower Silesia were mostly craftsmen and lower-ranking officials.[444] Those from Warsaw were undoubtedly more integrated into Polish society than those from Lower Silesia. Nevertheless the findings are revealing. Of the sample, 37 percent were brought up in mixed marriages in which, overwhelmingly, it was the father who was Jewish and the mother non-Jewish.[445] According to the sample, 84 percent of those who emigrated to Sweden did not know Yiddish and 95 percent did not

---

443 Archive of the Polish Institute for National Remembrance, AIPN BU MSW II 7161, Information about the meeting of women who were members at the Social and Cultural Association of Jews, this took place on 15 June 1963 in Łódź at the Social and Cultural Association of Jews.
444 Julian Ilicki, "Changing Identity Among Younger Polish Jews in Sweden after 1968," in *Polin* 4 (1990), 270-271.
445 Ibid.

know Hebrew. Those who knew either language tended to be among the oldest members of the sample. Only 12.2 percent had attended primary schools for Jews in Poland and even fewer (4.5 percent) had attended Jewish secondary school. Two percent had taken part in teaching organized by the Organization for the Development of Creativity (ORT, Organizacja Rozwoju Twóczości), an institution established in 1880 in Russia that prepared Jews for artisanal and commercial occupations (It was called the Society for the Promotion of Artisanal and Agricultural Work among the Jews in Russia). [446] Its aim was to help Jews to gain employment.[447] Among those who came to Sweden, no fewer than 50 percent had had no contact at all with Jewish organizations or centers in the cities in which they lived; indeed 18 percent did not even know of the existence of such Jewish institutions in the cities where they had lived. Nevertheless, it is interesting that only 24 percent estimated that their acquaintances and neighbors did not know that they were Jewish.[448] In other words, though they might be heavily assimilated into Polish society, they were aware of being marked as Jewish in the overwhelmingly Polish community around one.

The group who settled in Sweden was very secularized. 75 percent described themselves as atheists and 14 percent as agnostics. Moreover, as many as 84 percent of males were uncircumcised. The percentage of non-religious was higher among those whose parents were Jewish than among those from mixed marriages.[449] Though seemingly strange, this appears connected to the fact that all-Jewish families tended to have higher social status than mixed-marriage families. In general, religiosity was inversely proportional to the family's social status. Very few of the families of the emigrants had converted to Christianity, although 18 percent had been baptized. These latter, naturally, came from mixed-marriage rather than all-Jewish families and the former tended to be of lower social

---

446 Julian Ilicki, *Den föränderliga idenitieten: om identitetsförändringar hos den yngre generationen polska judar som invandrade till Sverige under åren 1968-1972* (Åbo: Sällskapet för judaistisk forskning, 1988), 288.
447 Szydzisz, *Społeczność*, 284.
448 Julian Ilicki, *Den föränderliga idenitieten* , 288, 290-1, 293, 295-7.
449 Ibid., 270-1.

status than the latter. In general, Christian traditions were not widespread among the emigrants. For instance, only 13 percent of them shared the sacramental wafers on Christmas Eve, a Polish Catholic tradition which obviously drew on the Eucharist, and only 11 percent sang carols.[450] At the same time, almost three quarters had adopted Polish traditions that might be described as 'cultural' rather than religious, such as putting up Christmas trees and giving Christmas gifts. This suggests that Poles of Jewish origin were selective in choosing which non-Jewish traditions they adopted. Again, there is some evidence that families with a higher social status from Warsaw were more likely to adopt the 'extrinsic' aspects of the Christian tradition than those from a lower social status, such as Jews in Lower Silesia. As one might expect, there is evidence that families from mixed marriages observed the 'intrinsic' aspects of Christmas more than families where both parents were Jews.[451]

The extent to which Jewish identity connected with national identity can be seen in the fact that in Wrocław there was some tension between those who had come to the city after the war, who saw themselves Polish Jews, and those who came to the city in the late 1950s under the terms of the repatriation agreement with the Soviet Union. The former considered themselves Polish and the latter to be Russian or Soviet rather than 'real' Poles.[452] Many of those who wished to emigrate were said to be from the Soviet Union and they, presumably, came to Poland in the hope that this would be the first stage on their journey to leave Eastern Europe. Those who had returned to Poland after the end of the war, by contrast, had had several opportunities before 1968 to leave Poland – in 1945-46, 1948-51 and again after 1956 – so the fact that they had stayed until 1968 was a sign that they wished to integrate into Polish society.[453] Nevertheless the testimony of those who moved to Sweden after 1968

---

450 Ibid., 288, 290, 291, 293, 295-297.
451 Małgorzata Melchior, "Facing Antisemitism in Poland during the Second World War and in March 1968," in *Polin*, 21 (2009),197.
452 Archive of the Polish Institute of National Remembrance, AIPN Wrocław 053 / 1480, 14.
453 Ibid.

suggests that even they had considered emigration in the years before the crisis erupted. Thirty percent said that they first considered leaving Poland between 1956 and 1958; 9.3 percent said they were thinking about leaving between 1958 and 1967; and almost half - 49.4 percent—said that they came to consider emigration when the crisis of 1967-1968 broke out.

5. The Six-Day War of 1967 and the Crisis of 1968

The crisis of 1968 emanated from the crackdown against the student movement and the liberal intelligentsia in spring of that year—against the backdrop of the 'Prague Spring' in Czechoslovakia—and it became entangled with a campaign against 'Zionism' that had originated the previous year and that was being instrumentalised by elements within the Polish United Workers' Party. Israel's war against Egypt, Jordan and Syria in the Six-Day War of 1967 had caused the Polish People's Republic to break off diplomatic relations with Israel on 12 June 1967. When Israeli diplomats left on 18 June, some 200 drunken Poles bid them farewell at the airport, an incident that was to get considerable press coverage in subsequent months. It proved to be the beginning of an antisemitic campaign in which a faction in the Polish Workers' Party led by General Mieczysław Moczar, the head of the Ministry of the Home Office and also of the Association of Veterans who Fought for Freedom and Democracy, used exclusivist nationalism in a bid to undermine the general secretary of the party, Władysław Gomułka.[454] The Polish Worker's Party had been split by the crisis of 1956, with the Puławian faction seeking greater liberalization and supporting Władysław Gomułka, and the Natolin faction opposing liberalization and using chauvinist slogans to strengthen its influence over the party.[455] The two factions had disappeared by 1960, and in the course of the 1960s Gomułka pursued an increasingly conservative

---

454 Eisler, *Polski rok 1968*, 106.
455 Stefan Garsztecki, "Poland," in *1968 in Europe: A History of Protest and Activism, 1956-1977*, ed. Joachim Klimke and Martin Scharloth (New York: Palgrave Macmillan, 2008), 79-180.

course, yet he continued to remain unacceptable to nationalists like Moczar.

Gomułka opted to defend his position on the same ideological ground of anti-Zionism as Moczar. In June 1967 and March 1968 he publicly stated that people who possessed two home countries should leave Poland as soon as possible, a clear allusion to Jews' attachment to Israel.[456] In June factories and other institutions were mobilized to denounce Israel's attack and Zionism in general.[457] Moczar proceeded to dismiss Jews from positions within the Ministry of Internal Affairs and to incite a purge of Jews from the Polish Workers' Party, who were accused of being the most hardline Stalinists during the postwar period (though the leading Jewish Stalinists had been forced out in 1956).[458] The 'events of March 1968' were triggered by controversies caused by the staging of the famous play 'Dziady' (Forefathers' Eve) by the nineteenth-century playwright, Adam Mickiewicz. The play was taken off the stage of the National Theatre in Warsaw because of the public's lively reaction to the anti-Russian statements in its text. When "Dziady" was performed on 30 January 1968 for the last time, students started to demonstrate around the statue of Mickiewicz. The demonstration resulted in 35 arrests. The student protests were quickly interpreted by General Moczar and the nationalistic fraction of the Polish United Workers' Party as being motivated by 'Zionists' as a means of distracting public attention from the dire political and economic situation in Poland. The logic was dubious since neither the student protests nor the poor economic situation had any connection to Jews, except for the fact that some of the student protestors came from Jewish families. However, antisemitism, disguised as anti-Zionism, had potential popular appeal, and the security organs stoked it by

---

456 Joanna Wiszniewicz, *Życie przecięte: opowieści pokolenia marca* (Wołowiec: Wydawnictwo Czarne, 2008), 769-771.
457 Eisler, *Polski rok 1968*, 109.
458 Dariusz Stola, "Antyżydowski nurt Marca 1968," in *Oblicza Marca 1968*, ed. Konrad Rokicki and Sławomir Stępień (Warszawa: Instytut Pamięci Narodowej, 2004), 66.

spreading rumours that Zionists were responsible for rising prices.[459]

A petition was drawn up with a request to recommence performances of 'Dziady'. By mid-February three thousand people in Warsaw and one thousand in Wrocław had signed it. At the end of February the Association of Polish Writers sharply criticized official policy on culture — a key event, given the public respect for intellectuals. On 3 March the decision was made to remove Michnik and Szlajfer from the University of Warsaw. On 8 March students started to demonstrate in front of the university library, but the protest was broken up by the security forces. Similar demonstration took place also in other Polish cities. The fears of the authorities were magnified by the events in Czechoslovakia, where a parallel attempt was being made to liberalise the communist regime.[460] In Czechoslovakia, too, diplomatic relations with Israel had been severed and the authorities made some use of anti-Zionism to blacken the reform movement.[461]

According to official propaganda, provocateurs who were supporters of Israel with no loyalty to the Polish state were whipping up the unrest. An article published on 11 March 1968 claimed that the children of the Jewish Communists who had brought Stalinist terror to Poland were now inspiring the student unrest.[462] Zionism was described as the conscious enemy of socialism and of Poland, more dangerous than American imperialism.[463] From the perspective of the security services all Jewish inhabitants of Poland were active or passive Zionists.[464] The imagined enemy of the state

---

459 Włodzimierz Suleja, *Dolnośląski Marzec '68: anatomia protestu*. Warszawa: Instytut Pamięci Narodowej Komisja Ścigania Zbrodni Przeciwko Narodowi Polskiemu, 2006), 231 and Dariusz Stola, *Kampania antysyjonistyczna w Polsce 1967-68* (Warszawa: Instytut Studiów Politycznych PAN, 2000).
460 Marcin Kula, *Uparta sprawa: Żydowska? Polska? Ludzka?* (Kraków: Universitas, 2004), 191.
461 Eisler, *Polski rok 1968*, 712.
462 Wiszniewicz, *Życie przecięte*, 769-771.
463 Piotr Osęka, *Syjoniści, inspiratorzy, wichrzyciele: obraz wroga w propagandzie Marca 1968* (Warszwa: Żydowski Instytut Historyczny, 1999), 77.
464 Suleja, *Dolnośląski Marzec '68*, 252.

thus came easily to acquire a Jewish face, although this was not directly stated in published texts, which were always careful to talk about 'Zionists' rather than 'Jews'.[465] Nevertheless Zionists were depicted in ways that drew directly on centuries-old antisemitic traditions, with the Polish press featuring a demonic Moshe Dajan, a witch-like Golda Meir, and the menorah as a rocket launcher.[466]

The attack on Zionists was the first official antisemitic campaign to occur on Polish soil, nothing similar having taken place under the Second Republic.[467] In contrast to the interwar period, however, Jews were no longer so publicly visible within Polish society due to the extensive assimilation that had taken place. As we have seen, Jews were highly Polonized and in the main did not cultivate their religion or maintain strong ties to Jewish organizations. Yet the stereotype of the 'commie Jew' proved to be extremely potent, and served to channel the widespread discontent with the system that had been building up among Poles during the 1960s away from the ruling party.[468] Moreover, however integrated they had become, non-Jews were still very much aware of the Jewish presence in their midst. The memories of the harsh early years of Communism — when Jews had been rather prominent in the upper reaches of the Polish United Workers' Party — facilitated the easy equation of economic and political problems with the ongoing influence of communist Jews.[469]

It is difficult to estimate just how much the largely secularized Jewish population identified with the Israeli victory. Zionist organizations had, of course, been banned in Poland since the 1948. And although there had been a steady exodus of Jews from Poland since 1945, the majority had not chosen to go to Israel. Nevertheless identification with Israel had become rather widespread since 1948, not

---

465 Waldemar Sęczyk, "Obraz Marca '68 w prasie lokalnej," *Sobótka* 1 (2001), 87-98.
466 Agnieszka Skalska, *Obraz wroga w antysemickich rysunkach prasowych Marca 68'* (Warszawa: Narodowe Centrum Kultury, 2007), 11.
467 Feliks Tych, "Das polnische Jahr 1968," in *Die Vertreibung von Juden aus Polen 1968: Antisemitismus und politisches Kalkül*, ed. Beate Kosmala (Berlin: Metropol, 2000), 65.
468 Dariusz Stola, "Antyżydowski nurt Marca 1968," 66.
469 Marci Shore, *Caviar and Ashes: a Warsaw Generation's Life and Death in Marxism 1918-1968* (New Haven: Yale University Press, 2006), 356.

least because initially the communist regime itself had encouraged this. The security organs in Wrocław reported that Jews were expressing solidarity with Israel and even collecting money to aid the state in its war against the Arab world.[470] This did not, of course, amount to 'Zionism' as it was depicted in official propaganda. It was more a matter of sympathy for Israel rather than a worked-out anti-Polish position. Nevertheless what such sympathy might mean for the majority of Jews who were otherwise rapidly losing any organized connection with Polish Jewry is hard to estimate.

In Wrocław national events played out on a smaller scale. Students protested the closing down of the performance of 'Dziady' which caused the security organs to move in. As in Warsaw, they particularly targeted students of Jewish descent, such as Szyja Bronsztejn, who was depicted in the press as a dangerous individual seeking to lead the country towards revisionism and Zionism.[471] In the poisoned atmosphere Jewish workers in state enterprises lost their jobs. The director of the state harbor in Wrocław was accused of Zionism for being in contact with members of his family in Israel. The director of the Pafawag plant was similarly accused of Zionism. Prior to 1 January 1968, i.e. before the student protests of spring, 50 persons from Wrocław who had held positions as directors in the state apparatus or in state industrial enterprises or in the regional party organization had applied to emigrate.[472] All in all, 184 people in the city lost their jobs, accused of working against the interests of Poland.[473]

The local Social and Cultural Association of Jews, of course, had no choice but to criticize the state of Israel publicly for its responsibility for the Six-Day War.[474] Its statement expressed opposition to all forms of nationalism, including Zionism, saying these ideologies were alien to socialism and served to alienate the Jewish population from the Polish motherland. The statement affirmed the

---

470 Archive of the Polish Institute of National Remembrance AIPN Wr 053 / 1481, 7.
471 Suleja, *Dolnośląski Marzec' 68*, 233-238.
472 Archive of the Institute for National Remembrance AIPN / Wr 053 / 1599 / 42-52.
473 Suleja, *Dolnośląski Marzec '68*, 245, 247-248, 257, 252.
474 Bronsztejn, *Z dziejów ludności żydowskiej*, 22.

patriotic love of Jews for Poland.[475] This, however, seems not to have been enough to satisfy the more nationalistic members of the Polish United Workers' Party. It appears that the Association came under intolerable pressure, for on 26 March 1968 it appears to have discussed the possibility of dissolving itself.[476] On 31 August 1968 the president of the Social and Cultural Association of Jews lost his post and was expelled from the Polish United Workers' Party. The charge against him was that he had been reluctant to publish propaganda critical of Israel and that he had urged Jews to listen not to the Polish government but to the Western media.[477]

The emigration of Jews from Wrocław badly undermined the viability of the Jewish Congregation in the city. As we have seen, the synagogue closed in 1968, without a rabbi. By September 1969 the situation was so grave that the members of the Congregation were having trouble finding ten people to meet at the prayer house on the Sabbath, a minimum of ten being required by Jewish law. Members of the Congregation even approached the Social and Cultural Organization of Jews to ask if it would be willing to join prayers.[478] Despite the depletion of the Jewish community, however, several hundred might still gather for major festivals. On 4 November 1968, for instance, 300 to 400 came to the White Stork synagogue to celebrate Yom Kippur.[479]

6. Jewish Emigration from Poland

At the start of 1968 there were approximately 25,000 – 30,000 Jews in Poland, around 0.1 percent of the population.[480] Between 1961

---

475 Archive of the Polish Institute of National Remembrance, AIPN BU MSW II 7198.
476 Archive of the Polish Institute of National Remembrance, AIPN 053/ 566, 279, reprinted in Łukasz Kamiński, "Wrocławski Marzec '68 w meldunkach służby bezpieczeństwa," in *Rocznik Wrocławski* 9 (2004), 265.
477 Archive of the Polish Institute of National Remembrance, AIPN BU MSW 7197, notatka służbowa.
478 Archive of the Institute of National Remembrance (Instytut Pamięci Narodowej) IPN Wrocław / 053 / 1481 Volume Five, 370.
479 Ibid., 381.
480 Dariusz Stola, "The Hate Campaign of March 1968: How it Did Became Anti-Jewish," *Polin* 21(2009): 18.

and 1967 the average rate of Jewish emigration from Poland had been 500 — 900 persons per year. Between January and August 1969, the number of Jews who left Poland reached 7,300, according to records of the Ministry of Interior Affairs, and a high level of migration continued until 1972.[481] In all about 13,000 Jews went into emigration. Up to the autumn of 1969, 30 percent of the emigrants were from Lower Silesia.[482] In Wrocław as many as 1,000 people — two-thirds of the Jewish population — may have emigrated, leaving a Jewish community of 400 to 500 in the region of Lower Silesia in 1992.[483] This corresponds with the research done by Szydzisz, who found out that the number of Jews in Wrocław who were members of the Social and Cultural Organization in 1967 was 1,140 yet this had collapsed to 77 by 1969. However, once again it has to be stressed that only a minority of Jews had ever been members of the Association.[484] The majority of emigrants were well educated, intellectuals like Krzysztof Pomian, Zygmunt Bauman and Leszek Kołakowski, or artists such as Ida Kamińska, who had been a theater director, and Alexander Ford, the film director.[485] Intellectuals like Bauman might be dismissed for ideological 'revisionism' rather than Zionism.[486] There were also many members of the Polish Workers' Party among those forced to emigrate. In the survey of emigrants to Sweden, the respondents gave the following answers to the question why they had left Poland (clearly some respondents cited several reasons): they or a member of their family had come under attack (40 percent); they or a family member had been dismissed from their job or expelled from university (31 percent); they feared for their professional future (34 percent); they were concerned to meet the deadline for applications to emigrate (25 percent); they were afraid for their physical safety (25 percent); they

---

481 http://en.wikipedia.org/wiki/1968_Polish_political_crisis#cite_note-ipn238-14 (last accessed 27 February 2012).
482 Stola, *Kampania antysyjonistyczna*, 210-213.
483 Bronsztejn, *Z dziejów ludności*, 23.
484 Szydzisz, *Społeczność żydowska*, 51.
485 Stola, *Kampania antysyjonistyczna*, 215.
486 Adam Ciołkosz, "Anti-Zionism in Polish Communist Party Politics," in *The Left Against the Zion: Communism, Israel and the Middle East*, ed. Robert Wistrich (Vallentine: Mitchell, 1979),137-152.

were concerned that 'all the others were leaving' (24 percent).[487] Those who left were given documents to travel abroad but not passports. So they lost their Polish citizenship and were not in a position to return to the country. In order to get permission to travel the applicants had to indicate Israel as their destination. From the 13,000 who left Poland, only 28 percent left for Israel. This suggests that if these people did indeed have sympathy for Israel, they were not Zionists in any serious way. Other destinations of the migrants were: Denmark, Sweden, Australia, Canada and the United States of America. There are no figures on the destinations of emigrants from Wrocław, but we know that 54 persons had contacted Israel up to December 1968.[488] The fact that many Jews had non-Jewish spouses made it difficult for them to go to Israel even had they wished to. But the military and political tension in the Middle East, the economic situation in Israel and cultural differences were factors that were also cited to justify not seeking Israel as a destination.[489]

7. Emigration of Jews from the Soviet Union in the 1970s

In the 1960s emigration from the Soviet Union was extremely difficult. Between 1959 and 1970, 7,256 of the 11,572 applications for exit visas to Israel from the Ukrainian SSR were rejected.[490] From 1970, however, Jewish emigration began to accelerate. The number of Jews in the Ukraine fell from 840,000 to 777, 000 between 1959 and 1979, the fall coming mostly in the 1970s. In L'viv the fall was slightly greater: from 25,800 in 1959, to 24,362 in 1970, to 17,952 in 1979, to 12,800 in 1989.[491] This decline, though clearly accelerated by emigration after 1971, was also a consequence of a low birth-rate

---

487 Ilicki, *Den föränderliga idenitieten,* 289.
488 Archive of the Institute for National Remembrance, Wrocław, IPN Wrocław 053 / 1482, 51-52.
489 Stankowski, *Nowe spojrzenie na statystyki,* 144.
490 TsDAHO, F. 1, OP. 25, D. 541, LL. 2-4, P.E. Shelest to the CPSU CC on 11-12 March 1971, reprinted in Khanin, *Documents,* 186.
491 http://www.eleven.co.il/article/12523 (accessed 31 January 2012).

and increased intermarriage with non-Jews. One assumes, since these figures were drawn from censuses, that the figures relate to those who were classed as being of Jewish nationality in their passports. Another factor, peculiar to the Soviet situation, which also may have limited the growth of the Jewish population is that children of mixed marriages were able when applying for a passport at the age of sixteen to chose which of their parent's nationalities they should adopt. It is clear that at that stage many chose not to take the Jewish nationality of the one parent. This was one mechanism of assimilation that was not available to Jews in Poland where citizenship was not defined by ethnic criteria. At the same time, however, the fact that one's nationality was registered in one's passport in the Soviet Union also served as a way to perpetuate Jewish identity in a way that was not possible in Poland. Nevertheless this state-imposed identity, along with government and popular discrimination against Jews, served to maintain boundaries between Jews and other nationalities long after a connection with Judaism and specifically Jewish traditions had disappeared.[492]

The Jewish population of Ukraine was almost entirely urban. In 1970, 99.1 percent of Jews in Ukraine lived in cities, and while they formed 1.6 percent of the population of the Soviet republic, they formed 3 percent of Ukraine's urban population. According to the 1970 census, 87.9 percent of Jews in L'viv oblast' lived in the capital.[493] The Jewish population of L'viv was some six times bigger than that of Wrocław, yet it lacked the cultural organizations that helped give meaning to Jewish identity in Poland. From 1960, moreover, as we have seen, it even lacked a synagogue, an institution central to Jewish identity even for the many non-observant Jews. The tie with Yiddish was still relatively strong, despite the absence of any provision to teach Yiddish in the school system, a marker of the fact that relatively speaking the community in L'viv was more 'traditional' than that in Wrocław. In 1959, 17.9 percent of the Jews

---

492 Zvi Y. Gitelman, *A Century of Ambivalence: The Jews of Russia and the Soviet Union, 1881 to the Present* (Bloomington: Indiana University Press, 2001), 270.
493 TsDAHO, F.1, OP 25, D. 695, LL 6-16, G. Kriuchkov et al., Report on Pro-emigration Sentiment among a Segment of the Jewish Population in the UKSSR, reprinted in Khanin, *Documents,* 246-256.

identified Yiddish as their mother tongue; however, this percentage fell to 13 percent by 1970.[494]

Despite the identification of Jews by passport, and despite what we know to have been rather extensive discrimination against Jews in relation to higher education and jobs, the Jewish community in L'viv, as in Wrocław, was relatively over-represented in responsible positions. In the Ukrainian Soviet republic as a whole, Jews comprised 4.1 percent (6,518) of specialists in the economic field; 6.8 percent in the scientific research institutes and in the construction and geological prospecting organizations; 5.9 percent in contract building organizations; 5.7 percent in industrial enterprises; 5.2 percent in medical institutions; 3.2 percent in organs of state and economic administration, credit and insurance institutions; 2.6 percent in educational institutions; and 2.4 percent of those studying in the daytime system — all percentages in excess of the 1.6 percent of the Ukraine population that they represented. By sharp contrast, they were underrepresented (0.06 percent) in the kolkhoz system.[495]

A report by the L'viv oblast' party organization in 1972 claimed that the 'great majority of Jewish workers' actively participated in the construction of communism, but it observed that 'a number of Jews' had fallen under the influence of Zionist organizations; and that they 'express their will to leave the USSR and emigrate to Israel'. It cited several examples. Izer' L'vovich Blank, an engineer in the L'viv insulation factory, in his late twenties, was quoted as saying 'Aren't they in the USA partially right? Don't they [the Soviet authorities, IK] in fact discriminate against Jews at every opportunity?' Moisei Iakovich Vittenberg, the head of the supply department at the Elektropobutprylad factory, described in the report as 'an active Jewish nationalist', was said to have called press articles against Zionism 'empty phrases'; and his son-in-law was said to have accused Professor R. Brods'kyi of L'viv university of

---

494 Ibid.
495 TsDAHO, F.1, OP 25, D. 699, LL.53-7, V. Kutsevol to the CPU CC, reprinted in Khanin, *Documents*, 229-231.

142   JEWS IN POST-WAR WROCŁAW AND L'VIV

'betraying' Jews for writing articles against Zionism.[496] The campaign against 'the intrigues of international Zionism' was more longstanding and persistent than the 1968 campaign in Poland, having never really ceased when the anti-cosmopolitan campaign was wound up following the death of Stalin. As in Poland, however, the Six-Day war awakened expressions of Jewish patriotism among Soviet Jews and spurred the regime to step up its rhetoric against the Zionist danger. The Zionist movement was accused of spreading bourgeois nationalism, instilling in Jewish youth a pro-Israeli spirit, writing and sending slanderous letters and petitions to various institutions and organizations, spreading pro-emigrationist sentiment among Jews, and organizing the study of Hebrew language, Israeli history and culture.[497]

This was the immediate context in which there was a surge in the number of Jews seeking to leave the Soviet Union. Between 1968 to 1976, 132,500 Jews emigrated from the USSR on Israeli visas, of whom 114,800 went to Israel. In 1971 14,300 Jews left the USSR for Israel; in 1972, 31,500; in 1973, 35,000; in 1974 approximately 21,000; in 1975, 11,700; and in 1976, more than 14,000. These figures do not include the small number of Jews who were granted visas for countries other than Israel.[498] The figures for Ukraine were even more telling. In 1970, 2,000 persons requested permission to leave Soviet Ukraine.[499] In 1972 this number soared to 10,031, of whom 7,633 were given permission, although only 6,567 left.[500] The figures were mirrored—on a slightly lesser scale—in L'viv oblast'. Here there

---

496   Ibid.
497   TsDAHO, F.1, OP.25, D. 514, LL. 17-20, A. Grigorenko to the CPU, reprinted in Khanin, *Documents*, 187-190.
498   Łukasz Hirszowicz, "The Soviet-Jewish Problem: Internal and International Developments, 1972-1976," in *Aspects of Religion in the Soviet Union 1917-1967*, ed. Richard H. Marshall (Chicago: University of Chicago, Chicago University Press, 1971), 367.
499   TsDAHO, F.1, OP.25, D. 514, LL. 17-20, A. Grigorenko to the CPU, reprinted in Khanin, *Documents*, 187-190.
500   TsDAHO, F.1, OP. 25, D. 890, LL. 43-5, Golovchenko to the CPU CC, reprinted in Khanin, *Documents*, 259-261.

THE DECLINE OF THE JEWISH COMMUNITIES   143

were 296 applications to the Office of Internal Affairs of L'viv oblast' in 1969; 70 in 1970; and 322 in 1971.[501] Between 1968 and 1976 the total number of Jews who emigrated from L'viv was about 3,800.[502] Among those who left for Israel in 1972 were 148 former members of the Communist Party of the Soviet Union, 413 former Komsomols, and 898 people with higher education, including 398 engineers, 211 teachers, 188 doctors and 15 lawyers.[503] The Soviets' own analysis of why so many Jews wished to emigrated centred on their supposed desire to engage in private commerce and business in Israel. Being the descendants of shopkeepers, petty traders and entrepreneurs, so the Soviets reasoned, they had over the centuries developed a private proprietorial mentality. They did concede, however, that for the intelligentsia more important was the desire to have greater access to Jewish culture and language and to send their children to Jewish schools.[504]

There had been steady emigration from Poland in the 1950s and early 1960s, but the surge in emigration from Poland between 1968 and 1971 was essentially provoked by the state. This was not the case in the Soviet Union, where the pressure to emigrate came from Jews themselves. What is noteworthy, however, is that there was a significantly larger emigration of Jews from the Ukrainian Soviet Republic than from the Russian Federation. Between 1970 and 1997 over 308,500 Jews emigrated from Russia but over 422,000 from Ukraine, despite the fact that the Jewish population in Russia had been somewhat larger than that of Ukraine for half a century.[505] Zvi Gitel'man points out that it is not easy to explain this in terms of economic 'push' factors. He suggests that it was due to the real or imagined perception of Jews that antisemitism was greater in Ukraine than in Russia (something that would probably prove true

---

[501] TsDAHO, F.1, OP 25, D. 699, LL.53-7, V. Kutsevol to the CPU CC, reprinted in Khanin, *Documents*, 229-231.
[502] Hirszowicz, "The Soviet-Jewish Problem," 371.
[503] TsDAHO, F.1, OP. 25, D. 890, LL. 43-5, Golovchenko to the CPU CC, reprinted in Khanin, *Documents*, 259-261.
[504] TsDAHO, F.1, OP.25, D. 699, LL. 34-7, V. Dykusarov to the CPU CC, reprinted in Khanin,*Documents*, 220-223.
[505] Gitel'man, *A Century*, 262

if one looked at this question in a longer historical perspective).[506] He contends that Jews were more integrated into the dominant culture in the RSFSR than in Ukraine, notwithstanding the fact that we have seen that Jews were somewhat overrepresented in higher-status positions. This, he suggests, is because in Ukraine there was greater pressure from increasingly nationalistically minded Ukrainians to ensure that high government and party positions and positions in the state economic apparatuses were occupied by Ukrainians.[507] As she shall see in the conclusion, however, post-communist surveys suggest that antisemitism in Ukraine may actually have been weaker than in Poland.

---

506 Ibid.
507 Ibid., 265.

Conclusion

This study has examined the attempt to re-establish Jewish communities after the Holocaust in two cities that once had a large Jewish presence and that after 1945 had passed, respectively, from Germany to Poland and from Poland to Soviet Ukraine. It has compared, in particular, the policies of the Polish communist regime and the policies of the Ukrainian Soviet republic as they affected the reconstruction of Jewish life at the level of the two cities of Wrocław and L'viv. Fundamentally, it has sought to explain why the Ukrainian attempts to recreate strong Jewish communities in the wake of the Holocaust ultimately failed.

As we saw in chapter 1, at the start of the 1930s the Jewish communities in Breslau and Lwów represented the third largest Jewish communities in Germany and Poland, respectively. At that time, Breslau had a Jewish population of more than 20,000, although this halved in the course of the 1930s as Jews fled Nazi Germany. Lwów at around the same time had a Jewish population of some 100,000, but this number swelled to about 240,000 by the end of 1940 as tens of thousands of Jews fled from the Nazi-occupied parts of Poland into the relative (and temporary) sanctuary of Soviet-occupied Poland in the wake of the Molotov-Rippentrop pact. As a result of the Holocaust, the Jewish communities of the two cities were virtually wiped out. After 1945, the transformation of Breslau into Wrocław saw the attempt to found a new Jewish community. This transformation possibly constitutes the biggest relocation of a city's population in the twentieth century. As many as 70,000 Jews may have come to the city in the immediate aftermath of the war, not least from L'viv, which had become part of the Soviet Union, and from other parts of southern Poland; others came to the city who had resided before the war in the Soviet Union or in the former eastern territories of Germany. Most of those who came to Wrocław in these years, however, were intent on emigrating from Poland. Statistics, which are on the conservative side, suggest that the Jewish community in Wrocław declined from 17,747 in 1946 to 3,800/4,000 in 1960, or from 9.8 percent of the city population to 0.9

percent.⁵⁰⁸ Despite this decline, from the mid-1950s, Wrocław overtook Łódź as the city in Poland with the largest Jewish community. The postwar Jewish community of L'viv was much larger. In 1945 many Polish Jews were forced to leave the city in order to be 'repatriated' to Poland, while Russian and Ukrainian Jews flocked to the city. It proved much harder for those Jews who did not leave the city during the turmoil that prevailed in the immediate postwar years subsequently to leave the Soviet Union. The exception were those Polish Jews who were 'repatriated' in the late 1950s. So the Jewish community of L'viv held up much better in terms of size than its Wrocław counterpart. Again according to statistics that err on the conservative side, L'viv's Jewish community numbered 25,800 in 1959 and more or less the same (24,362) in 1970; but proportionately, it fell from 6.3 percent of the city population of 410,678 in 1959 to 4.4 percent of the population of 553,452 in 1979. As Soviet policy on emigration relaxed in the 1970s, the Jewish population began to decline rather rapidly. By 1989, the Jewish community in L'viv comprised just 1.6 percent of the city's population, whereas in 1931 it had comprised 24.1 percent.⁵⁰⁹

As this suggests, emigration was the factor that most directly weakened the drive to reestablish numerically significant Jewish communities in Wrocław and L'viv, although until the 1970s the community in Wrocław was far more affected by emigration than that in L'viv. The push factors that encouraged Jews to emigrate were a desire to leave the territory on which the Holocaust had taken place, compounded by revulsion at outbursts of popular and official antisemitism (discussed below). The pull factors disposing Jews to emigrate were a desire to join families decimated by the Holocaust and a desire to join and help build the new state of Israel. In the Soviet case, as we saw in chapter four, Jews had to battle for the right to emigrate, and so emigration really only became significant when the regime began to relax its policy from the 1970s (and,

---

508 http://www.yivoencyclopedia.org/article.aspx/WrocpercentC5percent82aw (last accessed 4 February 2012).
509 http://ru.wikipedia.org/wiki/percentD0percent9BpercentD1percent8CpercentD0percentB2percentD0percentBEpercentD0percentB2 (last accessed 4 February 2012).

above all, once the Soviet regime collapsed). In Poland it remained easier for Jews to emigrate in the 1940s and 1950s and into the 1960s. Yet the key event that sparked mass Jewish emigration was the state's active expulsion of Jews in 1968, an action that had no parallel in the Soviet Union, even though the last years of Stalinism were marked, more or less for the first time, by ugly official antisemitism.

As this suggests, state policy was crucial in determining the fate of Jews in the two cities and a central concern of this study has been to compare official policy towards Jews at both central and local levels. We have seen that although local economies and social structures — and to some extent the vigour of local administrations — were factors that shaped the specific experience of Jews in the two cities, in general the very centralised nature of communist rule meant that in neither Wrocław nor L'viv did local policy differ greatly from that laid down in Warsaw or Kiiv/Moscow. Moreover, there were strong similarities in general policy between Poland and the Soviet Union, especially in the early years of communist rule when Stalinist policies were imposed from Moscow. That said, there were significant differences in official policy between the two countries as well.

Until the outbreak of official antisemitism in Poland in 1968 the policies of the Polish Communists were generally more tolerant of Jewish communal self-expression than those of either the Second Polish Republic or the Ukrainian Soviet Socialist Republic. During the Polonization of Wrocław and Lower Silesia, the priority of the Polish authorities was to find jobs and housing for the new residents of the city, and one solution was to encourage Jewish immigrants to form cooperatives. Until 1948, Jews in Poland could form their own Jewish political parties — Zionist parties experienced a new lease of life after the war — and could build up schools and religious communities as well as secular cultural institutions and printing houses. With the consolidation of a communist government things became more restricted. There was no longer any possibility for Zionist parties or the Bund to operate. At the same time, however, after 1945 there was no longer any possibility for the political parties that had actively campaigned on an antisemitic platform during the 1930s to operate. Similarly, in contrast to the 1930s, there were no economic boycotts and no numerus clausus in operation — at least officially — with regard to access to education and to senior positions in administration or industry. The government funded Jewish schools, Yiddish theatre, and tolerated a rather impressive Social and Cultural Association which, while working within the framework set by a one-party state, nevertheless promoted Jewish cultural life with some vigour.

If anything, Jews in Poland were over-represented in the party and state apparatuses — not least in the secret service, though probably not in the army — compared with their number in the population at large. The Polish Communists, moreover, did not indulge in the antisemitic purges that marred late-Stalinist Ukraine or Czechoslovakia. Bożena Szaynok argues that the Polish Communist Party's early support for the Palestine project was rooted in sympathy for Jewish claims to independence, and her analysis of the Polish press suggests that the project of a Jewish national homeland was supported by much of the Polish public.[510] As Carla Tonini points out, however, this may minimize the fact that not the least of the reasons for this support was the communist government's desire to create a mono-ethnic state.[511] Overall, although Jewish self-expression became more restricted after 1948, compared with the period 1945 to 1948, Communist policies were more favourable to Jewish cultural self-expression than they had been in interwar Poland or than they were in the Soviet Union at this time.

The policies of the Soviet government in Ukraine, by contrast, were altogether more restrictive, especially when compared with the progressive policies of promoting Jewish culture that had been in operation during the 1920s. The bilious campaign of official antisemitism in the last years of Stalin's rule did much to make Jews retreat from the public arena. Following Stalin's death, official dis-

---

510 Bożena Szaynok, *Z Historią i Moskwą w tle: Polska a Izrael, 1944-1968* (Wrocław: IPN, 2007).
511 Carla Tonini, "The Jews in Poland after the Second World War: Most Recent Contributions of Polish Historiography," *Quest. Issues in Contemporary Jewish History. Journal of Fondazione CDEC* 1 (2010) www.quest-cdecjournal.it/focus.php?id=211 (accessed 3 February 2012).

course insisted that Jews were equal citizens who should be integrated into the mainstream of economic and social life without any discrimination, yet the reality often deviated substantially from this ideal. Moreover, there were to be no special ways in which Jewish identity was marked, other than limited practice of Judaism. In contrast to Poland, there were no forms of Jewish economic cooperation, such as the cooperatives created in Lower Silesia; the Jewish theatre, which had been the most vibrant form of Yiddish cultural expression in the Soviet Union prior to the Second World War, was shut down in 1948; and by the early 1950s the last Jewish schools had disappeared. Jews in L'viv were thoroughly integrated into the Russian-language state education system and there was nothing akin to the Social and Cultural Association in Wrocław. In L'viv the only focus of Jewish life was the synagogue and, as we saw, this was shut down in 1962 after a nasty campaign. In practice, moreover, a tacit numerus clausus operated with respect to such organizations as universities or medical schools. Jews were nevertheless overrepresented in all professional and administrative spheres of Soviet life, as well as in higher education. Ironically, we can measure this because Jews were recognized in the Soviet Union as a fully-fledged national minority in a way that was not true in Poland. Jews in Poland had common Polish citizenship, which must have made assimilation easier (see below), whereas in the Soviet Union, the authorities, whilst shutting down Jewish cultural and religious organizations, encouraged in a strange sort of the way the reproduction of Jewish identity by insisting that those whose parents were Jews had no option to maintaining Jewish nationality in their passports.

Despite official antisemitism, which is discussed below, it seems that in the Soviet Union until the late 1940s and in Poland for a longer time, many Jews looked with some sympathy on Communism, especially on the record of the Red Army in liberating some extermination camps. In the Soviet Union Jews in the aftermath of the war had not yet forgotten the progressive policies that had been in place in the 1920s (as they would forget by the 1970s), and Jews in both Poland and the Soviet Union appreciated the role of the Soviet Union in defeating Nazism. Jewish perceptions of

Communism may have been more positive in Poland than in the Soviet Union since they had had no prior experience of communist rule (except those who had experienced Stalinism at first hand while in exile in the Soviet Union). Of course, no more than a small minority of Jews were active Communists, yet we should not allow our knowledge of the events to come—1968 in Poland, and the exodus of Jews from the Soviet Union in the 1970s—to blind us to the fact that in the immediate postwar period many Jews in the two countries confidently believed in the promises of the communist parties to bring civic equality and educational and professional opportunity to the Jewish population. And as the statistics on Jewish representation in the professions show, in spite of official antisemitism, these promises did not prove completely hollow.

Yet if official discourse put a heavy accent on the civic equality of Jews, both the Polish and the Soviet regimes succumbed to bouts of antisemitism that made this commitment hollow. We have covered the anticosmopolitan campaign in Ukraine in some detail. In Poland there were no significant signs of official antisemitism until 1956 (provoked by popular attacks on 'Jewish communism') and it was not until 1968 that this came to a head. Ironically, by this stage many Jews in Ukraine were dying to leave the Soviet Union but were unable to, whereas the Jews who were forced to leave Poland were broadly loyal and had hitherto showed little inclination to emigrate to Israel. What is perhaps most striking from a present-day point of view is how unwilling the two regimes were to recognise Jewish suffering in the Holocaust. Poles, Russians and Ukrainians had all suffered terribly at the hands of the Nazis and it is perhaps understandable that the majority ethnic populations of the two states did not wish to be reminded of the specific suffering of Jews. Yet the official media never gave them the opportunity to be so reminded. The dominant discourse stressed the role of the Soviet Union in the struggle against a generalized 'fascism', making no specific reference to the Holocaust. In Poland even references to the Auschwitz-Birkenau camps made only veiled reference to the ethnicity of the mass of those who had perished there. The context of the Cold War, moreover, also powerfully shaped official attitudes to the 'Jewish question'. Both the Soviet and Polish regimes initially looked favourably on the idea of a state of Israel, but the onset of the Cold War led them increasingly to believe that the establishment of Israel was an element in a campaign by US imperialism to destabilise the communist world. In Poland it may have required some pressure from Moscow to convince the Polish comrades to adopt this position, but they fell into line. In both Ukraine and Poland the secret services became ever watchful for signs of 'Zionism' in the Jewish population.

How far opposition to 'Zionism' and restrictions on Jewish self-expression can be labeled antisemitic remains somewhat contentious. Some point to the heavily ideological character of anti-Zionist discourse and note that it distinguished Jews who were loyal to the communist order from those who were stooges of Israel and the USA. Others point, too, to the fact that the attack on Judaism in the Soviet Union after 1959 was but one expression of a broader anti-religious campaign that hit the Orthodox Church at least as hard as Jews or Muslims. Certainly, official antisemitism, if that is what it was, was very different from 'traditional' antisemitism, in that it was purged of all Christian elements (Jews as 'Christ-killers') or of Nazi 'scientific' racism. And we should be wary of labeling all anti-Zionism as antisemitic (there had, after all, historically been many political tendencies within Jewry that had rejected Zionism). Nevertheless, if we look at the discourse that surrounded the closure of the L'viv synagogue in 1962, or at the speeches of General Mieczysław Moczar in 1968 in Poland, it is hard to ignore the extent to which they drew on many of the basest stereotypes of traditional antisemitism. There may have been truth to the claim that the L'viv synagogue was being used as a centre for foreign currency dealing and for other forms of 'speculation', yet official propaganda traded shamelessly on the age-old association of Jews with black marketeering and profiteering; just as Moczar, a few years later, played on the idea of the Jew as a traitor to the nation.

There is little evidence that popular antisemitism in either Poland or Ukraine had been diminished by the Holocaust. Moreover, expressions of antisemitism on the part of the communist regimes did little to dint the belief in large sections of the population, especially in Poland, that Communism was a Jewish plot. Certain strands of Polish nationalism, along with certain strands of Roman Catholicism, had always had an intimate relationship with antisemitism. And in a situation where Poland had emerged from the war as a largely mono-ethnic society, the tiny minority of Jews seemed even more alien to the Polish and Roman Catholic majority. Similarly, strands of Ukrainian nationalism had also been closely associated with antisemitism; and although the possibilities for the expression of Ukrainian nationalism in the Soviet Union were severely limited, there is indirect evidence that Ukrainian nationalism was making headway in the institutions of party and state in the postwar era. Popular antisemitism, however, was never simply an expression of national identity: it was always closely linked to economic conditions, such as lower-class grievances over high prices, shortages of basic goods, and poor living and working conditions. When pogroms occurred in Poland in the aftermath of the war, these were triggered by attempts by Jews to recover property that had passed to gentiles in the course of the war. Similarly, in the crisis of 1956 antisemitism expressed popular frustration with the Communist Party's rule. It was thanks to swift action by the local authorities that Wrocław and L'viv were spared the antisemitic pogroms that broke out in the aftermath of the war, and in general the authorities were keen to avoid outbreaks of antisemitism, since it threatened law and order. This still did not prevent the local authorities in the two cities from discriminating in subtle ways against Jews when it came to housing or jobs.

As noted in chapter two, the question of the extent to which Poles in general were antisemitic has proved extremely controversial. Indifference to, rather than active hatred of Jews was almost certainly what characterized the average Pole or Ukrainian, though there are no historical survey data on public attitudes. According to the census of 2002, only 0.0028 percent of the Polish population—just 1,100 people in all!—declared their nationality to be Jewish. According to the research of Polish sociologist Ireneusz Krzemiński, about 12 percent of Poles in 2002 believed that Jews were responsible for the death of Jesus.[512] According to the same research, antisemitism had increased in the 1990s. While in 1992, 8 percent of Poles expressed antisemitic views—seeing Germans as more of a threat to Polish national identity than Jews—in 2002 the percentage had risen to 16 percent, and Jews were now seen as more threatening than Germans. This research further showed that antisemitism was more widespread in the countryside and in small towns, and more widespread in former Galicia (south-eastern Poland) than elsewhere in the country. In cities with more than 200,000 inhabitants, only 4 percent of people blamed Jews for killing Christ.[513] Ukrainian scholars who collaborated with Ireneusz Krzemiński point out that in the western part of Ukraine, which had been part of Austro-Hungary and later part of the Polish Second Republic, Jews and other minorities were relatively more assimilated than in other parts of Ukraine.[514] Natalia Zajcewa is of the opinion that generally Poles were more antisemitic than Ukrainians, but that Western Ukrainians' historic contacts with Poles had had an impact on the attitudes of the population towards Jews.[515] The research of another Ukrainian sociologist, Natalia Czernysz, appears to confirm this. At the time she conducted her research in 2003-04, there were vastly more Jews in Ukraine than in Poland—some 104,000—although this was a shadow of that country's once large Jewish population.[516] She concludes that at the beginning of the twenty-first century, Ukrainians were considerably more tolerant of Jews than Poles, with Ukrainians more likely than Poles to see Jews as having played some positive role in the nation's history.[517] Her research

---

512 Ireneusz Krzemiński, *Antysemityzm w Polsce i na Ukrainie: raport z badań* (Warszawa: Scholar, 2004), 25.
513 Natalia Czernysz, "Specyfika stosunku ludności Ukrainy do Żydów: przeszłość i teraźniejszość, problemy i perspektywy," in *Antysemityzm w Polsce i na Ukrainie: raport z badań*, ed. Ireneusz Krzemiński (Warszawa: Scholar, 2004), 182.
514 Natalia Zajcewa, "Stosunki narodowościowe na Ukrainie: ujęcie regionalne," in *Antysemityzm w Polsce i na Ukrainie: raport z badań*, ed. Ireneusz Krzemiński (Warszawa: Scholar, 2004), 238.
515 Ibid., 242.
516 Czernysz, "Specyfika stosunku ludności," 178.
517 Ibid., 176-77.

shows that antisemitism exists in Ukraine, but that it is not clearly defined in ideological terms. There is no stable stereotype of Jews that exists in the minds of the majority of Ukrainians. It is rather an inchoate mix of prejudice and ignorance. Significantly, such antisemitism is stronger in the western parts of Ukraine, carved out of Poland after 1945, than elsewhere.[518] In contrast to Poland, at the time of the research the rural population in Ukraine was more tolerant towards non-Ukrainians in their country than the inhabitants of cities.[519] As in Poland, antisemites are mostly people with a low level of education, and unemployed people and people with low social status (such as unskilled workers, housekeepers, and pensioners) are more often antisemitic. The higher the social status of the respondents, the more positive their attitudes towards Jews and their rights.[520] Despite these findings, as mentioned in chapter four, some scholars have suggested that the higher levels of emigration of Jews from Ukraine as opposed to the RSFSR from the 1970s may reflect more widespread antisemitism in Ukraine than in the Russian parts of the Soviet Union. Though it is treacherous to read back such twenty-first century findings into the 1950s and 1960s, it is clear that popular antisemitism — perhaps especially in Poland — remained a fact of life for Jews who tried to settle in the two cities of our investigation.

The final factor explaining the failure of Jewish communities to thrive in the postwar communist regimes is in some ways the most difficult to evaluate. It relates, of course, to those objective processes we associate with modernization, including urbanization and industrial work, increased social mobility, rising living standards, rising levels of education, declining levels of religious observance, and increasing intermarriage. To what extent did these processes lead to the increasing assimilation of the Jewish popula-

---

518 Ibid., 183.
519 Dopowid Antypowicz, "Wpływ czynników społeczno-ekonomicznych na ocenę stosunków narodowościowych współcześnie na Ukrainie," in *Antysemityzm w Polsce i na Ukrainie: raport z badań*, ed. Ireneusz Krzemiński (Warszawa: Scholar, 2004), 191.
520 Ibid., 198-201.

tion into mainstream society? Had the policies of the two communist regimes been more supportive of Jewish self-expression, would these processes nevertheless have undermined the attempt to create vibrant Jewish communities? Prior to the Second World War, the Jewish population in Breslau—Germanised, socially differentiated and apparently integrated into the mainstream society—seemed to point towards the future of European Jewry as a whole. Yet the Holocaust confounded that vision. Nevertheless the postwar evolution of the Jewish community in a city such as L'viv was in certain respects similar to the evolution of the community in Breslau in the late-nineteenth and early-twentieth century: a Yiddish speaking and religiously conventional population, largely involved in retail and handicrafts, gave way to one that was far more integrated into Soviet society and far more socially and economically differentiated. Yet it was also one that still retained a sense of Jewishness, albeit one that was no longer tied to Yiddish culture or to the Jewish religion. This, in turn, raises the question of what it means to have high levels of social integration of Jews and yet for Jews to retain a sense of their own distinctiveness.

Given that the official policy of both regimes was unfavourable to the practice of religion—to put it mildly—it is not surprising that only a small minority of Jews in Wrocław and L'viv were regular attenders at synagogue; even if at holidays, such as Yom Kippur, more would attend, especially in Wrocław. To judge by attendance at the synagogue, and relative to the size of the community, Jews in Wrocław were more religious than their counterparts in L'viv. This would accord with the fact that secularization had been more intensively underway in Soviet Ukraine than in interwar Poland, as well as with the fact that the background of the Jews who settled in Wrocław after 1945 (and again following the 'repatriation' of Jews from the Soviet Union in 1957) tended to be more traditional than that of the Jews who returned to L'viv after the war. The overwhelming Catholic character of Poland, moreover, marked a key difference of political and social context. After 1956, at least, the Polish government could not afford to assail the religious sensibilities of its citizens in the way that Khrushchev did in the antireligious campaign. What is noticeable, however, is that assimilated

Jews in Poland did not show any inclination to become Catholic: yes, they might adopt certain Polish traditions, such as Christmas, and might adopt Polish names; yet they did not have their children baptised (although the circumcision of children of mixed marriages did decline). Even more than in Wrocław, Jews in L'viv were heavily non-religious. In that city, of course, there was no synagogue to which the relatively large community of Jews could go after 1962, so the option of expressing Jewish identity through religious observance simply did not exist.

In postwar Ukraine, Jews were denied any possibility to express their identity in officially approved cultural forms, such as they had enjoyed in the prewar period. There was no Yiddish theatre and the number of books published in Yiddish was limited. In Wrocław, by contrast, it was possible to express one's Jewish identity in a cultural form through the activities of the Social and Cultural Association, though only a small part of Wrocław's Jews chose to do so. This latter fact suggests that Jews in Wrocław in general did not make any great attempt to preserve their heritage, either through religion, language or culture. The Jewish schools from the late 1950s found it hard to keep up student enrolment and the Yiddish language fast gave way to Polish. The same was even more true in Ukraine. In areas where there were compact Jewish communities, Yiddish continued to be spoken, but in the absence of any special provision for education in Yiddish, young Jews recognized that to get on in life, to get oneself a technical training or higher education, one had to be competent in Russian. Finally, it is clear that mixed marriage became the norm in both cities, especially in L'viv; and in Soviet Ukraine as a whole more than 90 percent of the offspring of mixed marriages chose not to be classed as Jews in their passports. This high rate of intermarriage, combined with the necessity to get on in mainstream Polish or Ukrainian society, was a key driver of the process of assimilation.

Yet however much Polish Jews may have felt themselves to have become indistinguishable from their fellow citizens, it is clear that they retained some residual sense of themselves as Jews, although they did not always wish to pass this on to their children. It is also clear that it was not difficult for the regime in 1968 to identify

Jews once it chose to target them. So even if Polish Jews felt themselves to be 'almost Poles'; it is not clear that Poles in their turn saw them that way. In Soviet Ukraine the identification and self-identification of Jews was stronger, because the state reified nationality as a principle of socio-political organization: in everyday interactions one was constantly reminded of one's Jewishness. This level of everyday practice may have countered the effects of the (relative) absence of religious or cultural organization. Jews in L'viv nevertheless seem most commonly to have developed a joint Soviet and Jewish identity, but this Soviet identity was expressed in terms of identification with a Russian rather than Ukrainian culture. Many of those who had come to L'viv after the war were Russified Jews, and they remained so as L'viv underwent a process of Ukrainization. This was not the least reason why the subterranean forces of Ukrainian nationalism often showed little love for the Jews who happened to live on the territory of Soviet Ukraine, since their loyalties were assumed to lie more with the centre than with the periphery.

So a note of caution is in order. The ambient pressures for Jews to integrate into Polish and Soviet Ukrainian society were extremely strong and the rapid decline of traditional Jewish communities in the postwar era is striking. Nevertheless Jews in L'viv never lost a sense that they were Jews; and in Wrocław, notwithstanding very strong assimilationist pressures, those who had come to the city after the war appear to have retained a sense of Jewishness, even if their children did not. This was not least because of the continuing antisemitism. In the Soviet Union, moreover, in spite of more than thirty years of secularization and assimilation, Jews in the course of the 1950s and 1960s may actually have become more proud of their Jewishness, if the high level of official anxiety about 'Zionism' is any indicator. Of course, we should take official propaganda about the 'Zionist' threat with a large pinch of salt, yet it seems undeniable that many Jews, albeit more in the Soviet Union than in Poland, came to sympathise deeply with Israel. And, by the 1970s, it was this, combined with disaffection at being treated as a social problem, that led many to seek to emigrate from the Soviet Union.[521]

In conclusion, then, the project of rebuilding lively Jewish communities on the territory of the Holocaust after the war largely failed, owing to a combination of mainly voluntary emigration by Jews themselves, restrictive state policies including bouts of antisemitism, day-to-day discrimination and prejudice on the part of the majority population, and the strong pressures to assimilate into wider society. The failure was especially apparent in Wrocław, where following the antisemitic purge of 1968, the Jewish community was reduced to almost nothing. Yet the failure to create vibrant Jewish communities and the strong forms of assimilation of Jews into communist society did not mean that Jewish identity died. If there is a positive lesson to be drawn from this essentially dismal tale, it is that identity is resilient and that communities have immense capacity to survive the vicissitudes that fate deals out to them.

---

[521] Vladimir Khanin, *Documents on Ukrainian Jewish Identity and Emigration 1944 - 1990* (London: Cass, 2003), 20.

Bibliography

Articles

Aleksiun, Natalia. "The Situation of the Jews in the Polish People's Republic as Seen by the Soviet Security Forces in 1945." *Jews in Eastern Europe* 35-37 (1998): 52-68.

Altshuler, Mordechai. "Jewish Holocaust Commemoration Activity in the USSR under Stalin." *Yad Vashem Studies* XXX (2002): 271-296.

Amar, Tarik Cyril. "Yom Kippur in L'viv: The L'viv Synagogue and the Soviet Party-State, 1944-1962." *East European Jewish Affairs* 35/1 (2005): 91-110.

Azadovskii, Konstantin, and Boris Egorov. "From Anti-Westernism to Anti-Semitism." *Journal of Cold War Studies* 4:1 (2002): 66-80.

Blus-Węgrowska, Danuta. "Pogromstimmung." *Karta: Zeitzeugnisse aus Ostmitteleuropa* 3 (2002): 161-162.

Boeckh, Katrin. "Fallstudie: Lemberg in Galizien. Jüdisches Gemeindeleben in der Ukraine zwischen 1945 und 1953." *Glaube in der 2. Welt* 4 (2002): 20-25.

Bronsztejn, Szyja. "Ludność żydowska na Dolnym Śląsku po II wojnie światowej." *Sobótka* 2 (1991): 259-275.

Davies, Norman. "Ethnic Diversity in Twentieth Century Poland." *Polin* 4 (1990): 132-149.

Gansiniec, Ryszard. "Auf Post für die Stadt: Auszüge aus den Lemberger Notizen 1944- 1946." *Karta Historische Zeitschrift* 2 (2001): 105-129.

Goldsztejn, Arnold. "Produktywizacja ludności żydowskiej na Dolnym Śląsku w latach 1945-1948." *Acta Universitatis Wratislaviensis* 1182 (1991): 118-142.

Gołuchowski, Lech. "Gomułka writes to Stalin." *Polin* 17 (2004): 365-381.

Grabski, August. "Sytuacja Żydów w Polsce w latach 1950-1957." *Biuletyn ŻIH* 4 (2000): 515-519.

Grüner, Frank. "Jüdischer Glaube und religiöse Praxis unter dem stalinistischen Regime in der Sowjetunion während der Kriegs- und Nachkriegsjahre." *Jahrbücher für die Geschichte Osteuropas* 52 (2004): 534-556.

Himka, John-Paul. "Dimensions of a Triangle: Polish-Ukrainian-Jewish Relations in Austrian Galicia." *Polin* 12 (1999): 30-55.

Hurwic-Nowakowska, Irena. "Jeszcze raz o kwestii żydowskiej." *Więź* 7-8 (1986): 91-12.

Ilicki, Julian. "Changing Identity Among Younger Polish Jews in Sweden after 1968." *Polin* 4 (1990): 268-276.

Kenney, Padraic. "Whose Nation, Whose State? Working Class Nationalism and Antisemitism in the Polish People's Republic, 1945-1947." *Polin* 13 (2000): 224-235.

Khanin, Vladimir. "Judaism and Organized Jewish Movements in the USSR / CIS after World War II: The Ukrainian Case." *Jewish Political Studies Review* 11 (1999): 75-100.

Kos, Jerzy. "Synagoga pod Białym Bocianem we Wrocławiu." *Sobótka* 2 (1991): 191-203.

Koźmińska-Frejlak, Ewa. "Polen als Heimat von Juden: Strategien des Heimischwerdens von Juden im Nachkriegspolen 1944-1949." *Jahrbuch zur Geschichte und Wirkung des Holocaust* 2 (1997): 71-108.

Melchior, Małgorzata. "Facing Antisemitism in Poland during the Second World War and in March 1968." *Polin* 21 (2009): 189-203.

Michlic-Coren, Joanna. "Anti-Jewish Violence in Poland, 1918-1939 and 1945-1947." *Polin* 13 (2004): 35-61.

Mitzner, Piotr. "Die Säuberung Lembergs." *Karta* 2 (2001): 89-95.

Polonsky, Antony. "Introduction: The Jews of Galicia under the Habsburgs." *Polin* 12 (1999): 3-24.

Pudło, Kazimierz. "Wybrane problemy z organizacji życia zbiorowego ludności żydowskiej na Dolnym Śląsku 1950-1967." *Acta Universitatis Wratislaviensis* 1182 (1991): 149-161.

Sęczyk, Waldemar. "Obraz Marca '68 w prasie lokalnej." *Sobótka* 1 (2001): 87-98.

Skerpan, Alfred. "Aspects of Soviet Antisemitism." *The Antioch Review* 3:12 (1953): 287-328.

Stola, Dariusz. "The Hate Campaign of March 1968: How did it Become Anti-Jewish." *Polin* 21 (2009): 16-36.

Waszkiewicz, Ewa. "Program i działalność polityczna Frakcji żydowskiej Polskiej Partii Robotniczej we Wrocławiu w latach 1945-1948." *Sobótka* 3-4 (1994): 299-310.

Chapters or other parts of a book

Adelson, Józef. "W Polsce zwanej ludową." In *Najnowsze dzieje Żydów w Polsce w zarysie (do 1950)*, edited by Jerzy Tomaszewski, 387-477. Warszawa: Wydawnictwo Naukowe PWN, 1993.

Altshuler, Mordechai. "Ukrainian-Jewish Relations in the Soviet Milieu in the Interwar Period." In *Ukrainian-Jewish Relations in Historical Perspective,* edited by Peter Potichnyj et al., 280-295. Edmonton: Canadian Institute of Ukrainian Studies, 1988.

Amar, Tarik Cyril. "Sovietization as a Civilizing Mission in the West." In *The Sovietization of Eastern Europe: New Perspectives on the Postwar Period,* edited by Balázs Apor et al., 29-45. Washington: New Academia Publishing, 2008.

Antypowicz, Dopowid. "Wpływ czynników społeczno-ekonomicznych na ocenę stosunków narodowościowych współcześnie na Ukrainie." In *Antysemityzm w Polsce i na Ukrainie: raport z badań*, edited by Ireneusz Krzemiński, 186-203. Warszawa: Scholar, 2004.

Bauer, Jehuda. "Some Introductory Comments." In *Insiders and Outsiders: Dilemmas of East European Jewry*, edited by Jonathan Frankel et al., 1-16. Portland: Littman Library of Jewish Civilization, 2010.

Berendt, Grzegorz. "Udział Żydów polskich w walce o pamięć i rehabilitację twórców radzieckiej kultury żydowskiej - lata 1955-1956." In *Żydzi a lewica: Zbiór studiów historycznych*, edited by August Grabski, 279-305. Warszawa: Żydowski Instytut Historyczny, 2007.

—. "Życie od nowa: Instytucje i organizacje żydowskie 1944-1950." In *Następstwa zagłady Żydów: Polska 1944-2010,* edited by Feliks Tych and Monika Adamczyk-Garbowska, 191-214. Lublin: Wydawnictwo Uniwersytetu Marii Curii-Skłodowskiej i ŻIH, 2011.

Blatman, Daniel. "National Minority Policy, Bundist Social Organizations, and Jewish Women in the Interwar Period." In *The Emergence of Modern Jewish Politics: Bundism and Zionism in Eastern Europe,* edited by Zvi Gitelman, 54-70. Pittsburgh: University of Pittsburgh Press, 2003.

Borodziej, Włodzimierz, Stanisław Ciesielski and Jerzy Kochanowski. "Wstęp." In *Przesiedlenie ludności polskiej z kresów wschodnich do Polski, 1944-1947*, edited by Stanisław Ciesielski, 1-30. Warszawa: Neriton, 1999.

Boshyk,Yury, Jonathan Frankel, Yaroslav Bilinsky and Mordechai Altshuler. "Ukrainian-Jewish Relations in the Soviet Milieu in the Interwar Period." In *Ukrainian-Jewish Relations in Historical Perspective,* edited by Peter Potichnyj et al., 281-305. Edmonton: Canadian Institute of Ukrainian Studies, 1988.

Chimen, Abramsky. "The Birobidzhan Project, 1927-1959." In *The Jews in Soviet Russia since 1917*, edited by Lionel Kochan, 64-77. Southampton: The Camelot Press, 1978.

Ciołkosz, Adam. "Anti -Zionism' in Polish Communist Party Politics." In *The left against Zion: Communism,* edited by Robert Wistrich, 137- 152. London: Vallentine Michell, 1979.

Garsztecki, Stefan. "Poland." In *1968 in Europe: A History of Protest and Activism, 1956-1977*, edited by Martin Klimke and Joachim Scharloth, 79-180. New York: Palgrave Macmillan, 2008.

Czernysz, Natalia. "Specyfika stosunku ludności Ukrainy do Żydów: przeszłość i teraźniejszość, problemy i perspektywy." In *Antysemityzm w Polsce i na Ukrainie: raport z badań*, edited by Ireneusz Krzemiński, 171-185. Warszawa: Scholar, 2004.

Fitzpatrick, Sheila. "The Two Faces of Anastasia: Narratves and Counternarratives of Identity in Stalinist Everyday Life." In *Everyday Life in Early Soviet Russia: Taking the Revolution Inside*, edited by Christina Kiaer and Eric Naiman, 23-34. Bloomington: Indiana University Press, 2006.

Gitelman, Zvi. "Native Land, Promised Land, Golden Land: Jewish Emigration from Russia and Ukraine." In *Cultures and Nations of Central and Eastern Europe: Essays in Honor of Roman Szporluk*, edited by Zvi Gitelman et al., 137-164. Cambridge: Ukrainian Research Institute, 2000.

Gitelman, Zvi, Valeriy Chervyakov, and Vladimir Shapiro. "E pluribus unum? Post-Soviet Jewish Identities and their Implications for Communal Reconstruction." In *Jewish Life after the USSR*, edited by Zvi Gitelman et al., 61-76. Bloomington: Indiana University Press, 2003.

Głowacki, Albin. "Czy i dokąd wracać? Dylematy repatriacyjne Żydów polskich." In *Świat niepożegnany: Żydzi na dawnych ziemiach wschodnich Rzeczypospolitej w XVIII-XX wieku*, edited by Krzysztof Jasiewicz, 161-180. Warszawa: Instytut Studiów Politycznych PAN, 2004.

Grabski, August. "Działalność frakcji PPR w CKŻP: jesień 1944-czerwiec 1946." In *Między emigracją a trwaniem: komuniści i syjoniści żydowscy w Polsce po Holokauście*, edited by Grzegorz Berendt and August Grabski, 9-98. Warszawa: Żydowski Instytut Historyczny, 2003

—. "Kształtowanie się pierwotnego programu żydowskich komunistów w Polsce po Holocauście." In *Studia z historii Żydów w Polsce po 1945 roku*, edited by Grzegorz Berendt, August Grabski, and Albert Stankowski, 67-100. Warszawa: Żydowski Instytut Historyczny, 2000.

Grabski, August, and Albert Stankowski. "Życie religijne społeczności żydowskiej." In *Następstwa zagłady Żydów: Polska 1944-2010*, edited by Feliks Tych and Monika Adamczyk-Garbowska, 215-244. Lublin: Wydawnictwo Uniwersytetu Marii Curii-Skłodowskiej.

Himka, John-Paul. "Ukrainian Collaboration in the Extermination of Jews During the Second World War: Sorting Out the Long-term and Conjunctural Factors." In *The Fate of the European Jews 1939-1945: Continuity and Contingency*, edited by Jonathan Frankel, 170-90. New York: Oxford University Press,1997.

Hirszowicz, Łukasz. "The Soviet-Jewish Problem: Internal and International Developments, 1972-1976." In *Aspects of Religion in the Soviet Union 1917-1967*, edited by Richard H. Marshall, 366-381. Chicago: University of Chicago, Chicago University Press, 1971.

Kossak-Szczucka, Zofia. "Protest." In *Żegota: Rada Pomocy Żydom: wybór dokumentów*, edited by Andrzej Friszke, Warszawa: Rada Pamięci Walk i Męczeństwa, 2002.

Kurcz, Zbigniew. "Aussiedlungen und Umsiedlungen in den östlichen und westlichen Grenzgebieten Polens." In *Bevölkerungstransfer und Systemwandel. Ostmitteleuropäische Grenzen nach dem Zweiten Weltkrieg*, edited by Helga Schulz, 39-54. Berlin: Berlin-Verlag Spitz, 2001.

Kurtyka, Janusz. "Wstęp." In *Wokół pogromu kieleckiego*, edited by Łukasz Kamiński and Jan Żaryń, 7-8. Warszawa: Instytut Pamięci Narodowej Komisja Ścigania Zbrodni Przeciwko Narodowi Polskiemu, 2006.

Macagg, William. "The Soviet Union and the Habsburg Empire: Problems of Comparison." In *Nationalism and Empire: The Habsburg Monarchy and the Soviet Union,* edited by Richard L. Rudolph et al., 45-64. New York: St. Martin's Press, 1992.

Paczkowski, Andrzej. "Żydzi w UB: próba weryfikacji stereotypu." In *Komunizm: ideologia, system, ludzie*, edited by Tomasz Szarota, 192-204. Warszawa: Nerition, 2001.

Patek, Artur. "Projekt Birobidżan w teorii i praktyce ZSRR." In *Żydzi a lewica: Zbiór studiów historycznych,* edited by August Grabski, 65-84. Warszawa: Żydowski Instytut Historyczny, 2007

Polonsky, Antony. "Ukrainian Collaboration in the Extermination of Jews during the Second World War: Sorting out the Long-term and Conjunctural Factors." In *The Fate of the European Jews, 1939-1945: Continuity and Contingency*, edited by Jonathan Frankel, 170-90. New York: Oxford University Press, 1997.

Rothenberg, Joshua. "Jewish Religion in the Soviet Union." In *The Jews in Soviet Russia since 1917*, edited by Lionel Kochan, 168-196. Southampton: The Camelot Press, 1978.

Schulze-Rhonhof, Friedrich-Carl. "Anstelle eines Vorwortes." In *Geschichte der Juden in Schlesien im 19. und 20. Jahrhundert,* edited by Friedrich-Carl Schulze-Rhonhof, 1-8. Hannover: Stiftung Schlesien, 1995.

Shapiro, Leonard. "Introduction." In *The Jews In Soviet Russia Since 1917*, edited by Lionel Kochan, 1-11. Southampton: The Camelot Press, 1978.

Siudut, Grzegorz. "Pochodzenie wyznaniowo-narodowościowe ludności Małopolski Wschodniej i Lwowa wedle spisu ludności z 1931." In *Lwów: miasto, społeczeństwo, kultura*, edited by Kazimierz Karolczak et al., 261-280. Kraków: Wydawnictwo Naukowe WSP, 1995.

Stankowski, Albert. "Nowe spojrzenie na statystyki dotyczące emigracji Żydów z Polski po 1944." In *Studia z historii Żydów w Polsce po 1945 roku*, edited by Grzegorz Berendt, August Grabski, and Albert Stankowski, 107-111. Warszawa: ŻIH, 2000.

Stola, Dariusz. "Antyżydowski nurt Marca 1968." In *Oblicza Marca 1968*, edited by Konrad Rokicki and Sławomir Stępień, 65-72. Warszawa: IPN, 2004.

Szaynok, Bożena. "Sprawa Arie Lernera-nieznany fragment walki z syjonizmem w Polsce pierwszej połowie lat 1950." In *Polska w podzielonym świecie po II wojnie światowej do 1989 roku*, edited by Mieczysław Wojciechowski, 258-269. Toruń: Wydawnictwo Adam Marszałek, 2002.

—. "Walka z syjonizmem w Polsce: 1948-1953." In *Komunizm: ideologia, system, ludzie*, edited by Tomasz Szarota, 252-271. Warszawa: Nerition, 2001.

Ther, Philipp. "Chancen und Untergang einer multinationalen Stadt: Die Beziehungen zwischen den Nationalitäten in Lemberg in der ersten Hälfte des 20. Jahrhunderts." In *Nationalitiätenkonflikte im 20. Jahrhundert: Ursachen von interethnischen Gewalt im Vergleich*, edited by Philipp Ther et. al., 123-146. Wiesbaden: Harrassowitz, 2003.

Tomaszewski, Jerzy. "The Jews in Poland 1918-1939: An Emerging National Minority." In *Major Changes within the Jewish People in the Wake of the Holocaust*, edited by Yisrael Gutman, 111-127. Jerusalem: Yad Vashem, 1996.

Tych, Feliks. "Das polnische Jahr 1968." In *Die Vertreibung von Juden aus Polen 1968: Antisemitismus und politisches Kalkül*, edited by Beate Kosmala, 65-79. Berlin: Metropol, 2000.

Weinryb, Bernard. "Poland." In *The Jews in the Soviet Satellites*, edited by Meyer P. Duschinsky et al., 1970-220. New York: Syracuse University Press, 1953.

Wierzbieniec, Wacław. "Organizacje żydowskie o charakterze asymilatorskim we Lwowie w okresie II Rzeczypospolitej." In *Żydzi i Judaizm we współczesnych badaniach polskich. Tom III*, edited by Krzysztof Pilarczyk, 139-172. Kraków: Antykwa, 2003.

Wildt, Michael. "Violence against Jews in Germany 1933-1939." In *Probing the Depths of German Antisemitism: German Society and the Persecution of the Jews, 1933-1941*, edited by David Bankier, 181- 212. New York: Berghan Books, 2000.

Wylęgała, Anna. "Die Russen und die russischsprachige Minderheit im gegenwärtigen Lemberg." In *Eine neue Gesellschaft in einer alten Stadt: Erinnerung und Geschichtspolitik in Lemberg anhand der Oral History*, edited by Philipp Ther et al., 125-140. Wrocław: Atut, 2007.

Zajcewa, Natalia. "Stosunki narodowościowe na Ukrainie: ujęcie regionalne." In *Antysemityzm w Polsce i na Ukrainie: raport z badań*, edited by Ireneusz Krzemiński, 236- 251. Warszawa: Scholar, 2004.

Zielinski, Konrad. "To pacify, Populate and Polonise: Territorial Transformations and the Displacement of Ethnic Minorities in Communist Poland, 1944-1949." In *Warlands: Population Resettlement and State Reconstruction in the Soviet East European Borderlands, 1945- 50*, edited by Peter Gatrell and Nick Baron,188-209. London: Palgrave Macmillan, 2009.

Zimmerman, Joshua. "Introduction: Changing Perceptions in the Historiography of Polish-Jewish Relations during the Second World War." In *Contested Memories: Poles and Jews during the Holocaust and its Aftermath*, edited by Joshua D. Zimmerman, 1-18. New Brunswick: Rutgers University Press, 2003.

Żyndul, Jolanta. "Z Getta do asymilacji: Żydzi w poszukiwaniu tożsamości." In *Tematy żydowskie: historia, literatura, edukacja*, edited by Robert Traba et al., 56-68. Olsztyn: Wspólnota Kulturowa Borussia, 1999.

Monographs and edited volumes

Abramson, Henry. *A Prayer of the Government: Ukrainians and Jews in Revolutionary Times, 1917-1920*. Cambridge: Harvard University Press, 1999.

Albin, Janusz. *Wrocław: rozwój miasta w Polsce Ludowej*. Warszawa: Państwowy Instytut Wydawniczy, 1971.

Aleksiun, Natalia. *Dokąd dalej? Ruch syjonistyczny w Polsce 1944-1950*. Warszawa: Trio, 2002.

Altshuler, Mordechai. *Soviet Jewry since the Second World War: Population and Social Structure*. New York: Greenwood Press, 1987.

Amar, Tarik C. *The Making of Soviet L'viv*. PhD diss., Princeton Universtity, 2006.

Arad, Yitzhak. *The Holocaust in the Soviet Union*. Lincoln: University of Nebraska Press, 2009.

Ascher, Abraham. *A Community under Siege: The Jews of Breslau under Nazism*. Stanford: Stanford University Press, 2007.

Barkai, Avraham. *From Boycott to Annihilation: The Economic Struggle of German Jews, 1933-1943*. Hanover: University Press of New England, 1989.

Berendt, Grzegorz. *Życie żydowskie w Polsce w latach 1950-1956: z dziejów Towarzystwa Społeczno – Kulturalnego Żydów w Polsce*. Gdańsk: Wydawnictwo Uniwersytetu Wrocławskiego, 2006.

Bergman, Werner. *Geschichte des Antisemitismus*. München: Verlag C.H. Beck, 2004.

Berkhoff, Karel. *Harvest of Despair: Life and Death in Ukraine under Nazi Rule*. Cambridge: Belknap Press of Harvard University Press, 2004.

Bocheńska, Paulina. *Polish-Jewish Relations Between 1944-48 in the Light of Prejudices, Stereotypes and Myths*. PhD diss., European University Institute, 2006. Published version: Bocheńska, Paulina. *A Mythical Jew and a Real Pole – Polish-Jewish Relations Between 1944-48 in the Light of Prejudices, Stereotypes and Myths*. Saarbrücken: VDM Verlag, 2008.

Bociurkiw, Bohdan R. *Ukrainian Churches under Soviet rule: Two Case Studies*. Cambridge: Harvard University Press, 1984.

Brown, Kate. *A Biography of No Place: From Soviet Ethnic Borderland to Soviet Heartland*. Cambridge: Harvard University Press, 2005.

Brubaker, Rogers. *Nationalism Reframed: Nationhood and the National Question in the New Europe*. Cambridge: Cambridge University Press, 1996.

Cała, Alina, and Halina Datner. *Dzieje Żydów w Polsce, 1944-1986: Teksty źródłowe*. Warszawa: ŻIH, 1997.

Cichopek, Anna. *Jews, Poles and Slovaks: A Story of Encounters, 1944-1948*. Charleston: BiblioBaazar, 2011.

—. *Pogrom Żydów w Krakowie 11 sierpnia 1945 roku*. Warszawa: ŻIH, 2000.

Davies, Norman. *God's Playground: A History of Poland in Two Volumes*. Oxford: Clarendon Press, 1981.

—, and Roger Moorhouse. *Microcosm: Portrait of a Central European City*. New York: Random House, 2011.

Dobroszycki, Lucjan, and Jeffrey Gurock. *The Holocaust in the Soviet Union: Studies and Sources on the Destruction of the Jews in the Nazi-occupied Territories of the USSR, 1941-1945*. Armonk: M. E. Sharp,1993.

Eisler, Jerzy. *Polski rok 1968*. Warszawa: IPN, 2006.

Gellately, Robert. *Backing Hitler: Consent and Coercion in Nazi Germany*. Oxford: Oxford University Press, 2001.

Gerrits, Andre. *The Myth of Jewish Communism: A Historical Interpretation*. Brussels: Peter Lang, 2009.

Gitelman, Zvi. *A Century of Ambivalence: The Jews of Russia and the Soviet Union, 1881 to the Present.* Bloomington: Indiana University Press, 2001.

Grabski, August. *Działalność komunistów wśród Żydów w Polsce (1944-1949).* Warszawa: Trio, 2004.

—. *Żydowski ruch kombatancki w Polsce w latach 1944-1949.* Warszawa: Trio, 2002.

Gross, Jan Tomasz. *Fear: Anti-Semitism in Poland after Auschwitz, an Essay in Historical Interpretation.* New York: Random House, 2006.

—. *Sąsiedzi: Historia zagłady żydowskiego miasteczka.* Sejny: Pogranicze, 2000.

—. *Und wehe du hoffst...Die Sowjetisierung Ostpolens nach dem Hitler-Stalin-Pakt (1939-1941).* Freiburg: Herder, 1988.

—. *Upiorna dekada: trzy eseje na temat Żydów, Polaków, Niemców.* Kraków: Universitas, 2001.

—, and Irena Grudzińska-Gross. *Golden Harvest.* Oxford: Oxford University Press, 2011. Polish translation: *Złote żniwa: rzecz o tym, co się działo na obrzeżach zagłady Żydów.* Kraków: Wydawnictwo Znak, 2011.

Grüner, Frank. *Patrioten und Kosmopoliten: Juden im Sowjetstaat 1941-1953.* Köln: Böhlau, 2008.

Grynberg, Michał. *Żydowska spółdzielczość pracy w Polsce w latach 1945-1949.* Warszawa: PWN, 1986.

Haumann, Heiko. *A History of East European Jews.* Budapest: Central European University Press, 2002.

Hirszfeld, Ludwik. *Historia jednego życia.* Warszawa: PAX, 1989.

Hryciuk, Grzegorz. *Polacy we Lwowie 1939 -1944: życie codzienne.* Warszawa: Książka i Wiedza, 2000.

Hoffmann, Andreas. *Nachkriegszeit in Schlesien: Gesellschafts- und Bevölkerungspolitik in den polnischen Siedlungsgebieten 1945-1948.* Köln: Böhlau, 2000.

Hurwic-Nowakowska, Irena. *Żydzi polscy 1947-1950: analiza więzi społecznej ludności żydowskiej.* Warszawa: Wydawnictwo Instytutu Filozofii i Socjologii Polskiej Akademii Nauk, 1996.

Ilicki, Julian. *Den föränderliga idenitieten: om identitetsförändringar hos den yngre generationen polska judar som invandrade till Sverige under åren 1968-1972.* Åbo: Sällskapet för judaistisk forskning, 1988.

Kaganovich, Lazar. *Pamyatnye zapysky.* Moscow: Vagrius, 1996.

Kahane, Dawid. *L'viv ghetto diary.* Amherst: The University of Massachusetts Press, 1993.

Kamiński, Łukasz, and Jan Żaryń. *Wokół pogromu kieleckiego.* Warszawa: IPN, 2006.

Kazejak, Izabela. *Zwischen Assimilation und Emigration: die Breslauer jüdische Minderheit in den Jahren 1945-1968.* M.A. thesis, Europa-Universität Viadrinia, 2007.

Kenney, Padraic. *Rebuilding Poland: Workers and Communists 1945-1950.* Boulder: Cornell University Press, 1997.

Kersten, Krystyna. *Żydzi, Polacy, Komunizm: anatomia półprawd.* Warszawa: Niezależna Oficyna Wydawnicza,1992.

Khanin, Vladimir. *Documents on Ukrainian Jewish Identity and Emigration 1944-1990.* London: Cass, 2003.

Kochan, Lionel. *The Jews in Soviet Russia since 1917.* Oxford: Oxford University Press, 1978.

Kolarz, Walter. *Religion in the Soviet Union.* London: Macmillan, 1962.

Kula, Marcin. *Uparta sprawa: żydowska, Polska, ludzka?* Kraków: Universitas, 2004.

Krzemiński, Ireneusz. *Antysemityzm w Polsce i na Ukrainie.* Warszawa: Scholar, 2004.

Laqueur, Walter. *The Changing Face of Antisemitism: From Ancient Times to the Present Day.* Oxford: Oxford University Press, 2006.

Lasman, Noach. *Wspomnienia z Polski: 1 sierpnia 1944-30 kwietnia 1957.* Warszawa: Żydowski Instytut Historyczny, 1997.

Levin, Kurt. *Przeżyłem: saga świętego Jura spisana w 1946 przez syna rabina Lwowa.* Ciechanów: Fundacja Zeszytów Literackich, 2006.

Levin, Nora. *The Jews in the Soviet Union Since 1917: Paradox of Survival.* New York: New York University Press, 1988.

Lower, Wendy. *Nazi-Empire Building and the Holocaust in Ukraine.* Chapel Hill: University of North Carolina Press, 2005.

—, and Ray Brandon. *The Shoah in Ukraine: History, Testimony, Memorialization.* Bloomington: Indiana University Press, 2008.

Lukowski, Jerzy, and Hubert Zawadzki. *A Concise History of Poland.* Cambridge: Cambridge University Press, 2001.

Machcewicz, Paweł. *Polski rok 1956.* Warszawa: Mówią Wieki, 1993.

Magocsi, Paul Robert. *History of Ukraine.* Seattle: University of Washington Press, 1998.

Markus, Vasyl. *Religion and Nationalism in Soviet Ukraine after 1945.* Cambridge: Harvard University Press, 1985.

Marples, David. *Stalinism in Ukraine in the 1940s.* Edmonton: University of Alberta Press, 1992.

Marrus, Michael R. *The Unwanted: European Refugees in the Twentieth Century.* New York: Oxford University Press, 1985.

Martin, Terry. *The Affirmative Action Empire: Nations and Nationalism in the Soviet Union, 1923-1939.* London: Cornell University Press, 2001.

Mendelsohn, Ezra. *The Jews of East Central Europe between the World Wars.* Bloomington: Indiana University Press, 1983.

Mitsel, Mikhail. *Obshchiny iudeiskovo veroispovidaniia v Ukrainie, 1945-1981.* Kiev: Sfera, 1998.

Modras, Ronald. *Kościół Katolicki i antysemityzm w Polsce w latach 1933-1939.* Kraków: Homini, 2004.

Ordyłowski, Marek. *Życie codzienne we Wrocławiu 1945- 1948.* Wrocław: Zakład Narodowy im. Ossolińskich, 1991.

Osęka, Piotr. *Marzec '68.* Kraków: Znak, 2008.

—. *Syjoniści, inspiratorzy, wichrzyciele: Obraz wroga w propagandzie Marca 1968.* Warszawa: ŻIH, 1999.

Pinkus, Beniamin. *The Jews of the Soviet Union: The History of a National Minority.* Cambridge: Cambridge University Press, 1988.

Pufelska, Agnieszka. *Die 'Judäo-Kommune' — ein Feindbild in Polen: das polnische Selbstverständnis im Schatten des Antisemitismus.* Paderborn: Ferdinand Schöningh Verlag, 2007.

Pulzer, Peter. *Jews and the German State: The Political History of a Minority 1848-1933.* Cambridge: Harvard University Press, 1992.

Rahden, Till van. *Juden und andere Breslauer: die Beziehungen zwischen Juden, Protestanten und Katholiken in einer deutschen Großstadt von 1860 bis 1925.* Göttingen: Vandenhoeck & Ruprecht, 2000.

Redlich, Shimon. *War, Holocaust and Stalinizm: A Documented Study of the Jewish Anti- Fascist Committee in the USSR.* Luxembourg: Harwood Academic, 1995.

Ro'i, Yaacov. *The Struggle for Soviet Jewish Emigration.* Cambridge: Cambridge University Press, 1991.

Ro'i, Yaacov, ed. *Jews and Jewish Life in Russia and the Soviet Union.* Newbury Park: Frank Cass and Co., 1995.

Shore, Marci. *Caviar and Ashes: A Warsaw Generation's Life and Death in Marxism 1918-1968.* New Haven: Yale University Press, 2006.

Skalska, Agnieszka. *Obraz wroga w antysemickich rysunkach prasowych Marca 68'.* Warszawa: Narodowe Centrum Kultury, 2007.

Steer, Martina. *Bertha Badt-Strauss: eine jüdische Publizistin.* Frankfurt/Main: Campus, 2005.

Steffen, Katrin. *Jüdische Polonität: Ethnizität und Nation im Spiegel der polnischsprachigen jüdischen Presse 1918-1939.* Göttingen: Vandenhoeck & Ruprecht, 2004.

Steinlauf, Michael. *Pamięć nieprzyswojona.* Warszawa: Cyklady, 2001.

Stola, Dariusz. *Kampania antysyjonistyczna w Polsce 1967-1968*. Warszawa: Instytut Studiów Politycznych PAN, 2000.

Subtelny, Orest. *Ukraine: A History*. Toronto: University of Toronto Press, 1988.

Suleja, Włodzimierz. *Dolnośląski Marzec' 68: anatomia protestu*. Warszawa: IPN, 2006.

—. *Historia Wrocławia, Vol. 3: W Polsce Ludowej, PRL i III Rzeczypospolitej*. Wrocław: Wydawnictwo Dolnośląskie, 2001.

—. *Pogrom w Kielcach 4 lipca 1946 roku*. Warszawa: Bellona, 1992.

Szaynok, Bożena. *Ludność żydowska na Dolnym Śląsku 1945-1950*. Wrocław: Wydawnictwo Uniwersytetu Wrocławskiego, 2000.

—. *Z historią i z Moskwą w tle. Polska a Izrael 1944-1968*. Warszawa: IPN, 2007.

Szydzisz, Marcin. *Społeczność żydowska na Dolnym Śląsku w latach 1950-1989 w świetle działalności Towarzystwa Społeczno-Kulturalnego Żydów w Polsce*. PhD diss., University of Wrocław, 2005.

Thum, Gregor. *Die fremde Stadt – Breslau 1945*. Berlin: Siedler, 2003.

Tyszkiewicz, Jakub. *Sto wielkich dni Wrocławia: wystawa Ziem Odzyskanych we Wrocławiu a propaganda polityczna Ziem Zachodnich i Północnych w latach 1945-48*. Wrocław: Wydawnictwo Arboretum, 1997.

Vasyl, Markus. *Religion and Nationalism in Soviet Ukraine after 1945*. Cambridge: Harvard University Press, 1985.

Wajntraub-Busson, Magdalena. *Gesellschaftliche und politische Hintergründe des Judenpogroms in Kielce vom 4. Juli 1946*. M.A. thesis, Europa-Universität Viadrina, Frankfurt/Oder, 2005.

Waszkiewicz, Ewa. *Kongregacja Wyznania Mojżeszowego na Dolnym Śląsku na tle polityki wyznaniowej Polskiej Rzeczypospolitej Ludowej 1945-1968*. Wrocław: Wydawnictwo Uniwersytetu Wrocławskiego, 1999.

Weiner, Amir. *Making Sense of War: The Second World War and the Fate of the Bolshevik Revolution*. Princeton: Princeton University Press, 2001.

Wiszniewicz, Joanna. *Życie przecięte: opowieści pokolenia marca*. Wołowiec: Wydawnictwo Czarne, 2008.

Wolak, Artur. *Forced Out: The Fate of Polish Jewry in Communist Poland*. Tucson: Fenestra Books, 2004.

Yones, Eliahu. *Smoke in the Sand: The Jews of Lvov in the War Years, 1939-1944*. Jerusalem: Gafen Publishing House, 2004.

Zabarko, Boris. *Holocaust in Ukraine*. London: Vallentine Michell, 2005.

Ziątkowski, Leszek. *Dzieje Żydów we Wrocławiu*. Wrocław: Wydawnictwo Dolnośląskie, 2000.

Zubrzycki, Geneviéve. *The Crosses of Auschwitz: Nationalism and Religion in Post-Communist Poland.* Chicago: The University of Chicago Press, 2006.

Internet – sources

Czech, Mirosław. "Antysemityzm w ZSRR: rozjechani ciężarówką." *Gazeta Wyborcza*, http://wyborcza.pl/1,97737,7533270,Antysemityzm_w_ZSRR__rozjechani_ciezarowka.html.

Luvish, Ilya Eli. "Post World War 2 Pogroms." http://www.ilyaluvish.com/post-world-war-2-pogroms/#_ftn40.

Open Society Archives. Radio Free Europe News & Information Service, 'Emigration of Polish Jews', 6 June 1957. http://www.osaarchivum.org/files/holdings/300/8/3/text/39-1-175.shtml.

Osipova, I. I. "Presledovaniia Khasidov vo L'vove v 40-kh godov." *Khasidus po-russki*. http://chassidus.ru/history_of_chassidism/osipova/7.htm.

Tonini, Carla. "The Jews in Poland after the Second World War: Most Recent Contributions of Polish Historiography." *Quest. Issues in Contemporary Jewish History. Journal of Fondazione CDEC* 1 (2010). www.quest-cdecjournal.it/focus.php?id=211.

Tych, Feliks. "Deutsche, Juden, Polen: Der Holocaust und seine Spätfolgen," last modified August 2000. http://library.fes.de/fulltext/historiker/00809002.htm.

"L'vovskaia sinagoga na ulitse Ugol'noi."

http://clubs.ya.ru/4611686018427425093/replies.xml?item_no=421.

http://www.eleven.co.il/article/12523

http://en.wikipedia.org/wiki/1968_Polish_political_crisis#cite_note-ipn 238-14

http://jwa.org/encyclopedia/article/demography-soviet-union-russian-federation-and-other-successor-states

http://www.sbu.gov.ua/sbu/control/uk/publish/article?art_id=40380&cat_id=53081 http://www.sbu.gov.ua/sbu/doccatalog/document?id=42995

http://ru.wikipedia.org/wiki/percentD0percent9BpercentD1percent8CpercentD0percentB2percentD0percentBEpercentD0percentB2

http://www.yivoencyclopedia.org/article.aspx/WrocpercentC5percent82aw

http://www.yivoencyclopedia.org/article.aspx/Soviet_Yiddish-Language_Schools

Consulted Archives:

Warsaw

Archive of the Jewish Historical Institute:

There are several types of documents that relate to the life of Jews in Wrocław. For instance the Central Committee of Jews in Poland produced a range of documents on the life of Jews. It consisted of many departments, particularly: the Department of Repatriation (303/ VI / 63), the Department of Education (303 / IX/ 1584), the Department for Statistics and Records (303 / V/ 401) and the Department of Controlling and Organization (303/ 2/ 130). Files 61-62 consist of documents produced by the Social and Cultural Association of Jews in Poland at the Department of Organization and include for instance the correspondence with Jews who were living in Poland as well as letters from the Social and Cultural Association in the main Polish cities. I was concerned with analyzing documents that included information on Wrocław. The main office of the Social and Cultural Association of Jews in Warsaw had its own departments and dealt with many requests coming from the other Polish cities in which Jews were living. This material proved to be most important for the collection of important information on the life of Jews in Wrocław.

List of documents used:

324 / 1190, Letter of the Social and Cultural Association of Jews in Wrocław to the Main Executive Committee in Warsaw, March 31, 1954

817, TSKŻ Towarzystwo Społeczno-Kulturalne Żydów w Polsce

303 / IX/ 1584, Department of Education

77, Department of Organization, Notatka informacyjna o udziale TSKŻ w akcji wyborczej do Rad Narodowych, Protokoły z odbytego w dniu 12 October 1954 zebrania Żydów - pracowników Wrocławskiego Zjednoczenia Elektormontażowego, Notatka informacyjna o udziale TSKŻ w akcji wyborczej do Rad Narodowych

324 / 1184, Society for Health Care, Reports (TOZ Sprawozdania).

303 / II / 126, Report from 25 June 1948 written during the meeting of the Jewish Voivodship Committee

- 73 Social and Cultural Association of Jews, Protokół narady aktywu z udziałem Egita, analiza przeprowadzonej kampanii Jidysz Buch na rok 1952 i wytyczne na rok 1953.
- 303/ II/ 133, Central Committee of Jews in Poland, Department of Organization and Controling, 8 Report of the Jewish Voivodship Committee in Wrocław.
- 303/ II/ 127, Report from 25 October 1949 of the Jewish Voivodship Committee and the Jewish Association of Culture, 21.
- 324 / 1180, Society for Health Care, Reports (Sprawozdania TOZ).
- 324/ 1172 (TOZ Sprawozdania) Society for the Healthcare, 54
- 324 / 1190 Society for Health Care, Reports (TOZ Sprawozdania).
- 303/ VI / 63, Department of Repatriation, Report summarizing the situation of the incoming migrants for the period of time from January to 1 July 1946.
- 303 / V/ 401, CKŻP - Central Committee of Jews in Poland, Department of Statistics and Records, 16. Report for the first half of the year 1946.
- 303 / V / 401, CKŻP Central Committee of Jews in Poland, Department of Statistics and Records, Report on conducted local briefings.
- 303/ V/ 683, Central Committee of Jews in Poland, Department of Statistics and Records.
- 61- 62, Documents produced by the Social and Cultural Association of Jews in Poland, Department of Organization, Correspondence
- 303 / V / 401, Department of Statistics and Records, 44. Report on the work of the schools with Yiddish language as a language of instruction at the Jewish Committee of the Lower Silesian Voivodship for the period of time: 1 January -1 June 1946.
- 303/ 2/ 130, Central Committee of Jews in Poland, Department of Controlling and Organization, Report on the activities of this department written in 1946, 16.
- 303-2-130, Central Committee of Jews, Department of Controlling and Organization, 43.
- 61-62, Social and Cultural Association of Jews, Department of Organization, Wyciąg z protokołu posiedzenia Prezydium Wojewódzkiego TSKZ z dnia 22 sierpnia 1951.
- 65, Section: The Social and Cultural Organization of Jews, Correspondence
- 67, Department of Organization, Social and Cultural Association of Jews, TSKŻ, documents written on 23 and 19 December 1955

115, Social and Cultural Association of Jews, Department of Organization, page 3. Letter to the Communal Police Station (Militia) written by the Social and Cultural Association of Jews in Wrocław on 3 November 1956.

118, Social and Cultural Association of Jews, Letter to the Prime Minister Józef Cyrankiewicz.

118, Social and Cultural Association of Jews in Wrocław, document dated: 31 July 1957

2, Social and Cultural Association of Jews, AŻIH, letter written on 8 October 1956

4, TSKŻ, Uwagi i wnioski o szkolnictwie żydowskim.

Wrocław

State Archive in Wrocław

The material stored in this archive consists of documents produced by the local administration. It also includes material produced by the Jewish Voivodship Committee in Wrocław. This material is very important for the understanding of the history of Jewish settlement in Lower Silesia after 1945. The material produced by the main Jewish organization in Lower Silesia, the Jewish Voivodship Committee, was produced by Jews themselves, and consists of monthly reports on the activities of the Jewish Voivodship Committee in Lower Silesia concerning the settlement of Jews and their work in Wrocław and other Lower Silesian cities.

List of documents used:

AP WKŻ 17, Information concerning the Yiddish language at the kindergarten, from 22 April 1947.

AP Wr., WKŻ (Jewish Voivodship Committee) 17, Protocol of the meeting of the City Jewish Committee on 11 December 1946

AP Wr., WKŻ 17, Protocol of the meeting of the City Jewish Committee on 23 January 1947.

AP Wr., Jewish Voivodship Committee, Taśma nr T932 14.

AP Wr., WKŻ Department of Settlement Protocol number 001, 002

AP Wr., WKŻ 17, Jewish City Committee of Wrocław, Report written on 9 July 1948,

AP Wr., WKŻ, Jewish Voivodship Committee for Lower Silesia of 23 May 1949

AP Wr., WKŻ Jewish Committee of Lower Silesian Voivodship, 12th Protocol 27 July 1946.

AP Wr., C.S.W. "Solidarność", 2/2,5 / 67.

AP Wr., Jewish Voivodship Committee, Protocols of the Jewish Committee of the Wrocław Voivodship, 8 August 1945 (number of the Zespół 415).

AP Wr., WKŻ 17, (Jewish Voivodship Committee) Protocol from 4 December 1945 from the meeting of the City Committee of Jews.

AP Wr., Department of Settlement, 4, Report about controlling the districts of Rychbach (Dzierżoniów), Wałbrzych, and Kłodzko.

AP Wr., WKŻ Jewish Voivodship Committee, Report written on 21 May 1948,222.

AP Wr., WKŻ Jewish Voivodship Committee, Protocols of the main body of the Jewish Voivodship Committee and other meetings number 415, Protocol of 17 March 1946

AP, Wr., 74/ 04 / 76

AP, Wr., 74 / 04/ 72

AP, Wr., Komitet Wojewódzki PZPR, 74/ XIV/ 17

Warsaw, Wrocław

AIPN, Archive of the Polish Institute for National Remembrance:

This archive stores material produced by important Polish institutions. Hence it includes material produced for and by the Security Service and other institutions. This is a very important source of knowledge of the history of Poland after 1944. This is because the institutions of the state, including the militia, wrote reports to Warsaw about their activity and about potential problems, for instance concerning the minority issues. I examined the material produced for the Ministry of Education and the Ministry of Internal Affairs (MSW Ministerstwo Spraw Zagranicznych).

List of documents used

AIPN Wr. 053/ 346, 133

AIPN KGMO 35/ 922, Report of the Militia of the Wrocław Voivodship for the period from 15 April to 15 May 1946.

KGMO 35/922, Report about the situation in Wrocław between 25 October and 10 November 1945.

AIPN BU MSW II 829

AIPN BU MSW II 7148, Information about projects for organizing primary and secondary schools with the additional teaching of the Yiddish language for the academic year 1967/ 68.

AIPN BU MSW II 7161, Information about the meeting of women who were members at the Social and Cultural Association of Jews. This took place on 15 June 1963 in Łódź at the Social and Cultural Association of Jews.

AIPN BU MSW II 7268, Information on the expulsion of JOINT.

AIPN Wrocław 053 / 1480.

AIPN Wr 053 / 1481

AIPN / Wr 053 / 1599

AIPN BU MSW II 7198

AIPN 053/ 566, 279, reprinted in Łukasz Kamiński, "Wrocławski Marzec '68 w meldunkach służby bezpieczeństwa," *Rocznik Wrocławski* 9 (2004), 265.

AIPN BU MSW 7197, notatka służbowa.

AIPN Wrocław / 053 / 1481 Volume Five.

AIPN Wrocław 053 / 1482

Ukrainian Archives

State Archive of the L'viv Region

This archive contains material produced by the institutions of the state in the L'viv region. I worked there with material produced by the Plenipotentiary for Religious Cults in L'viv on the activities of the L'viv Jewish community.

List of documents used

State Archive of the L'viv Region, p-1332/2/25

State Archive of the L'viv Region, p - 3/ 8/ 120

State Archive of the L'viv Region, Documents produced by the Plenipotentiary of Religious Cults, p- 1332-2-6-57.

State Archive of the L'viv Region, Documents produced by the Plenipotentiary of Religious Cults, p- 1332-2-15.

State Archive of L'viv Region, Documents produced by the Plenipotentiary of Religious Cults, p-1332.

State Archive of the L'viv Region, Documents produced by the Plenipotentiary for Religious Cults in L'viv, p-3/8/446.

State Security Archive in Kiev and in L'viv

This archive contains material on the activities of the Security Service. This material concerns the security of the state with regard to problems in the Soviet period connected to the presence of Jews in Ukraine. For instance, the international contacts of Jews were perceived as a problem, which is why the reports on these issues were produced by the Security Service.

State Security Service Archive of Ukraine, Kiev, 105, 23, April 1946.

State Security Service Archive of Ukraine, Kiev, 16, o- 7/ 4, 1948, vol. 6.

A pamphlet written by the KGB in 1956. State Security Service Archive in Kiev: 13/ 535.

Archive of the State Security Service of the L'viv region, p- 7290.

Central State Archive of Public Organizations of Ukraine

This archive consists of material that was produced by the institutions of the state in the Soviet period. This material also concerns the problems of the Jewish organizations and the struggle of Jews to emigrate.

List of documents used:

TsDAGO, 1/ 23/ 3851.

TsDAGO, Report on the work of the UKSSR Commissioner of the council for the affairs of religious cults.

TsDAGO, 1/ 23/ 4556, 109. Documents produced by the Plenipotentiary for Religious Cults.

TsDAGO, 1/ 70/ 1281, 7.

TsDAGO F.1, OP 23. D. 1640, LL 155A, 176-180, Report on the work of the UKSSR Commissioner of the council for the affairs of religious cults for 1945, reprinted in Khanin, Documents, 68-72.

TsDAGO, 1/ 23/ 5070, 17. Documents produced by the Plenipotentiary for Religious Cults.

TsDAGO, f.1. op. 24. d. 5488, II. 57- 9, reprinted in Khanin, Documents, 172

TsDAGO, F. 1, OP. 25, D. 541, LL. 2-4, P.E. Shelest to the CPSU CC on 11-12 March 1971, reprinted in Khanin, Documents, 186.

TsDAGO 1/ 24/ 4265/ Document Concerning Mass Political Work among the Population of L'viv oblast, reprinted in Khanin, Documents, 149.

TsDAGO, F.1, OP 25, D. 695, LL 6-16, G. Kriuchkov et al., Report on Pro-emigration Sentiment among a Segment of the Jewish Population in the UKSSR, reprinted in Khanin, Documents, 246-256.

TsDAGO, F.1, OP 25, D. 699, LL.53-7, V. Kutsevol to the CPU CC, reprinted in Khanin, Documents, 229-231.

TsDAGO, F.1, OP. 25, D. 514, LL. 17-20, A. Grigorenko to the CPU, reprinted in Khanin, Documents, 187-190.

TsDAGO, F.1, OP. 25, D. 890, LL. 43-5, Golovchenko to the CPU CC, reprinted in Khanin, Documents, 259-261.

TsDAGO, F.1, OP. 25, D. 699, LL. 34-7, V. Dykusarov to the CPU CC, reprinted in Khanin,Documents, 220-223.

SOVIET AND POST-SOVIET POLITICS AND SOCIETY
Edited by Dr. Andreas Umland | ISSN 1614-3515

1   Андреас Умланд (ред.) | Воплощение Европейской конвенции по правам человека в России. Философские, юридические и эмпирические исследования | ISBN 3-89821-387-0

2   Christian Wipperfürth | Russland – ein vertrauenswürdiger Partner? Grundlagen, Hintergründe und Praxis gegenwärtiger russischer Außenpolitik | Mit einem Vorwort von Heinz Timmermann | ISBN 3-89821-401-X

3   Manja Hussner | Die Übernahme internationalen Rechts in die russische und deutsche Rechtsordnung. Eine vergleichende Analyse zur Völkerrechtsfreundlichkeit der Verfassungen der Russländischen Föderation und der Bundesrepublik Deutschland | Mit einem Vorwort von Rainer Arnold | ISBN 3-89821-438-9

4   Matthew Tejada | Bulgaria's Democratic Consolidation and the Kozloduy Nuclear Power Plant (KNPP). The Unattainability of Closure | With a foreword by Richard J. Crampton | ISBN 3-89821-439-7

5   Марк Григорьевич Меерович | Квадратные метры, определяющие сознание. Государственная жилищная политика в СССР. 1921 – 1941 гг | ISBN 3-89821-474-5

6   Andrei P. Tsygankov, Pavel A. Tsygankov (Eds.) | New Directions in Russian International Studies | ISBN 3-89821-422-2

7   Марк Григорьевич Меерович | Как власть народ к труду приучала. Жилище в СССР – средство управления людьми. 1917 – 1941 гг. | С предисловием Елены Осокиной | ISBN 3-89821-495-8

8   David J. Galbreath | Nation-Building and Minority Politics in Post-Socialist States. Interests, Influence and Identities in Estonia and Latvia | With a foreword by David J. Smith | ISBN 3-89821-467-2

9   Алексей Юрьевич Безугольный | Народы Кавказа в Вооруженных силах СССР в годы Великой Отечественной войны 1941-1945 гг. | С предисловием Николая Бугая | ISBN 3-89821-475-3

10 Вячеслав Лихачев и Владимир Прибыловский (ред.) | Русское Национальное Единство, 1990-2000. В 2-х томах | ISBN 3-89821-523-7

11 Николай Бугай (ред.) | Народы стран Балтии в условиях сталинизма (1940-е – 1950-е годы). Документированная история | ISBN 3-89821-525-3

12 Ingmar Bredies (Hrsg.) | Zur Anatomie der Orange Revolution in der Ukraine. Wechsel des Elitenregimes oder Triumph des Parlamentarismus? | ISBN 3-89821-524-5

13 Anastasia V. Mitrofanova | The Politicization of Russian Orthodoxy. Actors and Ideas | With a foreword by William C. Gay | ISBN 3-89821-481-8

14 Nathan D. Larson | Alexander Solzhenitsyn and the Russo-Jewish Question | ISBN 3-89821-483-4

15 Guido Houben | Kulturpolitik und Ethnizität. Staatliche Kunstförderung im Russland der neunziger Jahre | Mit einem Vorwort von Gert Weisskirchen | ISBN 3-89821-542-3

16 Leonid Luks | Der russische „Sonderweg"? Aufsätze zur neuesten Geschichte Russlands im europäischen Kontext | ISBN 3-89821-496-6

17 Евгений Мороз | История «Мёртвой воды» – от страшной сказки к большой политике. Политическое неоязычество в постсоветской России | ISBN 3-89821-551-2

18 Александр Верховский и Галина Кожевникова (ред.) | Этническая и религиозная интолерантность в российских СМИ. Результаты мониторинга 2001-2004 гг. | ISBN 3-89821-569-5

19 Christian Ganzer | Sowjetisches Erbe und ukrainische Nation. Das Museum der Geschichte des Zaporoger Kosakentums auf der Insel Chortycja | Mit einem Vorwort von Frank Golczewski | ISBN 3-89821-504-0

20 Эльза-Баир Гучинова | Помнить нельзя забыть. Антропология депортационной травмы калмыков | С предисловием Кэролайн Хамфри | ISBN 3-89821-506-7

21 Юлия Лидерман | Мотивы «проверки» и «испытания» в постсоветской культуре. Советское прошлое в российском кинематографе 1990-х годов | С предисловием Евгения Марголита | ISBN 3-89821-511-3

22 Tanya Lokshina, Ray Thomas, Mary Mayer (Eds.) | The Imposition of a Fake Political Settlement in the Northern Caucasus. The 2003 Chechen Presidential Election | ISBN 3-89821-436-2

23 Timothy McCajor Hall, Rosie Read (Eds.) | Changes in the Heart of Europe. Recent Ethnographies of Czechs, Slovaks, Roma, and Sorbs | With an afterword by Zdeněk Salzmann | ISBN 3-89821-606-3

24　*Christian Autengruber* | Die politischen Parteien in Bulgarien und Rumänien. Eine vergleichende Analyse seit Beginn der 90er Jahre | Mit einem Vorwort von Dorothée de Nève | ISBN 3-89821-476-1

25　*Annette Freyberg-Inan with Radu Cristescu* | The Ghosts in Our Classrooms, or: John Dewey Meets Ceauşescu. The Promise and the Failures of Civic Education in Romania | ISBN 3-89821-416-8

26　*John B. Dunlop* | The 2002 Dubrovka and 2004 Beslan Hostage Crises. A Critique of Russian Counter-Terrorism | With a foreword by Donald N. Jensen | ISBN 3-89821-608-X

27　*Peter Koller* | Das touristische Potenzial von Kam"janec'–Podil's'kyj. Eine fremdenverkehrsgeographische Untersuchung der Zukunftsperspektiven und Maßnahmenplanung zur Destinationsentwicklung des „ukrainischen Rothenburg" | Mit einem Vorwort von Kristiane Klemm | ISBN 3-89821-640-3

28　*Françoise Daucé, Elisabeth Sieca-Kozlowski (Eds.)* | Dedovshchina in the Post-Soviet Military. Hazing of Russian Army Conscripts in a Comparative Perspective | With a foreword by Dale Herspring | ISBN 3-89821-616-0

29　*Florian Strasser* | Zivilgesellschaftliche Einflüsse auf die Orange Revolution. Die gewaltlose Massenbewegung und die ukrainische Wahlkrise 2004 | Mit einem Vorwort von Egbert Jahn | ISBN 3-89821-648-9

30　*Rebecca S. Katz* | The Georgian Regime Crisis of 2003-2004. A Case Study in Post-Soviet Media Representation of Politics, Crime and Corruption | ISBN 3-89821-413-3

31　*Vladimir Kantor* | Willkür oder Freiheit. Beiträge zur russischen Geschichtsphilosophie | Ediert von Dagmar Herrmann sowie mit einem Vorwort versehen von Leonid Luks | ISBN 3-89821-589-X

32　*Laura A. Victoir* | The Russian Land Estate Today. A Case Study of Cultural Politics in Post-Soviet Russia | With a foreword by Priscilla Roosevelt | ISBN 3-89821-426-5

33　*Ivan Katchanovski* | Cleft Countries. Regional Political Divisions and Cultures in Post-Soviet Ukraine and Moldova | With a foreword by Francis Fukuyama | ISBN 3-89821-558-X

34　*Florian Mühlfried* | Postsowjetische Feiern. Das Georgische Bankett im Wandel | Mit einem Vorwort von Kevin Tuite | ISBN 3-89821-601-2

35　*Roger Griffin, Werner Loh, Andreas Umland (Eds.)* | Fascism Past and Present, West and East. An International Debate on Concepts and Cases in the Comparative Study of the Extreme Right | With an afterword by Walter Laqueur | ISBN 3-89821-674-8

36　*Sebastian Schlegel* | Der „Weiße Archipel". Sowjetische Atomstädte 1945-1991 | Mit einem Geleitwort von Thomas Bohn | ISBN 3-89821-679-9

37　*Vyacheslav Likhachev* | Political Anti-Semitism in Post-Soviet Russia. Actors and Ideas in 1991-2003 | Edited and translated from Russian by Eugene Veklerov | ISBN 3-89821-529-6

38　*Josette Baer (Ed.)* | Preparing Liberty in Central Europe. Political Texts from the Spring of Nations 1848 to the Spring of Prague 1968 | With a foreword by Zdeněk V. David | ISBN 3-89821-546-6

39　*Михаил Лукьянов* | Российский консерватизм и реформа, 1907-1914 | С предисловием Марка Д. Стейнберга | ISBN 3-89821-503-2

40　*Nicola Melloni* | Market Without Economy. The 1998 Russian Financial Crisis | With a foreword by Eiji Furukawa | ISBN 3-89821-407-9

41　*Dmitrij Chmelnizki* | Die Architektur Stalins | Bd. 1: Studien zu Ideologie und Stil | Bd. 2: Bilddokumentation | Mit einem Vorwort von Bruno Flierl | ISBN 3-89821-515-6

42　*Katja Yafimava* | Post-Soviet Russian-Belarussian Relationships. The Role of Gas Transit Pipelines | With a foreword by Jonathan P. Stern | ISBN 3-89821-655-1

43　*Boris Chavkin* | Verflechtungen der deutschen und russischen Zeitgeschichte. Aufsätze und Archivfunde zu den Beziehungen Deutschlands und der Sowjetunion von 1917 bis 1991 | Ediert von Markus Edlinger sowie mit einem Vorwort versehen von Leonid Luks | ISBN 3-89821-756-5

44　*Anastasija Grynenko in Zusammenarbeit mit Claudia Dathe* | Die Terminologie des Gerichtswesens der Ukraine und Deutschlands im Vergleich. Eine übersetzungswissenschaftliche Analyse juristischer Fachbegriffe im Deutschen, Ukrainischen und Russischen | Mit einem Vorwort von Ulrich Hartmann | ISBN 3-89821-691-8

45　*Anton Burkov* | The Impact of the European Convention on Human Rights on Russian Law. Legislation and Application in 1996-2006 | With a foreword by Françoise Hampson | ISBN 978-3-89821-639-5

46　*Stina Torjesen, Indra Overland (Eds.)* | International Election Observers in Post-Soviet Azerbaijan. Geopolitical Pawns or Agents of Change? | ISBN 978-3-89821-743-9

47　*Taras Kuzio* | Ukraine – Crimea – Russia. Triangle of Conflict | ISBN 978-3-89821-761-3

48　*Claudia Šabić* | „Ich erinnere mich nicht, aber L'viv!" Zur Funktion kultureller Faktoren für die Institutionalisierung und Entwicklung einer ukrainischen Region | Mit einem Vorwort von Melanie Tatur | ISBN 978-3-89821-752-1

49   *Marlies Bilz* | Tatarstan in der Transformation. Nationaler Diskurs und Politische Praxis 1988-1994 | Mit einem Vorwort von Frank Golczewski | ISBN 978-3-89821-722-4

50   *Марлен Ларюэль (ред.)* | Современные интерпретации русского национализма | ISBN 978-3-89821-795-8

51   *Sonja Schüler* | Die ethnische Dimension der Armut. Roma im postsozialistischen Rumänien | Mit einem Vorwort von Anton Sterbling | ISBN 978-3-89821-776-7

52   *Галина Кожевникова* | Радикальный национализм в России и противодействие ему. Сборник докладов Центра «Сова» за 2004-2007 гг. | С предисловием Александра Верховского | ISBN 978-3-89821-721-7

53   *Галина Кожевникова и Владимир Прибыловский* | Российская власть в биографиях I. Высшие должностные лица РФ в 2004 г. | ISBN 978-3-89821-796-5

54   *Галина Кожевникова и Владимир Прибыловский* | Российская власть в биографиях II. Члены Правительства РФ в 2004 г. | ISBN 978-3-89821-797-2

55   *Галина Кожевникова и Владимир Прибыловский* | Российская власть в биографиях III. Руководители федеральных служб и агентств РФ в 2004 г. | ISBN 978-3-89821-798-9

56   *Ileana Petroniu* | Privatisierung in Transformationsökonomien. Determinanten der Restrukturierungs-Bereitschaft am Beispiel Polens, Rumäniens und der Ukraine | Mit einem Vorwort von Rainer W. Schäfer | ISBN 978-3-89821-790-3

57   *Christian Wipperfürth* | Russland und seine GUS-Nachbarn. Hintergründe, aktuelle Entwicklungen und Konflikte in einer ressourcenreichen Region| ISBN 978-3-89821-801-6

58   *Togzhan Kassenova* | From Antagonism to Partnership. The Uneasy Path of the U.S.-Russian Cooperative Threat Reduction | With a foreword by Christoph Bluth | ISBN 978-3-89821-707-1

59   *Alexander Höllwerth* | Das sakrale eurasische Imperium des Aleksandr Dugin. Eine Diskursanalyse zum postsowjetischen russischen Rechtsextremismus | Mit einem Vorwort von Dirk Uffelmann | ISBN 978-3-89821-813-9

60   *Олег Рябов* | «Россия-Матушка». Национализм, гендер и война в России XX века | С предисловием Елены Гощило | ISBN 978-3-89821-487-2

61   *Ivan Maistrenko* | Borot'bism. A Chapter in the History of the Ukrainian Revolution | With a new Introduction by Chris Ford | Translated by George S. N. Luckyj with the assistance of Ivan L. Rudnytsky | Second, Revised and Expanded Edition ISBN 978-3-8382-1107-7

62   *Maryna Romanets* | Anamorphosic Texts and Reconfigured Visions. Improvised Traditions in Contemporary Ukrainian and Irish Literature | ISBN 978-3-89821-576-3

63   *Paul D'Anieri and Taras Kuzio (Eds.)* | Aspects of the Orange Revolution I. Democratization and Elections in Post-Communist Ukraine | ISBN 978-3-89821-698-2

64   *Bohdan Harasymiw in collaboration with Oleh S. Ilnytzkyj (Eds.)* | Aspects of the Orange Revolution II. Information and Manipulation Strategies in the 2004 Ukrainian Presidential Elections | ISBN 978-3-89821-699-9

65   *Ingmar Bredies, Andreas Umland and Valentin Yakushik (Eds.)* | Aspects of the Orange Revolution III. The Context and Dynamics of the 2004 Ukrainian Presidential Elections | ISBN 978-3-89821-803-0

66   *Ingmar Bredies, Andreas Umland and Valentin Yakushik (Eds.)* | Aspects of the Orange Revolution IV. Foreign Assistance and Civic Action in the 2004 Ukrainian Presidential Elections | ISBN 978-3-89821-808-5

67   *Ingmar Bredies, Andreas Umland and Valentin Yakushik (Eds.)* | Aspects of the Orange Revolution V. Institutional Observation Reports on the 2004 Ukrainian Presidential Elections | ISBN 978-3-89821-809-2

68   *Taras Kuzio (Ed.)* | Aspects of the Orange Revolution VI. Post-Communist Democratic Revolutions in Comparative Perspective | ISBN 978-3-89821-820-7

69   *Tim Bohse* | Autoritarismus statt Selbstverwaltung. Die Transformation der kommunalen Politik in der Stadt Kaliningrad 1990-2005 | Mit einem Geleitwort von Stefan Troebst | ISBN 978-3-89821-782-8

70   *David Rupp* | Die Rußländische Föderation und die russischsprachige Minderheit in Lettland. Eine Fallstudie zur Anwaltspolitik Moskaus gegenüber den russophonen Minderheiten im „Nahen Ausland" von 1991 bis 2002 | Mit einem Vorwort von Helmut Wagner | ISBN 978-3-89821-778-1

71   *Taras Kuzio* | Theoretical and Comparative Perspectives on Nationalism. New Directions in Cross-Cultural and Post-Communist Studies | With a foreword by Paul Robert Magocsi | ISBN 978-3-89821-815-7

72   *Christine Teichmann* | Die Hochschultransformation im heutigen Osteuropa. Kontinuität und Wandel bei der Entwicklung des postsowjetischen Universitätswesens | Mit einem Vorwort von Oskar Anweiler | ISBN 978-3-89821-842-9

73 Julia Kusznir | Der politische Einfluss von Wirtschaftseliten in russischen Regionen. Eine Analyse am Beispiel der Erdöl- und Erdgasindustrie, 1992-2005 | Mit einem Vorwort von Wolfgang Eichwede | ISBN 978-3-89821-821-4

74 Alena Vysotskaya | Russland, Belarus und die EU-Osterweiterung. Zur Minderheitenfrage und zum Problem der Freizügigkeit des Personenverkehrs | Mit einem Vorwort von Katlijn Malfliet | ISBN 978-3-89821-822-1

75 Heiko Pleines (Hrsg.) | Corporate Governance in post-sozialistischen Volkswirtschaften | ISBN 978-3-89821-766-8

76 Stefan Ihrig | Wer sind die Moldawier? Rumänismus versus Moldowanismus in Historiographie und Schulbüchern der Republik Moldova, 1991-2006 | Mit einem Vorwort von Holm Sundhaussen | ISBN 978-3-89821-466-7

77 Galina Kozhevnikova in collaboration with Alexander Verkhovsky and Eugene Veklerov | Ultra-Nationalism and Hate Crimes in Contemporary Russia. The 2004-2006 Annual Reports of Moscow's SOVA Center | With a foreword by Stephen D. Shenfield | ISBN 978-3-89821-868-9

78 Florian Küchler | The Role of the European Union in Moldova's Transnistria Conflict | With a foreword by Christopher Hill | ISBN 978-3-89821-850-4

79 Bernd Rechel | The Long Way Back to Europe. Minority Protection in Bulgaria | With a foreword by Richard Crampton | ISBN 978-3-89821-863-4

80 Peter W. Rodgers | Nation, Region and History in Post-Communist Transitions. Identity Politics in Ukraine, 1991-2006 | With a foreword by Vera Tolz | ISBN 978-3-89821-903-7

81 Stephanie Solywoda | The Life and Work of Semen L. Frank. A Study of Russian Religious Philosophy | With a foreword by Philip Walters | ISBN 978-3-89821-457-5

82 Vera Sokolova | Cultural Politics of Ethnicity. Discourses on Roma in Communist Czechoslovakia | ISBN 978-3-89821-864-1

83 Natalya Shevchik Ketenci | Kazakhstani Enterprises in Transition. The Role of Historical Regional Development in Kazakhstan's Post-Soviet Economic Transformation | ISBN 978-3-89821-831-3

84 Martin Malek, Anna Schor-Tschudnowskaja (Hgg.) | Europa im Tschetschenienkrieg. Zwischen politischer Ohnmacht und Gleichgültigkeit | Mit einem Vorwort von Lipchan Basajewa | ISBN 978-3-89821-676-0

85 Stefan Meister | Das postsowjetische Universitätswesen zwischen nationalem und internationalem Wandel. Die Entwicklung der regionalen Hochschule in Russland als Gradmesser der Systemtransformation | Mit einem Vorwort von Joan DeBardeleben | ISBN 978-3-89821-891-7

86 Konstantin Sheiko in collaboration with Stephen Brown | Nationalist Imaginings of the Russian Past. Anatolii Fomenko and the Rise of Alternative History in Post-Communist Russia | With a foreword by Donald Ostrowski | ISBN 978-3-89821-915-0

87 Sabine Jenni | Wie stark ist das „Einige Russland"? Zur Parteibindung der Eliten und zum Wahlerfolg der Machtpartei im Dezember 2007 | Mit einem Vorwort von Klaus Armingeon | ISBN 978-3-89821-961-7

88 Thomas Borén | Meeting-Places of Transformation. Urban Identity, Spatial Representations and Local Politics in Post-Soviet St Petersburg | ISBN 978-3-89821-739-2

89 Aygul Ashirova | Stalinismus und Stalin-Kult in Zentralasien. Turkmenistan 1924-1953 | Mit einem Vorwort von Leonid Luks | ISBN 978-3-89821-987-7

90 Leonid Luks | Freiheit oder imperiale Größe? Essays zu einem russischen Dilemma | ISBN 978-3-8382-0011-8

91 Christopher Gilley | The 'Change of Signposts' in the Ukrainian Emigration. A Contribution to the History of Sovietophilism in the 1920s | With a foreword by Frank Golczewski | ISBN 978-3-89821-965-5

92 Philipp Casula, Jeronim Perovic (Eds.) | Identities and Politics During the Putin Presidency. The Discursive Foundations of Russia's Stability | With a foreword by Heiko Haumann | ISBN 978-3-8382-0015-6

93 Marcel Viëtor | Europa und die Frage nach seinen Grenzen im Osten. Zur Konstruktion ‚europäischer Identität' in Geschichte und Gegenwart | Mit einem Vorwort von Albrecht Lehmann | ISBN 978-3-8382-0045-3

94 Ben Hellman, Andrei Rogachevskii | Filming the Unfilmable. Casper Wrede's 'One Day in the Life of Ivan Denisovich' | Second, Revised and Expanded Edition | ISBN 978-3-8382-0044-6

95 Eva Fuchslocher | Vaterland, Sprache, Glaube. Orthodoxie und Nationenbildung am Beispiel Georgiens | Mit einem Vorwort von Christina von Braun | ISBN 978-3-89821-884-9

96 Vladimir Kantor | Das Westlertum und der Weg Russlands. Zur Entwicklung der russischen Literatur und Philosophie | Ediert von Dagmar Herrmann | Mit einem Beitrag von Nikolaus Lobkowicz | ISBN 978-3-8382-0102-3

97 Kamran Musayev | Die postsowjetische Transformation im Baltikum und Südkaukasus. Eine vergleichende Untersuchung der politischen Entwicklung Lettlands und Aserbaidschans 1985-2009 | Mit einem Vorwort von Leonid Luks | Ediert von Sandro Henschel | ISBN 978-3-8382-0103-0

98 *Tatiana Zhurzhenko* | Borderlands into Bordered Lands. Geopolitics of Identity in Post-Soviet Ukraine | With a foreword by Dieter Segert | ISBN 978-3-8382-0042-2

99 *Кирилл Галушко, Лидия Смола (ред.)* | Пределы падения – варианты украинского будущего. Аналитико-прогностические исследования | ISBN 978-3-8382-0148-1

100 *Michael Minkenberg (Ed.)* | Historical Legacies and the Radical Right in Post-Cold War Central and Eastern Europe | With an afterword by Sabrina P. Ramet | ISBN 978-3-8382-0124-5

101 *David-Emil Wickström* | Rocking St. Petersburg. Transcultural Flows and Identity Politics in the St. Petersburg Popular Music Scene | With a foreword by Yngvar B. Steinholt | Second, Revised and Expanded Edition | ISBN 978-3-8382-0100-9

102 *Eva Zabka* | Eine neue „Zeit der Wirren"? Der spät- und postsowjetische Systemwandel 1985-2000 im Spiegel russischer gesellschaftspolitischer Diskurse | Mit einem Vorwort von Margareta Mommsen | ISBN 978-3-8382-0161-0

103 *Ulrike Ziemer* | Ethnic Belonging, Gender and Cultural Practices. Youth Identitites in Contemporary Russia | With a foreword by Anoop Nayak | ISBN 978-3-8382-0152-8

104 *Ksenia Chepikova* | ‚Einiges Russland' - eine zweite KPdSU? Aspekte der Identitätskonstruktion einer postsowjetischen „Partei der Macht" | Mit einem Vorwort von Torsten Oppelland | ISBN 978-3-8382-0311-9

105 *Леонид Люкс* | Западничество или евразийство? Демократия или идеократия? Сборник статей об исторических дилеммах России | С предисловием Владимира Кантора | ISBN 978-3-8382-0211-2

106 *Anna Dost* | Das russische Verfassungsrecht auf dem Weg zum Föderalismus und zurück. Zum Konflikt von Rechtsnormen und -wirklichkeit in der Russländischen Föderation von 1991 bis 2009 | Mit einem Vorwort von Alexander Blankenagel | ISBN 978-3-8382-0292-1

107 *Philipp Herzog* | Sozialistische Völkerfreundschaft, nationaler Widerstand oder harmloser Zeitvertreib? Zur politischen Funktion der Volkskunst im sowjetischen Estland | Mit einem Vorwort von Andreas Kappeler | ISBN 978-3-8382-0216-7

108 *Marlène Laruelle (Ed.)* | Russian Nationalism, Foreign Policy, and Identity Debates in Putin's Russia. New Ideological Patterns after the Orange Revolution | ISBN 978-3-8382-0325-6

109 *Michail Logvinov* | Russlands Kampf gegen den internationalen Terrorismus. Eine kritische Bestandsaufnahme des Bekämpfungsansatzes | Mit einem Geleitwort von Hans-Henning Schröder und einem Vorwort von Eckhard Jesse | ISBN 978-3-8382-0329-4

110 *John B. Dunlop* | The Moscow Bombings of September 1999. Examinations of Russian Terrorist Attacks at the Onset of Vladimir Putin's Rule | Second, Revised and Expanded Edition | ISBN 978-3-8382-0388-1

111 *Андрей А. Ковалёв* | Свидетельство из-за кулис российской политики I. Можно ли делать добро из зла? (Воспоминания и размышления о последних советских и первых послесоветских годах) | With a foreword by Peter Reddaway | ISBN 978-3-8382-0302-7

112 *Андрей А. Ковалёв* | Свидетельство из-за кулис российской политики II. Угроза для себя и окружающих (Наблюдения и предостережения относительно происходящего после 2000 г.) | ISBN 978-3-8382-0303-4

113 *Bernd Kappenberg* | Zeichen setzen für Europa. Der Gebrauch europäischer lateinischer Sonderzeichen in der deutschen Öffentlichkeit | Mit einem Vorwort von Peter Schlobinski | ISBN 978-3-89821-749-1

114 *Ivo Mijnssen* | The Quest for an Ideal Youth in Putin's Russia I. Back to Our Future! History, Modernity, and Patriotism according to Nashi, 2005-2013 | With a foreword by Jeronim Perović | Second, Revised and Expanded Edition | ISBN 978-3-8382-0368-3

115 *Jussi Lassila* | The Quest for an Ideal Youth in Putin's Russia II. The Search for Distinctive Conformism in the Political Communication of Nashi, 2005-2009 | With a foreword by Kirill Postoutenko | Second, Revised and Expanded Edition | ISBN 978-3-8382-0415-4

116 *Valerio Trabandt* | Neue Nachbarn, gute Nachbarschaft? Die EU als internationaler Akteur am Beispiel ihrer Demokratieförderung in Belarus und der Ukraine 2004-2009 | Mit einem Vorwort von Jutta Joachim | ISBN 978-3-8382-0437-6

117 *Fabian Pfeiffer* | Estlands Außen- und Sicherheitspolitik I. Der estnische Atlantizismus nach der wiedererlangten Unabhängigkeit 1991-2004 | Mit einem Vorwort von Helmut Hubel | ISBN 978-3-8382-0127-6

118 *Jana Podßuweit* | Estlands Außen- und Sicherheitspolitik II. Handlungsoptionen eines Kleinstaates im Rahmen seiner EU-Mitgliedschaft (2004-2008) | Mit einem Vorwort von Helmut Hubel | ISBN 978-3-8382-0440-6

119 *Karin Pointner* | Estlands Außen- und Sicherheitspolitik III. Eine gedächtnispolitische Analyse estnischer Entwicklungskooperation 2006-2010 | Mit einem Vorwort von Karin Liebhart | ISBN 978-3-8382-0435-2

120 *Ruslana Vovk* | Die Offenheit der ukrainischen Verfassung für das Völkerrecht und die europäische Integration | Mit einem Vorwort von Alexander Blankenagel | ISBN 978-3-8382-0481-9

121 *Mykhaylo Banakh* | Die Relevanz der Zivilgesellschaft bei den postkommunistischen Transformationsprozessen in mittel- und osteuropäischen Ländern. Das Beispiel der spät- und postsowjetischen Ukraine 1986-2009 | Mit einem Vorwort von Gerhard Simon | ISBN 978-3-8382-0499-4

122 *Michael Moser* | Language Policy and the Discourse on Languages in Ukraine under President Viktor Yanukovych (25 February 2010–28 October 2012) | ISBN 978-3-8382-0497-0 (Paperback edition) | ISBN 978-3-8382-0507-6 (Hardcover edition)

123 *Nicole Krome* | Russischer Netzwerkkapitalismus Restrukturierungsprozesse in der Russischen Föderation am Beispiel des Luftfahrtunternehmens „Aviastar" | Mit einem Vorwort von Petra Stykow | ISBN 978-3-8382-0534-2

124 *David R. Marples* | 'Our Glorious Past'. Lukashenka's Belarus and the Great Patriotic War | ISBN 978-3-8382-0574-8 (Paperback edition) | ISBN 978-3-8382-0675-2 (Hardcover edition)

125 *Ulf Walther* | Russlands „neuer Adel". Die Macht des Geheimdienstes von Gorbatschow bis Putin | Mit einem Vorwort von Hans-Georg Wieck | ISBN 978-3-8382-0584-7

126 *Simon Geissbühler (Hrsg.)* | Kiew – Revolution 3.0. Der Euromaidan 2013/14 und die Zukunftsperspektiven der Ukraine | ISBN 978-3-8382-0581-6 (Paperback edition) | ISBN 978-3-8382-0681-3 (Hardcover edition)

127 *Andrey Makarychev* | Russia and the EU in a Multipolar World. Discourses, Identities, Norms | With a foreword by Klaus Segbers | ISBN 978-3-8382-0629-5

128 *Roland Scharff* | Kasachstan als postsowjetischer Wohlfahrtsstaat. Die Transformation des sozialen Schutzsystems | Mit einem Vorwort von Joachim Ahrens | ISBN 978-3-8382-0622-6

129 *Katja Grupp* | Bild Lücke Deutschland. Kaliningrader Studierende sprechen über Deutschland | Mit einem Vorwort von Martin Schulz | ISBN 978-3-8382-0552-6

130 *Konstantin Sheiko, Stephen Brown* | History as Therapy. Alternative History and Nationalist Imaginings in Russia, 1991-2014 | ISBN 978-3-8382-0665-3

131 *Elisa Kriza* | Alexander Solzhenitsyn: Cold War Icon, Gulag Author, Russian Nationalist? A Study of the Western Reception of his Literary Writings, Historical Interpretations, and Political Ideas | With a foreword by Andrei Rogatchevski | ISBN 978-3-8382-0589-2 (Paperback edition) | ISBN 978-3-8382-0690-5 (Hardcover edition)

132 *Serghei Golunov* | The Elephant in the Room. Corruption and Cheating in Russian Universities | ISBN 978-3-8382-0570-0

133 *Manja Hussner, Rainer Arnold (Hgg.)* | Verfassungsgerichtsbarkeit in Zentralasien I. Sammlung von Verfassungstexten | ISBN 978-3-8382-0595-3

134 *Nikolay Mitrokhin* | Die „Russische Partei". Die Bewegung der russischen Nationalisten in der UdSSR 1953-1985 | Aus dem Russischen übertragen von einem Übersetzerteam unter der Leitung von Larisa Schippel | ISBN 978-3-8382-0024-8

135 *Manja Hussner, Rainer Arnold (Hgg.)* | Verfassungsgerichtsbarkeit in Zentralasien II. Sammlung von Verfassungstexten | ISBN 978-3-8382-0597-7

136 *Manfred Zeller* | Das sowjetische Fieber. Fußballfans im poststalinistischen Vielvölkerreich | Mit einem Vorwort von Nikolaus Katzer | ISBN 978-3-8382-0757-5

137 *Kristin Schreiter* | Stellung und Entwicklungspotential zivilgesellschaftlicher Gruppen in Russland. Menschenrechtsorganisationen im Vergleich | ISBN 978-3-8382-0673-8

138 *David R. Marples, Frederick V. Mills (Eds.)* | Ukraine's Euromaidan. Analyses of a Civil Revolution | ISBN 978-3-8382-0660-8

139 *Bernd Kappenberg* | Setting Signs for Europe. Why Diacritics Matter for European Integration | With a foreword by Peter Schlobinski | ISBN 978-3-8382-0663-9

140 *René Lenz* | Internationalisierung, Kooperation und Transfer. Externe bildungspolitische Akteure in der Russischen Föderation | Mit einem Vorwort von Frank Ettrich | ISBN 978-3-8382-0751-3

141 *Juri Plusnin, Yana Zausaeva, Natalia Zhidkevich, Artemy Pozanenko* | Wandering Workers. Mores, Behavior, Way of Life, and Political Status of Domestic Russian Labor Migrants | Translated by Julia Kazantseva | ISBN 978-3-8382-0653-0

142 *David J. Smith (Eds.)* | Latvia – A Work in Progress? 100 Years of State- and Nation-Building | ISBN 978-3-8382-0648-6

143 *Инна Чувычкина (ред.)* | Экспортные нефте- и газопроводы на постсоветском пространстве. Анализ трубопроводной политики в свете теории международных отношений | ISBN 978-3-8382-0822-0

144 *Johann Zajaczkowski* | Russland – eine pragmatische Großmacht? Eine rollentheoretische Untersuchung russischer Außenpolitik am Beispiel der Zusammenarbeit mit den USA nach 9/11 und des Georgienkrieges von 2008 | Mit einem Vorwort von Siegfried Schieder | ISBN 978-3-8382-0837-4

145 *Boris Popivanov* | Changing Images of the Left in Bulgaria. The Challenge of Post-Communism in the Early 21st Century | ISBN 978-3-8382-0667-7

146 *Lenka Krátká* | A History of the Czechoslovak Ocean Shipping Company 1948-1989. How a Small, Landlocked Country Ran Maritime Business During the Cold War | ISBN 978-3-8382-0666-0

147 *Alexander Sergunin* | Explaining Russian Foreign Policy Behavior. Theory and Practice | ISBN 978-3-8382-0752-0

148 *Darya Malyutina* | Migrant Friendships in a Super-Diverse City. Russian-Speakers and their Social Relationships in London in the 21st Century | With a foreword by Claire Dwyer | ISBN 978-3-8382-0652-3

149 *Alexander Sergunin, Valery Konyshev* | Russia in the Arctic. Hard or Soft Power? | ISBN 978-3-8382-0753-7

150 *John J. Maresca* | Helsinki Revisited. A Key U.S. Negotiator's Memoirs on the Development of the CSCE into the OSCE | With a foreword by Hafiz Pashayev | ISBN 978-3-8382-0852-7

151 *Jardar Østbø* | The New Third Rome. Readings of a Russian Nationalist Myth | With a foreword by Pål Kolstø | ISBN 978-3-8382-0870-1

152 *Simon Kordonsky* | Socio-Economic Foundations of the Russian Post-Soviet Regime. The Resource-Based Economy and Estate-Based Social Structure of Contemporary Russia | With a foreword by Svetlana Barsukova | ISBN 978-3-8382-0775-9

153 *Duncan Leitch* | Assisting Reform in Post-Communist Ukraine 2000–2012. The Illusions of Donors and the Disillusion of Beneficiaries | With a foreword by Kataryna Wolczuk | ISBN 978-3-8382-0844-2

154 *Abel Polese* | Limits of a Post-Soviet State. How Informality Replaces, Renegotiates, and Reshapes Governance in Contemporary Ukraine | With a foreword by Colin Williams | ISBN 978-3-8382-0845-9

155 *Mikhail Suslov (Ed.)* | Digital Orthodoxy in the Post-Soviet World. The Russian Orthodox Church and Web 2.0 | With a foreword by Father Cyril Hovorun | ISBN 978-3-8382-0871-8

156 *Leonid Luks* | Zwei „Sonderwege"? Russisch-deutsche Parallelen und Kontraste (1917-2014). Vergleichende Essays | ISBN 978-3-8382-0823-7

157 *Vladimir V. Karacharovskiy, Ovsey I. Shkaratan, Gordey A. Yastrebov* | Towards a New Russian Work Culture. Can Western Companies and Expatriates Change Russian Society? | With a foreword by Elena N. Danilova | Translated by Julia Kazantseva | ISBN 978-3-8382-0902-9

158 *Edmund Griffiths* | Aleksandr Prokhanov and Post-Soviet Esotericism | ISBN 978-3-8382-0963-0

159 *Timm Beichelt, Susann Worschech (Eds.)* | Transnational Ukraine? Networks and Ties that Influence(d) Contemporary Ukraine | ISBN 978-3-8382-0944-9

160 *Mieste Hotopp-Riecke* | Die Tataren der Krim zwischen Assimilation und Selbstbehauptung. Der Aufbau des krimtatarischen Bildungswesens nach Deportation und Heimkehr (1990-2005) | Mit einem Vorwort von Swetlana Czerwonnaja | ISBN 978-3-89821-940-2

161 *Olga Bertelsen (Ed.)* | Revolution and War in Contemporary Ukraine. The Challenge of Change | ISBN 978-3-8382-1016-2

162 *Natalya Ryabinska* | Ukraine's Post-Communist Mass Media. Between Capture and Commercialization | With a foreword by Marta Dyczok | ISBN 978-3-8382-1011-7

163 *Alexandra Cotofana, James M. Nyce (Eds.)* | Religion and Magic in Socialist and Post-Socialist Contexts. Historic and Ethnographic Case Studies of Orthodoxy, Heterodoxy, and Alternative Spirituality | With a foreword by Patrick L. Michelson | ISBN 978-3-8382-0989-0

164 *Nozima Akhrarkhodjaeva* | The Instrumentalisation of Mass Media in Electoral Authoritarian Regimes. Evidence from Russia's Presidential Election Campaigns of 2000 and 2008 | ISBN 978-3-8382-1013-1

165 *Yulia Krasheninnikova* | Informal Healthcare in Contemporary Russia. Sociographic Essays on the Post-Soviet Infrastructure for Alternative Healing Practices | ISBN 978-3-8382-0970-5

166 *Peter Kaiser* | Das Schachbrett der Macht. Die Handlungsspielräume eines sowjetischen Funktionärs unter Stalin am Beispiel des Generalsekretärs des Komsomol Aleksandr Kosarev (1929-1938) | Mit einem Vorwort von Dietmar Neutatz | ISBN 978-3-8382-1052-0

167 *Oksana Kim* | The Effects and Implications of Kazakhstan's Adoption of International Financial Reporting Standards. A Resource Dependence Perspective | With a foreword by Svetlana Vlady | ISBN 978-3-8382-0987-6

168 *Anna Sanina* | Patriotic Education in Contemporary Russia. Sociological Studies in the Making of the Post-Soviet Citizen | With a foreword by Anna Oldfield | ISBN 978-3-8382-0993-7

169 *Rudolf Wolters* | Spezialist in Sibirien Faksimile der 1933 erschienenen ersten Ausgabe | Mit einem Vorwort von Dmitrij Chmelnizki | ISBN 978-3-8382-0515-1

170 *Michal Vít, Magdalena M. Baran (Eds.)* | Transregional versus National Perspectives on Contemporary Central European History. Studies on the Building of Nation-States and Their Cooperation in the 20th and 21st Century | With a foreword by Petr Vágner | ISBN 978-3-8382-1015-5

171 *Philip Gamaghelyan* | Conflict Resolution Beyond the International Relations Paradigm. Evolving Designs as a Transformative Practice in Nagorno-Karabakh and Syria | With a foreword by Susan Allen | ISBN 978-3-8382-1057-5

172 *Maria Shagina* | Joining a Prestigious Club. Cooperation with Europarties and Its Impact on Party Development in Georgia, Moldova, and Ukraine 2004–2015 | With a foreword by Kataryna Wolczuk | ISBN 978-3-8382-1084-1

173 *Alexandra Cotofana, James M. Nyce (Eds.)* | Religion and Magic in Socialist and Post-Socialist Contexts II. Baltic, Eastern European, and Post-USSR Case Studies | With a foreword by Anita Stasulane | ISBN 978-3-8382-0990-6

174 *Barbara Kunz* | Kind Words, Cruise Missiles, and Everything in Between. The Use of Power Resources in U.S. Policies towards Poland, Ukraine, and Belarus 1989–2008 | With a foreword by William Hill | ISBN 978-3-8382-1065-0

175 *Eduard Klein* | Bildungskorruption in Russland und der Ukraine. Eine komparative Analyse der Performanz staatlicher Antikorruptionsmaßnahmen im Hochschulsektor am Beispiel universitärer Aufnahmeprüfungen | Mit einem Vorwort von Heiko Pleines | ISBN 978-3-8382-0995-1

176 *Markus Soldner* | Politischer Kapitalismus im postsowjetischen Russland. Die politische, wirtschaftliche und mediale Transformation in den 1990er Jahren | Mit einem Vorwort von Wolfgang Ismayr | ISBN 978-3-8382-1222-7

177 *Anton Oleinik* | Building Ukraine from Within. A Sociological, Institutional, and Economic Analysis of a Nation-State in the Making | ISBN 978-3-8382-1150-3

178 *Peter Rollberg, Marlene Laruelle (Eds.)* | Mass Media in the Post-Soviet World. Market Forces, State Actors, and Political Manipulation in the Informational Environment after Communism | ISBN 978-3-8382-1116-9

179 *Mikhail Minakov* | Development and Dystopia. Studies in Post-Soviet Ukraine and Eastern Europe | With a foreword by Alexander Etkind | ISBN 978-3-8382-1112-1

180 *Aijan Sharshenova* | The European Union's Democracy Promotion in Central Asia. A Study of Political Interests, Influence, and Development in Kazakhstan and Kyrgyzstan in 2007–2013 | With a foreword by Gordon Crawford | ISBN 978-3-8382-1151-0

181 *Andrey Makarychev, Alexandra Yatsyk (Eds.)* | Boris Nemtsov and Russian Politics. Power and Resistance | With a foreword by Zhanna Nemtsova | ISBN 978-3-8382-1122-0

182 *Sophie Falsini* | The Euromaidan's Effect on Civil Society. Why and How Ukrainian Social Capital Increased after the Revolution of Dignity | With a foreword by Susann Worschech | ISBN 978-3-8382-1131-2

183 *Valentyna Romanova, Andreas Umland (Eds.)* | Ukraine's Decentralization. Challenges and Implications of the Local Governance Reform after the Euromaidan Revolution | ISBN 978-3-8382-1162-6

184 *Leonid Luks* | A Fateful Triangle. Essays on Contemporary Russian, German and Polish History | ISBN 978-3-8382-1143-5

185 *John B. Dunlop* | The February 2015 Assassination of Boris Nemtsov and the Flawed Trial of his Alleged Killers. An Exploration of Russia's "Crime of the 21st Century" | ISBN 978-3-8382-1188-7

186 *Vasile Rotaru* | Russia, the EU, and the Eastern Partnership. Building Bridges or Digging Trenches? | ISBN 978-3-8382-1134-3

187 *Marina Lebedeva* | Russian Studies of International Relations. From the Soviet Past to the Post-Cold-War Present | With a foreword by Andrei P. Tsygankov | ISBN 978-3-8382-0851-0

188 *Tomasz Stępniewski, George Soroka (Eds.)* | Ukraine after Maidan. Revisiting Domestic and Regional Security | ISBN 978-3-8382-1075-9

189 *Petar Cholakov* | Ethnic Entrepreneurs Unmasked. Political Institutions and Ethnic Conflicts in Contemporary Bulgaria | ISBN 978-3-8382-1189-3

190 *A. Salem, G. Hazeldine, D. Morgan (Eds.)* | Higher Education in Post-Communist States. Comparative and Sociological Perspectives | ISBN 978-3-8382-1183-1

191 *Igor Torbakov* | After Empire. Nationalist Imagination and Symbolic Politics in Russia and Eurasia in the Twentieth and Twenty-First Century | With a foreword by Serhii Plokhy | ISBN 978-3-8382-1217-3

192 *Aleksandr Burakovskiy* | Jewish-Ukrainian Relations in Late and Post-Soviet Ukraine. Articles, Lectures and Essays from 1986 to 2016 | ISBN 978-3-8382-1210-4

193 *Natalia Shapovalova, Olga Burlyuk (Eds.)* | Civil Society in Post-Euromaidan Ukraine. From Revolution to Consolidation | With a foreword by Richard Youngs | ISBN 978-3-8382-1216-5

194 *Franz Preissler* | Positionsverteidigung, Imperialismus oder Irredentismus? Russland und die „Russischsprachigen", 1991–2015 | ISBN 978-3-8382-1262-3

195 *Marian Madeła* | Der Reformprozess in der Ukraine 2014-2017. Eine Fallstudie zur Reform der öffentlichen Verwaltung | Mit einem Vorwort von Martin Malek | ISBN 978-3-8382-1266-1

196 *Anke Giesen* | „Wie kann denn der Sieger ein Verbrecher sein?" Eine diskursanalytische Untersuchung der russlandweiten Debatte über Konzept und Verstaatlichungsprozess der Lagergedenkstätte „Perm'-36" im Ural | ISBN 978-3-8382-1284-5

197 *Victoria Leukavets* | The Integration Policies of Belarus and Ukraine vis-à-vis the EU and Russia. A Comparative Analysis Through the Prism of a Two-Level Game Approach | ISBN 978-3-8382-1247-0

198 *Oksana Kim* | The Development and Challenges of Russian Corporate Governance I. The Roles and Functions of Boards of Directors | With a foreword by Sheila M. Puffer | ISBN 978-3-8382-1287-6

199 *Thomas D. Grant* | International Law and the Post-Soviet Space I. Essays on Chechnya and the Baltic States | With a foreword by Stephen M. Schwebel | ISBN 978-3-8382-1279-1

200 *Thomas D. Grant* | International Law and the Post-Soviet Space II. Essays on Ukraine, Intervention, and Non-Proliferation | ISBN 978-3-8382-1280-7

201 *Slavomír Michálek, Michal Štefansky* | The Age of Fear. The Cold War and Its Influence on Czechoslovakia 1945–1968 | ISBN 978-3-8382-1285-2

202 *Iulia-Sabina Joja* | Romania's Strategic Culture 1990–2014. Continuity and Change in a Post-Communist Country's Evolution of National Interests and Security Policies | With a foreword by Heiko Biehl | ISBN 978-3-8382-1286-9

203 *Andrei Rogatchevski, Yngvar B. Steinholt, Arve Hansen, David-Emil Wickström* | War of Songs. Popular Music and Recent Russia-Ukraine Relations | With a foreword by Artemy Troitsky | ISBN 978-3-8382-1173-2

204 *Maria Lipman (Ed.)* | Russian Voices on Post-Crimea Russia. An Almanac of Counterpoint Essays from 2015–2018 | ISBN 978-3-8382-1251-7

205 *Ksenia Maksimovtsova* | Language Conflicts in Contemporary Estonia, Latvia, and Ukraine. A Comparative Exploration of Discourses in Post-Soviet Russian-Language Digital Media | With a foreword by Ammon Cheskin | ISBN 978-3-8382-1282-1

206 *Michal Vít* | The EU's Impact on Identity Formation in East-Central Europe between 2004 and 2013. Perceptions of the Nation and Europe in Political Parties of the Czech Republic, Poland, and Slovakia | With a foreword by Andrea Pető | ISBN 978-3-8382-1275-3

207 *Per A. Rudling* | Tarnished Heroes. The Organization of Ukrainian Nationalists in the Memory Politics of Post-Soviet Ukraine | ISBN 978-3-8382-0999-9

208 *Kaja Gadowska, Peter Solomon (Eds.)* | Legal Change in Post-Communist States. Progress, Reversions, Explanations | ISBN 978-3-8382-1312-5

209 *Pawel Kowal, Georges Mink, Iwona Reichardt (Eds.)* | Three Revolutions: Mobilization and Change in Contemporary Ukraine I. Theoretical Aspects and Analyses on Religion, Memory, and Identity | ISBN 978-3-8382-1321-7

210 *Pawel Kowal, Georges Mink, Adam Reichardt, Iwona Reichardt (Eds.)* | Three Revolutions: Mobilization and Change in Contemporary Ukraine II. An Oral History of the Revolution on Granite, Orange Revolution, and Revolution of Dignity | ISBN 978-3-8382-1323-1

211 *Li Bennich-Björkman, Sergiy Kurbatov (Eds.)* | When the Future Came. The Collapse of the USSR and the Emergence of National Memory in Post-Soviet History Textbooks | ISBN 978-3-8382-1335-4

212 *Olga R. Gulina* | Migration as a (Geo-)Political Challenge in the Post-Soviet Space. Border Regimes, Policy Choices, Visa Agendas | With a foreword by Nils Muižnieks | ISBN 978-3-8382-1338-5

213 *Sanna Turoma, Kaarina Aitamurto, Slobodanka Vladiv-Glover (Eds.)* | Religion, Expression, and Patriotism in Russia. Essays on Post-Soviet Society and the State. ISBN 978-3-8382-1346-0

214 *Vasif Huseynov* | Geopolitical Rivalries in the "Common Neighborhood". Russia's Conflict with the West, Soft Power, and Neoclassical Realism | With a foreword by Nicholas Ross Smith | ISBN 978-3-8382-1277-7

215 *Mikhail Suslov* | Geopolitical Imagination. Ideology and Utopia in Post-Soviet Russia | With a foreword by Mark Bassin | ISBN 978-3-8382-1361-3

216 *Alexander Etkind, Mikhail Minakov (Eds.)* | Ideology after Union. Political Doctrines, Discourses, and Debates in Post-Soviet Societies | ISBN 978-3-8382-1388-0

217 *Jakob Mischke, Oleksandr Zabirko (Hgg.)* | Protestbewegungen im langen Schatten des Kreml. Aufbruch und Resignation in Russland und der Ukraine | ISBN 978-3-8382-0926-5

218 *Oksana Huss* | How Corruption and Anti-Corruption Policies Sustain Hybrid Regimes. Strategies of Political Domination under Ukraine's Presidents in 1994-2014 | With a foreword by Tobias Debiel and Andrea Gawrich | ISBN 978-3-8382-1430-6

219 *Dmitry Travin, Vladimir Gel'man, Otar Marganiya* | The Russian Path. Ideas, Interests, Institutions, Illusions | With a foreword by Vladimir Ryzhkov | ISBN 978-3-8382-1421-4

220 *Gergana Dimova* | Political Uncertainty. A Comparative Exploration | With a foreword by Todor Yalamov and Rumena Filipova | ISBN 978-3-8382-1385-9

221 *Torben Waschke* | Russland in Transition. Geopolitik zwischen Raum, Identität und Machtinteressen | Mit einem Vorwort von Andreas Dittmann | ISBN 978-3-8382-1480-1

222 *Steven Jobbitt, Zsolt Bottlik, Marton Berki (Eds.)* | Power and Identity in the Post-Soviet Realm. Geographies of Ethnicity and Nationality after 1991 | ISBN 978-3-8382-1399-6

223 *Daria Buteiko* | Erinnerungsort. Ort des Gedenkens, der Erholung oder des Einkehr? Kommunismus-Erinnerung am Beispiel der Gedenkstätte Berliner Mauer sowie des Soloveckij-Klosters und -Museumsparks | ISBN 978-3-8382-1367-5

224 *Olga Bertelsen (Ed.)* | Russian Active Measures. Yesterday, Today, Tomorrow | With a foreword by Jan Goldman | ISBN 978-3-8382-1529-7

225 *David Mandel* | "Optimizing" Higher Education in Russia. University Teachers and their Union "Universitetskaya solidarnost'" | ISBN 978-3-8382-1519-8

226 *Mikhail Minakov, Gwendolyn Sasse, Daria Isachenko (Eds.)* | Post-Soviet Secessionism. Nation-Building and State-Failure after Communism | ISBN 978-3-8382-1538-9

227 *Jakob Hauter (Ed.)* | Civil War? Interstate War? Hybrid War? Dimensions and Interpretations of the Donbas Conflict in 2014–2020 | With a foreword by Andrew Wilson | ISBN 978-3-8382-1383-5

228 *Tima T. Moldogaziev, Gene A. Brewer, J. Edward Kellough (Eds.)* | Public Policy and Politics in Georgia. Lessons from Post-Soviet Transition | With a foreword by Dan Durning | ISBN 978-3-8382-1535-8

229 *Oxana Schmies (Ed.)* | NATO's Enlargement and Russia. A Strategic Challenge in the Past and Future | With a foreword by Vladimir Kara-Murza | ISBN 978-3-8382-1478-8

230 *Christopher Ford* | Ukapisme – Une Gauche perdue. Le marxisme anti-colonial dans la révolution ukrainienne 1917-1925 | Avec une préface de Vincent Présumey | ISBN 978-3-8382-0899-2

231 *Anna Kutkina* | Between Lenin and Bandera. Decommunization and Multivocality in Post-Euromaidan Ukraine | With a foreword by Juri Mykkänen | ISBN 978-3-8382-1506-8

232 *Lincoln E. Flake* | Defending the Faith. The Russian Orthodox Church and the Demise of Religious Pluralism | With a foreword by Peter Martland | ISBN 978-3-8382-1378-1

233 *Nikoloz Samkharadze* | Russia's Recognition of the Independence of Abkhazia and South Ossetia. Analysis of a Deviant Case in Moscow's Foreign Policy | With a foreword by Neil MacFarlane | ISBN 978-3-8382-1414-6

234 *Arve Hansen* | Urban Protest. A Spatial Perspective on Kyiv, Minsk, and Moscow | With a foreword by Julie Wilhelmsen | ISBN 978-3-8382-1495-5

235 *Eleonora Narvselius, Julie Fedor (Eds.)* | Diversity in the East-Central European Borderlands. Memories, Cityscapes, People | ISBN 978-3-8382-1523-5

236 *Regina Elsner* | The Russian Orthodox Church and Modernity. A Historical and Theological Investigation into Eastern Christianity between Unity and Plurality | With a foreword by Mikhail Suslov | ISBN 978-3-8382-1568-6

237 *Bo Petersson* | The Putin Predicament. Problems of Legitimacy and Succession in Russia | With a foreword by J. Paul Goode | ISBN 978-3-8382-1050-6

238 *Jonathan Otto Pohl* | The Years of Great Silence. The Deportation, Special Settlement, and Mobilization into the Labor Army of Ethnic Germans in the USSR, 1941–1955 | ISBN 978-3-8382-1630-0

239 *Mikhail Minakov (Ed.)* | Inventing Majorities. Ideological Creativity in Post-Soviet Societies | ISBN 978-3-8382-1641-6

240 *Robert M. Cutler* | Soviet and Post-Soviet Foreign Policies I. East-South Relations and the Political Economy of the Communist Bloc, 1971–1991 | With a foreword by Roger E. Kanet | ISBN 978-3-8382-1654-6

241 *Izabella Agardi* | On the Verge of History. Life Stories of Rural Women from Serbia, Romania, and Hungary, 1920–2020 | With a foreword by Andrea Pető | ISBN 978-3-8382-1602-7

242 *Sebastian Schäffer (Ed.)* | Ukraine in Central and Eastern Europe. Kyiv's Foreign Affairs and the International Relations of the Post-Communist Region | With a foreword by Pavlo Klimkin and Andreas Umland| ISBN 978-3-8382-1615-7

243 *Volodymyr Dubrovskyi, Kalman Mizsei, Mychailo Wynnyckyj (Eds.)* | Eight Years after the Revolution of Dignity. What Has Changed in Ukraine during 2013–2021? | With a foreword by Yaroslav Hrytsak | ISBN 978-3-8382-1560-0

244 *Rumena Filipova* | Constructing the Limits of Europe Identity and Foreign Policy in Poland, Bulgaria, and Russia since 1989 | With forewords by Harald Wydra and Gergana Yankova-Dimova | ISBN 978-3-8382-1649-2

245 *Oleksandra Keudel* | How Patronal Networks Shape Opportunities for Local Citizen Participation in a Hybrid Regime A Comparative Analysis of Five Cities in Ukraine | With a foreword by Sabine Kropp | ISBN 978-3-8382-1671-3

246 *Jan Claas Behrends, Thomas Lindenberger, Pavel Kolar (Eds.)* | Violence after Stalin Institutions, Practices, and Everyday Life in the Soviet Bloc 1953–1989 | ISBN 978-3-8382-1637-9

247 *Leonid Luks* | Macht und Ohnmacht der Utopien Essays zur Geschichte Russlands im 20. und 21. Jahrhundert | ISBN 978-3-8382-1677-5

248 *Iuliia Barshadska* | Brüssel zwischen Kyjiw und Moskau Das auswärtige Handeln der Europäischen Union im ukrainisch-russischen Konflikt 2014-2019 | Mit einem Vorwort von Olaf Leiße | ISBN 978-3-8382-1667-6

249 *Valentyna Romanova* | Decentralisation and Multilevel Elections in Ukraine Reform Dynamics and Party Politics in 2010–2021 | With a foreword by Kimitaka Matsuzato | ISBN 978-3-8382-1700-0

250 *Alexander Motyl* | National Questions. Theoretical Reflections on Nations and Nationalism in Eastern Europe | ISBN 978-3-8382-1675-1

251 *Marc Dietrich* | A Cosmopolitan Model for Peacebuilding. The Ukrainian Cases of Crimea and the Donbas | With a foreword by Rémi Baudouï | ISBN 978-3-8382-1687-4

252 *Eduard Baidaus* | An Unsettled Nation. Moldova in the Geopolitics of Russia, Romania, and Ukraine | With forewords by John-Paul Himka and David R. Marples | ISBN 978-3-8382-1582-2

253 *Igor Okunev, Petr Oskolkov (Eds.)* | Transforming the Administrative Matryoshka. The Reform of Autonomous Okrugs in the Russian Federation, 2003–2008 | With a foreword by Vladimir Zorin | ISBN 978-3-8382-1721-5

254 *Winfried Schneider-Deters* | Ukraine's Fateful Years 2013–2019. Vol. I: The Popular Uprising in Winter 2013/2014 | ISBN 978-3-8382-1725-3

255 *Winfried Schneider-Deters* | Ukraine's Fateful Years 2013–2019. Vol. II: The Annexation of Crimea and the War in Donbas | ISBN 978-3-8382-1726-0

256 *Robert M. Cutler* | Soviet and Post-Soviet Russian Foreign Policies II. East-West Relations in Europe and the Political Economy of the Communist Bloc, 1971–1991 | With a foreword by Roger E. Kanet | ISBN 978-3-8382-1727-7

257 *Robert M. Cutler* | Soviet and Post-Soviet Russian Foreign Policies III. East-West Relations in Europe and Eurasia in the Post-Cold War Transition, 1991–2001 | With a foreword by Roger E. Kanet | ISBN 978-3-8382-1728-4

258 *Paweł Kowal, Iwona Reichardt, Kateryna Pryshchepa (Eds.)* | Three Revolutions: Mobilization and Change in Contemporary Ukraine III. Archival Records and Historical Sources on the 1990 Revolution on Granite | ISBN 978-3-8382-1376-7

259 *Mikhail Minakov (Ed.)* | Philosophy Unchained. Developments in Post-Soviet Philosophical Thought. | With a foreword by Christopher Donohue | ISBN 978-3-8382-1768-0

260 *David Dalton* | The Ukrainian Oligarchy After the Euromaidan. How Ukraine's Political Economy Regime Survived the Crisis | With a foreword by Andrew Wilson | ISBN 978-3-8382-1740-6

261 *Andreas Heinemann-Grüder (Ed.)* | Who are the Fighters? Irregular Armed Groups in the Russian-Ukrainian War in 2014-2015 | ISBN 978-3-8382-1777-2

262 *Taras Kuzio (Ed.)* | Russian Disinformation and Western Scholarship. Bias and Prejudice in Journalistic, Expert, and Academic Analyses of East European, Russian and Eurasian Affairs | ISBN 978-3-8382-1685-0

263 *Darius Furmonavicius* | LithuaniaTransforms the West. Lithuania's Liberation from Soviet Occupation and the Enlargement of NATO (1988–2022) | With a foreword by Vytautas Landsbergis | ISBN 978-3-8382-1779-6

264 *Dirk Dalberg* | Politisches Denken im tschechoslowakischen Dissens. Egon Bondy, Miroslav Kusý, Milan Šimečka und Petr Uhl (1968-1989) | ISBN 978-3-8382-1318-7

265 *Леонид Люкс* | К столетию «философского парохода». Мыслители «первой» русской эмиграции о русской революции и о тоталитарных соблазнах XX века | ISBN 978-3-8382-1775-8

266 *Daviti Mtchedlishvili* | The EU and the South Caucasus. European Neighborhood Policies between Eclecticism and Pragmatism, 1991-2021 | With a foreword by Nicholas Ross Smith | ISBN 978-3-8382-1735-2

267 *Bohdan Harasymiw* | Post-Euromaidan Ukraine. Domestic Power Struggles and War of National Survival in 2014–2022 | ISBN 978-3-8382-1798-7

268 *Nadiia Koval, Denys Tereshchenko (Eds.)* | Russian Cultural Diplomacy under Putin. Rossotrudnichestvo, the "Russkiy Mir" Foundation, and the Gorchakov Fund in 2007–2022 | ISBN 978-3-8382-1801-4

269 *Izabela Kazejak* | Jews in Post-War Wrocław and L'viv. Official Policies and Local Responses in Comparative Perspective, 1945-1970s | ISBN 978-3-8382-1802-1

270 *Jakob Hauter* | Russia's Overlooked Invasion. The Causes of the 2014 Outbreak of War in Ukraine's Donbas | With a foreword by Hiroaki Kuromiya | ISBN 978-3-8382-1803-8

271 *Anton Shekhovtsov* | Russian Political Warfare. Essays on Kremlin Propaganda in Europe and the Neighbourhood, 2020-2023 | With a foreword by Nathalie Loiseau | ISBN 978-3-8382-1821-2

272 *Андреа Пето* | Насилие и Молчание. Красная армия в Венгрии во Второй Мировой войне | ISBN 978-3-8382-1636-2

273 *Winfried Schneider-Deters* | Russia's War in Ukraine. Debates on Peace, Fascism, and War Crimes, 2022–2023 | With a foreword by Klaus Gestwa | ISBN 978-3-8382-1876-2

ibidem.eu